Latin America's Middle Class

Latin America's Middle Class

Unsettled Debates and New Histories

Edited by David S. Parker and
Louise E. Walker

LEXINGTON BOOKS
Lanham • Boulder • New York • Toronto • Plymouth, UK

Published by Lexington Books
A wholly owned subsidiary of The Rowman & Littlefield Publishing Group, Inc.
4501 Forbes Boulevard, Suite 200, Lanham, Maryland 20706
www.rowman.com

10 Thornbury Road, Plymouth PL6 7PP, United Kingdom

British Library Cataloguing in Publication Information Available

Library of Congress Cataloging-in-Publication Data

Latin America's middle class : unsettled debates and new histories / edited by David S. Parker and
Louise E. Walker.
pages cm
Includes bibliographical references and index.
ISBN 978-0-7391-6848-6 (cloth : alkaline paper) -- ISBN 978-0-7391-6853-0 (paper : alkaline
paper) -- ISBN 978-0-7391-6849-3 (electronic) (print)
1. Middle class--Latin America--History--20th century. 2. Latin America--Social conditions--20th
century. 3. Latin America--Economic conditions--20th century. 4. Latin America--Politics and
government--20th century. I. Parker, D. S. (David Stuart), 1960- II. Walker, Louise E., 1977-
HT690.L3L28 2013
305.5'50980904--dc23
2012038448

Printed in the United States of America

Contents

Acknowledgments

This book takes a retrospective look at some of the most influential scholarship and writing on Latin America's middle class, and the debts we have incurred over the course of the project are many and varied. Our first thanks go to the contributors, both for sharing their research and for their patience. Because several selections are the work of authors now deceased, we must express our heartfelt appreciation to their families and heirs. We are grateful as well to the Lexington Books division of Rowman and Littlefield Publishers for their enthusiasm and support. Over the past several years the project has benefited from the insights of Ezequiel Adamovsky, William Beezley, John Charles Chasteen, Iñigo Garcia-Bryce, Enrique Garguin, Colin McLachlan, and Sergio Visacovsky. Maureen Garvie proofread and copyedited the original manuscript. Claire Woodside provided assistance at an earlier stage in the editorial process.

This book could not have been completed without the support of our institutions, and we are beholden to our colleagues at Queen's University in Kingston, Ontario, Louisiana State University in Baton Rouge, the New School for Social Research in New York, and Northeastern University in Boston.

We want to thank those who allowed us to reproduce the chapters that have appeared previously elsewhere. The *Hispanic American Historical Review* granted permission to reprint John J. Johnson's "Middle Groups in National Politics in Latin America," *Hispanic American Historical Review* 37:3 (Aug. 1957), 313–29; Fredrick B. Pike's "Aspects of Class Relations in Chile, 1850–1960," *Hispanic American Historical Review* 43:1 (Feb. 1963), 14–33; and David S. Parker's "White-Collar Lima, 1910–1929: Commercial Employees and the Rise of the Peruvian Middle Class," *Hispanic American Historical Review* 72:1 (Feb. 1992), 47–72.

"Community Pillars: The Middle Class," first appeared in Andrew H. Whiteford, *Two Cities of Latin America: A Comparative Description of Social Classes* (Garden City, NY: Anchor Books, 1964). We are grateful to the Whiteford estate for permission to reprint this section.

Penguin Books granted permission to reprint the Gerald Brown translation of Mario Benedetti's "The Budget," which appears in *Spanish Short Stories I/Cuentos Hispánicos I*, Jean Franco, editor (London: Penguin Books, 1966), 27–41.

Francisco López Cámara's "Middle-Class Rebels" was originally published in his *El desafío de la clase media* (Mexico City: Editorial Joaquín Mortiz, 1971). We are grateful to the López Cámara estate for reprint permission.

Charles Wagley's "The Dilemma of the Latin American Middle Class," was originally published as chapter 7 of *The Latin American Tradition: Essays on the Unity and the Diversity of Latin American Culture* (New York: Columbia University Press, 1968). Permission to reprint was granted by Conrad Kottak and Isabel Wagley Kottak for Charles Wagley's estate.

William E. French's "Moralizing the Masses" first appeared as chapter 3 of his *A Peaceful and Working People: Manners, Morals, and Class Formation in Porfirian Mexico* (Albuquerque: University of New Mexico Press, 1996). We thank the University of New Mexico Press for permission to reprint.

Brian P. Owensby's "Domesticating Modernity: Markets, Home, and Morality in the Middle Class in Rio de Janeiro and São Paulo, 1930s and 1940s" was originally published in the *Journal of Urban History* 24:3 (March 1998), 337–63. Sage Publishers granted reprint rights through the Copyright Clearance Center.

"We Were the Middle Class" by Rodolfo Barros is excerpted from his book *Fuimos: aventuras y desventuras de la clase media* (Buenos Aires: Aguilar, Altea, Taurus, Alfaguara, 2005). We are grateful to the author for permission to translate and reprint.

Finally, we wish to thank our families. This book would not have been possible without their unwavering support, patience, and humor.

Introduction

The Making and Endless Remaking of the Middle Class

David S. Parker

By most measurements Latin America is the region of the world where wealth is most unequally distributed.[1] Although a few countries stand as exceptions, the popular image of a Latin America where the walled compounds of the rich turn their backs on the shantytowns of the poor holds a significant measure of truth. It is not unreasonable, therefore, to question the premise of a book about the Latin American middle class.

Yet tens of millions of Latin Americans identify themselves as middle class and live lives that most outside observers are comfortable calling middle class. Moreover, the middle class has long figured centrally in debates about Latin America's history and destiny. In the decades following World War II, scholars wrote extensively about the impact a growing middle class might have on the region: would it spearhead economic development and bring "modernity"? Would it promote democracy? Would it be a force for stability or instability? What kinds of values would it hold? What kinds of politics would it embrace? In the so-called lost decade of the 1980s, as a region beset by debt and financial crises began to accept the tough medicine of unbridled free-market neoliberalism, many wondered aloud whether the middle class had become an endangered species.[2] Yet since about 2000, demonstrations and even riots led by apparently middle-class people have captured headlines in Argentina, Venezuela, Ecuador, and elsewhere, bringing the class again to the center of political debate.[3]

Class, as a general concept, has long informed scholarly thinking about Latin America. In their search to explain everything from underdevelopment to militarism, analysts have often focused on shifts in the balance of power between elites, middle classes, and working classes, or on the state's ability or failure to incorporate specific social classes into a governing coalition.[4] Yet too seldom do theorists connect abstract classes to real human beings, and too seldom do competing interpretations share comparable methodologies, assumptions, or terminology. Despite a vague consensus that Latin America's middle class is somehow important, the class remains an elusive subject that never seems to stay in one place. It is always rising, falling, emerging, declining, consolidating its position or descending into crisis.

Who makes up this Latin American middle class, and how numerous is it? This most basic empirical question turns out to be among the most difficult to answer, because so much depends upon how we define *class* and how we define *middle*. We could, for example, describe as middle class the 20 or 30 percent of the population whose income lies closest to the statistical mean, though that measure would exclude most people who are thought of as middle class by their peers and would include many who are not. We might approximate by limiting the middle class to high school graduates who work in nonmanual jobs, who live in certain neighborhoods and send their children to certain schools, who own a car and employ a maid, or who meet some other similar standards. Depending on the country and the criteria, we might estimate a middle class ranging somewhere between 10 and 40 percent of the population, large enough to be a significant political force, though rarely a dominating one.[5]

Beyond those roughest of ballpark estimates, however, little more can be said with confidence because so much resides in the eye of the beholder. For most of the countries of Latin America for most of the period covered by this book, it would be a safe bet to include in the middle class most liberal professionals, government bureaucrats, engineers, white-collar workers in commerce and industry, and entrepreneurs in medium-sized businesses. One might easily add to the list teachers, writers, artists, salesmen, high-tech workers, military officers, prosperous farmers, or any number of other possibilities. But the class divisions that Latin Americans themselves perceive often bear little resemblance to the sociologist's neat categories. On close inspection, the middle class is rarely defined just by occupation or income: skin color, education, talents, lifestyle, last name, connections, even political loyalties are just as likely to enter the calculation.[6] To complicate matters further, membership requirements were (and are) ever changing, the goalposts constantly moving. Skilled independent craftsmen would have qualified as middle class in 1870; by the 1930s or 1940s, that was no longer the case.[7] In the 1950s, "middle class" in São Paulo, Brazil, presumed light skin, while the connection between class and color was less clear cut in Salvador, Bahia.[8] A native Quechua speaker could be middle class in 1950s Cuzco, Peru, but not in Lima.[9] Readers seeking a constant, unambiguous definition of Latin America's middle class should prepare to be frustrated. The subject is a slippery one, its boundaries both fuzzy and unstable.

In the face of such instability, this book examines the lives of people who are or were middle class *according to accepted understandings of "middle class" in their own time and place.* Their middle-class status (how others defined them) and identity (how they defined themselves) derived from a perception that they were, by some measure, below the elite yet above the poor and working masses. What differed from one place and time to another was not the sense of being in between but the location of the dividing lines and the rules by which they were drawn. Changes in who gets defined as middle class are key to the process by which a middle class is perceived to "rise" or "decline," "emerge" or "fall into crisis." One objective of this book is to help us understand how and why those lines shift and those rules change.

The book spends a fair amount of time focused on the everyday lives of ordinary men and women who inhabited this social middle, but it also examines how scholars, public officials, and educated Latin Americans thought and talked about the middle class, paying close attention to the politics of class labeling. A typical engineer or teacher or retail clerk might have no greater concern than making the mortgage payment or providing his or her children with an education, but it still means something that he considers himself and that others consider him part of "*the* middle class." It means something a bit different to be defined as a member of "middle classes" in the plural. Labels matter, because the middle class as a concept plays such a key role in how Latin Americans have interpreted their society and their history and has had an incalculable influence on politics and policy-making. We will return to this crucial point later.

For some, the middle class embodies a golden mean of moderation, compromise, and stability. As early as 350 BC, Aristotle wrote that the healthiest communities were those in which extremes of rich and poor are mitigated by the presence of a large middle class.[10] Many have described the middle class as a force for modernity, the champion of forward-looking change. After all, the bourgeoisie was the revolutionary protagonist long deemed responsible for the demise of feudalism and the birth of capitalism.[11] Scholars of many ideological stripes have associated the middle class with rational, secular, entrepreneurial, cosmopolitan, modern ideas and lifestyles.[12] At the same time, others have described the middle class as the guardian of family, patriotism, and bedrock moral values, supposedly less susceptible to vice than the dissolute rich or the undisciplined poor.[13] There are negative stereotypes of the middle class as well, as we will see, but in general people have tended to assume that a society that has a large middle class is healthier than a society that does not. This explains the power of political arguments couched in terms of protecting or promoting the middle class.

In thinking about the relationship between everyday middle-class lives and "*the* middle class" as a historical force, we should not be surprised that

Chilean businessmen or Peruvian bank employees often behaved in ways that confounded expert conceptions of how a middle class should behave. Even so, middle-class men and women were hardly unaware of their assigned role in society as part of "*the* middle class," and many embraced middle-classness as badge of honor and a source of distinction. Ideas of the middle class, including ideas imported from abroad, could give meaning to people's lives, shaping their sense of self and influencing their everyday decisions: where to live, where to send their children to school, whether to buy a car or hire a domestic servant.

The first part of this book reprints six classic views of the Latin American middle class, first published between the late 1940s and the middle-to-late 1960s. Four of these six pieces are by U.S. academics who challenged old stereotypes of a Latin America peopled only by peasants and aristocrats. Writing in the midst of Cold War tensions and witness to the region's dizzying urban transformation, these authors sought to understand how a rising middle class might reshape the region's economy, society, culture, and politics. While they agree that the middle class should, in theory, contribute to a triumph of progressive, entrepreneurial, and democratic values, they disagree on whether or not Latin America's actual middle class embraced those ideals, and whether or not they had the power to put their stamp on the societies in which they lived. The two other pieces in this section, the first by Uruguayan novelist and poet Mario Benedetti and the second by Mexican sociologist Francisco López Cámara, give Latin American perspectives on the hopes and disappointments of a government employee in the 1940s and the challenge of alienated middle-class youth in the 1960s.

The book's second half takes an empirical look at middle-class people in specific times and places, drawing on original research. On the one hand, the selections in part II immerse us in the everyday concerns of the Mexican industrialist, the Brazilian housewife, the young female Colombian office worker. On the other hand, these selections all have something to say about the culture and values of people in the middle, about how they perceived themselves as a class and drew distinctions between themselves and others. In so doing, they provide new, if tentative, answers to the more general questions that the earlier authors raised about "*the* middle class" and its likely impact on Latin American society.

THE MIDDLE CLASS DEBATE IN LATIN AMERICA'S MID-TWENTIETH CENTURY

In the late 1950s and early 1960s, when Latin America was one of the key hot spots in a world polarized by the Cold War, many U.S. scholars and policymakers invested hope in the benefits that might come from a growing middle class. Bolstering that hope was the fact that dictatorships in the region seemed to be weakening, ceding ground to less malignant forms of constitutional authoritarianism or, in several places, to genuine democracies.[14] Those who saw good times ahead for Latin America focused not only on the recent fall of dictatorial regimes in Argentina, Peru, Colombia, Cuba, and Venezuela but also on longer trends toward secularization, the expansion of suffrage and citizenship rights, the mushrooming of public education, industrializing economies, emerging consumer markets, and the declining political power of landholding elites.

On the side of pessimism, observers pointed to the radicalization of the Cuban Revolution in 1960 and 1961, though warning bells had already been ringing for some time. On a 1958 goodwill trip to South America, Vice-President Richard Nixon had confronted jeering crowds in Lima and an attack on his motorcade in Caracas. Many experts, particularly in the U.S. government, arrived at the conviction that change in Latin America was inevitable; it might come peacefully or violently, it might be reasonable or extremist, democratic or totalitarian, but change would come, and the longer the wait, the worse the likely outcome.[15] This attitude of "reform now or face revolution later" became the guiding principle behind the Alliance for Progress, John F. Kennedy's Latin American aid and development program, designed to promote economic growth and moderate social reform in order to take the wind out of communist sails.[16]

This was the larger political context in which the first two selections in this volume were originally published. For those who embraced the goals of the Alliance for Progress and believed in Latin America's potential for democratic development, it was important to be able to locate a middle class that could fulfill a moderating, modernizing, democratizing role. A strong and growing middle class would confirm the optimistic vision of a region well on the path to democracy and development.[17] That is not to say that the historians, sociologists, anthropologists, political scientists, and economists who began looking for, and at, Latin America's middle class in the 1950s and 1960s were driven by U.S. foreign policy goals rather than their own intellectual curiosity. It was clear to anyone looking that Latin America after World War II was not the same place it had once been. São Paulo, Buenos Aires, and Mexico City were becoming major industrial centers, "populist" leaders like Juan Perón and Getulio Vargas had ushered in a new age of mass politics, urban labor had become a powerful force, and change was in the air in hundreds of other ways. Many scholars saw behind these changes the hand of a rising middle class, and they sought to understand what was happening and where those developments were ultimately heading.

The first watershed moment in the academic study of Latin America's middle class came in 1948, when the newly created Social Sciences Section of the Pan American Union chose as its inaugural project an ambitious multinational study of the region's middle class, and enlisted twenty-seven social scientists (twenty of them Latin American) to carry out research in as many countries as possible.[18] The resulting six-volume compilation, *Materiales para el estudio de la clase media en la América Latina*, came to no grand conclusions: indeed the various contributors agreed on little at all, not even on whether such a thing as a "middle class" could be said to exist in the region.[19] In a review of the first four volumes, B. R. Wilson noted some of the unanswered questions:

> It is . . . apparent that these writers often mean very different things by the term Middle Class, and in the diverse nature of the societies on which they write this must be so. . . . More problems are raised than are solved by these studies—if, indeed, any are solved—but that was the intention of the promoters. Must a class be aware of its own existence to be considered a class at all? Must class members conduct themselves differently toward members of other classes? Must class members share similar chances in life?[20]

As this book will show, many of those questions remain as unresolved today as they were a half-century ago, though we will also see the strides that have been made, at very least in thinking about *how* scholars should go about asking and answering them.

The Pan American Union compilation was of enduring interest to Latin American social scientists, but was not widely distributed. For English-speaking audiences, the breakthrough book that launched the middle class debate was John J. Johnson's *Political Change in Latin America: The Emergence of the Middle Sectors*, published in 1958.[21] A year earlier the *Hispanic American Historical Review* published Johnson's preliminary findings in the piece reprinted here.

By deliberately choosing terms like *sectors* and *groups* rather than *class*, Johnson did two things. First, he highlighted the diversity of forces at work in Latin America's transformation and the unpredictability of its outcome. *Sectors* did not require unity of origin or purpose. They did not require class consciousness or even an awareness of themselves as a distinct social group. They did not require similar sources or levels of income, lifestyles in common, or shared ideology. By talking about sectors, Johnson could lump long-standing occupants of the social middle (such as priests and lawyers) together with newly emerging groups such as small business owners, skilled technicians, and white-collar workers. He was thus able to make his case that these new and traditional middle elements, though by no means comprising a unified *class*, had combined to create a new politics in the region. Wresting power from entrenched elites, they promoted such modernizing reforms as the expansion of public education, industrialization, state intervention in the economy, and protective legislation for workers and employees.

Sector v. Class

The second great virtue of words like *sectors* or *groups* lay in their ability to provide a flexible vocabulary that scholars could use to describe Latin American society in all its complexity. Deliberately rejecting traditional categories of European social analysis, Johnson freed himself from having to define *class*. Perhaps this was 1950s anti-Marxist empiricism at its purest, but one can argue that it was a useful way to look at third world realities without being straight-jacketed by first world categories.[22] For all of these reasons, the term *middle sectors* caught on among scholars and for decades dominated the literature in both English and Spanish, even among scholars who disagreed with Johnson's conclusions.[23]

Johnson's early critics questioned whether Latin America's middle sectors really embraced modern values and reformist politics. Bert Hoselitz, a development economist, argued in an influential 1960 paper that middle-class Latin Americans lacked entrepreneurial drive and were less concerned with creating wealth than with lobbying governments to redistribute wealth their way.[24] Historian Fredrick Pike, whose case study of Chile appears in this volume, contends that the middle sectors were beholden to the aristocracy, preoccupied with individual mobility, and indifferent or even hostile to the needs of society's majority. Pike describes a cultural fusion between an upper class that was open to new money and a middle class that desperately aspired to join high society; together, he argues, they circled the wagons against change.

Who was right? Did the middle class (or sectors, if you prefer) embrace or oppose reform? Clearly the question was not that simple: much depended upon whom you looked at, where, and when. Because *middle class* could denote people of widely varying occupations, lifestyles, and aspirations, it should come as no surprise that "middle-class" values are not so easily identified. Andrew Hunter Whiteford's anthropological study of Querétaro, Mexico, and Popayán, Colombia, illustrates this perfectly. In Querétaro, Whiteford's informants spoke not of one middle class but three: the "comfortable middle class," the "middle class without money," and the "middle class without culture." All were considered middle class by local standards, but what made them middle class—in some cases income, in other cases education or family name or something else—belied any single common interest. In Popayán, a smaller, more isolated and more traditional city, Whiteford's informants saw fewer divisions within the middle class and fewer differences between the middle and upper classes. Instead, they perceived a much sharper line between the middle and lower classes than did the people of Querétaro. Whiteford's findings point out the futility of efforts to identify a single, timeless middle class with certain axiomatic qualities. Yet it remained clear all the same that Querétaro, like the rest of Mexico, had been changed by this growing number of middle-class people, however difficult they were to define. Johnson's challenge, to assess where those changes were leading politically, did not go away.

One major question was the relationship between the middle sectors and the armed forces, whose own contribution to Latin American development was equally under debate at the time. Johnson, among others, saw both analogies and links between the rise of the middle sectors and the rise of a professionally trained officer corps. These upwardly mobile young officers, according to Johnson, generally shared nationalistic, pro-modernization values that coincided with the middle sectors' own technocratic, developmentalist agenda.[25] Indeed, some went further to argue that on several occasions in the twentieth century, military men had stepped into politics in service of middle-sector interests: threatening a coup in Chile in 1924 to force Congress to pass progressive social legislation; intervening in Brazil in 1930 and Bolivia in 1936; supporting Argentina's Juan Perón. In all of these cases, the argument goes, the military had the power that the middle sectors on their own lacked, to overcome the resistance of the old aristocratic order and to bring sought-after change.[26]

This twin vision of a rising progressive middle class and an emerging, forward-looking professional officer corps inspired great hope in Latin America in the late Eisenhower and early Kennedy years. But by the late 1960s hope had given way to disillusion. In theory, the Alliance for Progress had been predicated on the idea that democracy and moderate reform were the best defense against Communism. In practice, the hope (for some) and fear (for others) of a repeat of the Cuban revolution ended up undermining the democratic center and strengthening the extremes. Young leftists, inspired by Fidel Castro and Ché Guevara, repudiated the moderate reformers who had once been their allies. *Fidelista* insurgencies broke out in the early 1960s in Guatemala, Venezuela, Colombia, and Peru, among other places. Meanwhile, conservatives became convinced that civilian regimes were unwilling or unable to repress "subversion," broadly defined. They called on the military to intervene and cheered when elected governments were overthrown in Brazil (1964) and Argentina (1966), the first wave of what would later become an authoritarian tsunami.[27]

As Latin America polarized and several countries stumbled toward virtual civil war, the middle sectors polarized as well (some might even say they led the way). On the one side, as Francisco López Cámara argues in his selection, the youth movement that embraced sex, drugs, and revolution was a product of distinctly middle-class frustrations, particularly the uncertain career prospects of university students trained for liberal professions that the economy no longer required. On the other side, as Charles Wagley points out for Brazil in 1964, other members of the middle class so feared violent upheaval that they welcomed, and even clamored for, military takeovers and a clampdown on subversives. Gone was the faith that the middle class necessarily formed the backbone of a moderate, democratic political center.[28]

Over time, as middle-sector reformism languished as a political project, young scholars influenced by dependency theory embraced new grand historical narratives dominated by the idea of middle class failure. Building on elements of Pike's critique but recasting them in a more Marxist language, writers such as James Petras, Maurice Zeitlin, Dale Johnson, and José Nun argued that the weakness and/or conservatism of Latin America's middle class was in large measure responsible for the region's economic and political troubles.[29] They contended that Latin America strayed from the path blazed by successful Western democracies because it never had its "bourgeois revolution." The concentration of land, money, and power in the hands of a tiny oligarchy supposedly typified nations whose middle class was unable or unwilling to assume its assigned role as the bringer of capitalist modernity. Unlike the classic bourgeoisies of Britain or France, the argument went, Latin America's middle class had grown up in the embrace of the state, appropriating the fruits of economic development that they themselves had done little to create. Foreigners had provided Latin America's investment capital, so the middle sectors did not need to develop a Protestant ethic of frugality, efficiency, and savings. Nor did they need to destroy the power of the old feudal aristocracy: their advancement required no fundamental social upheaval.[30]

Political scientist José Nun reasoned, along the same lines, that the military coups of the 1960s were in fact *middle-class* coups. Drawing on earlier work by Edwin Lieuwen and others,[31] Nun argued that the middle sectors lacked the power, unity, and consciousness of the historical European bourgeoisie, so they enlisted the armed forces to act in their class interest. At first, military interventions had helped the middle groups break into power, by dismantling the social and political barriers of a crumbling aristocratic order. But winning a place at the table was not the same as imposing their middle-class values and ideology on society as a whole. In face of the resulting social and political stalemate (what Nun called a "hegemonic crisis"), with the oligarchy not yet destroyed and the urban and rural proletariat ever more insistent, Latin America's middle sectors turned again to the armed forces to defend them. This time, however, they sought protection against a working class clamoring for the very same rights and privileges that the middle class had so recently and precariously won.[32]

As the late 1960s/early 1970s critique of middle-class failure, weakness, and conservatism became dominant in academia, interest in the middle class as a research topic diminished. Entrepreneurs and technocrats no longer captured the imagination of young scholars who might be middle class themselves but who drew their inspiration from the bearded revolutionaries of the mountains and the peasant and working masses in whose name those rebels

fought. Even those who hesitated to embrace Ché Guevara found it hard to
see middle groups as the main actor driving Latin American history. By the
late 1970s and 1980s almost no one remained interested in Latin America's
middle class. The debate was apparently finished, Johnson had lost, the middle sectors did not hold the region's future in their hands, and perhaps nothing else needed to be said.

RETHINKING CLASS: CULTURAL HISTORY AND
THE LINGUISTIC TURN

Ironically, just at the moment the middle class fell off the scholarly map in
Latin America, European and North American social and cultural historians
had begun to craft new tools with which to understand class, tools that would
ultimately make possible a renaissance in scholarship on the middle sectors.
E. P. Thompson in his 1963 classic *The Making of the English Working Class*
emphasized how workers interpreted their everyday experiences of struggle
in cultural terms, and in so doing "made" themselves into a class as they
developed a shared sense of community and identity. Class, for Thompson,
was thus not an economic fact that preceded and gave rise to consciousness
and action; class was instead the outcome, the product of that consciousness
and of those actions.[33] Cultural historians who followed Thompson, most
notably Gareth Stedman Jones, challenged his understanding of the relationship between experience, culture, and class. Jones argued that even *experience* could not be considered a purely objective fact, because what men and
women experience is shaped by the ideas, concepts, beliefs, and even words
they use to try to make sense of reality.[34]

   For our purposes, two insights of the new cultural history stand out above
the others. First is the debunking of the presumption that European history
was in fact transformed by the revolutionary action of a victorious middle
class. In the case of the French Revolution, long considered the defining
example of middle-class revolution, the familiar story was challenged by the
finding that there was no real "bourgeois" class in pre-Revolutionary France
with economic interests distinct from those of the aristocracy, and that there
was no correlation whatsoever between the source of a Frenchman's income
and the side he took in the Revolution.[35] In England and Germany as well,
the portrait that has emerged over past decades is of a hybrid elite, involved
in commerce but sharing the interests and values of the aristocracy—indeed,
an elite remarkably like the Chileans portrayed by Fredrick Pike.[36] So if
scholars now believe that there was no bourgeois revolution in revolutionary
France, no triumphant middle class in middle-class Britain, then Latin America is no longer captive to historical narratives couched in terms of its devi-
ance from some universal norm.[37]

Second and more important is the interrogation of the concept of class itself. The authors in Part 1 may all have given different answers to the question of who belonged to the middle class and what its characteristics were. But Johnson, Pike, Whiteford, Wagley, and López Cámara all agreed that there was such a thing as a middle class—or at least such a thing as diverse middle sectors—and that the job of the social scientist was to discover and describe that reality as accurately as possible. The authors in part II of this book are not so unanimously confident that "the middle class," "middle classes," "middle sectors," or any similar collectivity actually exists as an unproblematic, objective fact.

Sure, out there in the real world there are people of median incomes, people with white-collar and professional occupations, people who fit traditional sociological descriptions of the middle class. But advocates of the new social and cultural history view those facts as only a point of departure, the place where the serious research begins. A Thompson-influenced social historian would go on to ask whether and how those white-collar and professional people, over the course of their everyday lives, crafted bonds of solidarity among themselves and a sense of being distinct from—and potentially in conflict with—members of other classes. Cultural historians would interrogate even deeper premises. Why do people perceive meaningful social boundaries in some places but not others? On what basis does a certain income range or set of occupations qualify as "middle class"? How much should we take into account what people themselves thought and said about their own membership in one or another class? If we do take into account what people think and say, how do we interpret those ideas and words? For example, if up to 80 percent of U.S. citizens, including many of the wealthiest, describe themselves in opinion polls as "middle class," does that make them so?[38] Alternatively, can a middle class exist in a society where the words "middle class" have never been uttered?[39]

Many of the writers of the 1950s and 1960s were aware of these kinds of questions (recall Wilson's review of the Pan American Union collection). But whereas those earlier scholars thought that vagueness and ill-definition were somehow unique and aberrant attributes of Latin America's middle class, those who embrace linguistic approaches to history are likely to believe that the same holds true universally: that class, like race or nation, is everywhere and always an abstraction, an idea, a rhetorical argument, what many scholars call a discourse.[40]

Lost in approaches rooted in the new cultural history is the analytical precision that comes when the scholar defines class categories and boundaries and assigns people to one pigeonhole or another following objective criteria. But gained is a greater sense of the categories that people in specific times and places used to describe one another, the often subtle meanings and subtexts of particular social descriptors, and what these class discourses say about how ordinary people imagined the world and their place in it, the rights they claimed and how they claimed them, with whom they felt common cause or emphasized difference and distance. My article "White-Collar Lima" in this volume, for example, explains when and why striking commercial employees in Peru first started to describe themselves as middle class and what those words meant to them. Ricardo A. López recounts how male and female office employees in 1940s Bogotá manipulated class and gender stereotypes to distinguish themselves as better than their blue-collar counterparts. J. Pablo Silva describes how competing visions of who constituted the Chilean middle class served opposing partisan political agendas. Rodolfo Barros looks at the deep connection that Argentines believed to exist between the middle class and aspirations of upward mobility through education. These kinds of insights only become possible when scholars jettison their own classifications and listen to how people themselves talked about class, no matter how imprecise, unscientific, and contradictory those discourses might be.

LIVES IN THE MIDDLE: CHANGING TRAJECTORIES AND SOME CONSTANTS

Starting, then, from the premise that the scholar's task is not so much to define the middle class as to uncover the shifting standards by which people imagined themselves and others as middle class, several important themes emerge. These include the competition among diverse groups for recognition as the class's standard-bearers, and major shifts over time in the kinds of people who come to be seen as typically middle class. These changes—sometimes gradual, sometimes sudden—are often interpreted in terms of a declining "old middle class" pitted against a rising "new middle class." Yet what is "old" and what is "new" itself changes. In the 1950s, when Johnson was writing, the new middle class comprised those occupational groups closely tied to state-supported industries and mushrooming public bureaucracies. Latin Americans employed in highly skilled technical and professional jobs in those sectors enthusiastically embraced the "middle class" label to describe themselves, and outside observers agreed: indeed, for many scholars, what uniquely defined Latin America's middle class was its deep roots in the state.[41] These employees, poignantly portrayed in Mario Benedetti's short story "The Budget" and analyzed in selections by Owensby and López, were easily distinguished from an older middle class of lawyers, doctors, priests, estate administrators, and import-house clerks who had flourished in an earlier, less industrial economy with a smaller public sector.

Beginning in the late 1970s and 1980s, the model of state-led development increasingly came under attack. Government growth was tamed, albeit more in some places than in others; industries saw their protective tariffs and subsidies taken away and found themselves unable to compete against cheaper foreign imports; publicly owned assets were sold off to private investors. These changes intensified in the rollercoaster years of the late twentieth century, during the transition from military dictatorship to restored democracy and in the context of recurrent economic crises and advancing globalization. The various crises, whether they took the form of 200-percent-a-month hyperinflation, drastic currency devaluations, or austerity and unemployment, did much to undermine the security of salaried employees already threatened by the retreat of the big state of the World War II era.[42] The selection by Rodolfo Barros chronicles how four Argentinian families experienced this loss of stability and predictability in their middle-class lives. Their stories contrast with Benedetti's 1947 portrait.

For some observers, neoliberal globalization destroyed the middle class, end of story. Others, however, contend that the class did not disappear but merely changed. The economic crises took as victims the educated salaried employees who had once formed the heart of the postwar "new" middle class. They now became the "old," declining middle class, supplanted by a *new* "new" middle class of self-employed entrepreneurs large and small, particularly in importing-exporting, computing, telecommunications, and services. Compared to their parents' generation, this middle class was defined less by education and stable employment in the public sector and more by their income and possessions. Some built homes in secure gated communities and spearheaded the rampant consumerism that characterized the neoliberal boom years of the late 1980s and 1990s.[43] Others, though also well off, came from diverse ethnic-racial origins and chose to remain in neighborhoods that had once been shantytowns: this *cholo* middle class, as they were called in Peru, included people who two decades earlier would never have been imagined as middle class.[44]

Other economic and social changes equally transformed the lives of men and women in the middle. One key trend was urbanization: as Latin American cities exploded, lost was the face-to-face familiarity that had once characterized town life, and social position came to be less ascribed than acquired. Family antecedents counted for little when people no longer knew exactly who was who. Whereas in the early 1900s it had been possible for a Peruvian housing inspector to lament the suffering of the "middle-class poor" whose respectable surnames and social standing contrasted with the economic misery in which they actually lived, by the 1950s such a radical disconnect between wealth and status would have seemed bizarre.[45] Instead, the post–World War II urban middle class increasingly identified one another by the new neighborhoods they lived in, the schools their children attended, the clubs they belonged to, and their material possessions. By the 1970s or so, to be middle class in Mexico meant to have a used Fiat or VW in the garage and a son or daughter in the UNAM, the National Autonomous University. A class defined by lifestyle, however, was more than ever at the mercy of the ups and downs of the market. The availability of consumer goods to an ever-expanding number of people also meant that status goalposts were continually moving. Products that had once distinguished the elite became available to the middle class, but products that had once distinguished the middle class were now available to workers, and so on down the line. It was like an escalator built on sand: as individuals slowly rose, the whole mechanism slowly sank. And with the triumph of free-market neoliberalism, that escalator became ever more unpredictable, carrying some (but not others) upward at breakneck speed in the boom years, stopping altogether or shifting into reverse in years of crisis. [46]

Education followed a similar trajectory. According to Barros, what had long set Argentina apart as a "middle-class" society was the fact that an immigrant meatpacker or metalworker could aspire to give his children a better education than he had had, and in so doing could realistically hope to catapult them into professional or white-collar jobs with higher salaries and social prestige. The journey might take a generation or more, and not everyone succeeded, but to the extent that intergenerational mobility occurred, its path went through the classroom. While Argentina in its heyday was a more fluid society than most, all Latin American societies similarly equated learning with upward mobility. As a result, Latin American universities mushroomed in response to the intense demand, and in many countries the national universities accepted all qualified applicants. The inevitable effect was credential inflation. By the 1960s a university degree was what a high-school diploma had been in the 1940s, and by the 1990s even a university degree could no longer guarantee a middle-income job. Even so, education remained a value fervently clung to, a value, some argued, that distinguished the middle class from all others. [47]

Not all was change, to be sure. There are perhaps as many continuities as there are ruptures, and certain themes seem to recur no matter what the country or time period. For example, middle-class identity in Latin America, as in Europe and North America, was very often tied up with a sense of cultural distinction, even superiority. For members of Mexico's turn-of-the-twentieth-century *sociedad culta* described in the selection by William French, their social position derived as much from their morality and behavior (non-drinking, chaste, modest, hard-working, stable, respectable) as it did from their wealth or education. This values-based sense of self could foster an impulse toward class segregation, to avoid mixing with the promiscuous rabble, but it could also foster a crusading, missionary impulse to "civilize" the lower classes and instill in them the same moral norms. Either way, "decency" in public and private life became the quality that people believed distinguished them as middle class.

Women in particular saw themselves and were seen by others as the guardians of middle-class respectability. They were the ones who in public led campaigns against alcohol and prostitution and who in private upheld the ideals of decency in their own meticulously cared-for homes. Middle-class wives in postwar Brazil, and female office workers in postwar Colombia (as portrayed by Brian Owensby and A. Ricardo López, respectively) took on responsibility for upholding or improving their families' social position. They were the ones whose upstanding personal behavior counted (men could be pardoned for occasional lapses into drunkenness or infidelity). They were the ones responsible for the moral education of their children. It was to their sense of taste that advertisers appealed, because they were the ones expected to understand fashion and to consume elegantly without breaking the family budget. And, as López notes for Colombia, if women worked outside the home, it was because they were bringing in that little extra that made a middle-class lifestyle possible.

If positive stereotypes of the middle class centered on responsibility, manners, sobriety, self-control, thrift, and education, negative stereotypes emphasized the opposite. For critics, "middle class" conjured up images of greed, poor taste, crass consumerism, flexible ethics, and a hypocritical preoccupation with "what people will say." In Latin America in particular, the postwar middle class was often associated in the popular mind with bloated and unresponsive government bureaucracies manned by legions of inefficient, oftentimes corrupt patronage appointees.[48] Early twentieth-century social critics coined the term *empleomanía* to describe the phenomenon of proliferating public-sector jobs created not to serve a public need but to win votes and political allies, by satisfying a brimming middle class's appetite for respectable employment.

No matter which stereotype is closer to the truth, the sober, thrifty, industrious middle class or the status-obsessed middle class keeping up appearances while living beyond its means, lifestyle and consumption appear again and again as the defining profiles of those in the social middle. In "White-Collar Lima" I describe how Peruvian employees in the 1910s and 1920s claimed an inherent right to a "middle-class" standard of living. They took what had long been a criticism—that they refused to live within their means—and turned it on its head: if white-collar salaries could not support a lifestyle befitting their social standing, the answer was not for them to consume more frugally but for employers to raise their salaries. Brian Owensby, too, finds that middle-class identities in mid-twentieth-century Brazil were tied up with the possession of certain defining status goods, goods that members of the working class allegedly did not expect, deserve, or need.

"*THE* MIDDLE CLASS" AND ITS CONTESTED MEANINGS

Against the backdrop of the rise and fall of state-led development followed by the rise and recurrent crises of free-market neoliberalism, conceptions of "*the* middle class" in Latin America also changed, because society's ideas of who was middle class and what defined that middle class changed. As noted earlier, one key contention in the new cultural history is that classes, because they are at some level collectively agreed upon abstractions, are really ideas and discourses rather than objective things. They provide a shorthand that people use to make sense of social reality. But as ideas, as discourses, understandings of class are forever evolving and are often bones of contention. They are also infused with heavy doses of mythology and moralizing. Very wealthy people may define themselves and be accepted by others as middle class, not upper class, if in their society the words "upper class" conjure up images of inherited landed estates and the pampered offspring of families tracing back generations. People of very low incomes may define themselves and be accepted by others as middle class, not poor or working or lower class, if in their society those other terms evoke only negative images of people with bad moral character and poor work discipline, people lacking education and the drive to improve themselves. Class labels not only describe and categorize, they value and stigmatize.[49] So who identifies as middle class will depend heavily on whether society attaches a positive or negative value to middle-classness.

Furthermore, how ideas of class change over time is an eminently political process. The British historian Dror Wahrman has gone so far as to argue that "the middle class" was in fact *created* in political debate. Britons in the eighteenth century either spoke of the middle class or they recognized only rich and poor, bourgeois and proletarians, elites and people—not because British society *was* one way or the other but because they chose to *see* British society one way or the other, as best served their political goals. People make deliberate political choices when they decide to invoke "the middle class," in how they define who belongs to it, in their assertions of what "the middle class" supposedly needs and deserves.

Those political choices have political effects. In "White-Collar Lima," for example, I argue that a certain vision of who the middle class was fueled by white-collar unionization and underpinned reformist labor legislation. A. Ricardo López shows how female office workers fought long and hard against an ideology that equated "middle class" with "male head of household," much to the detriment of white-collar women. In both cases, people invoked "*the* middle class" consciously and explicitly as an argument in pursuit of specific goals. In "Domesticating Modernity," Brian Owensby puts a somewhat different spin on things, making the case that a key characteristic of middle-class politics in Brazil was a deliberate retreat from the loud public demonstrations for which blue-collar unions and populist politicians were famous. Instead, spokesmen for the middle class claimed to long for the quiet life centered around the home and embraced either a cynical "plague-on-all-your-houses" anti-politics or a crusading sense of moral indignation. In "Re-thinking Aspects of Class Relations in Chile," J. Pablo Silva argues that the definition of "the middle class" in Chile changed between the 1920s and 1960s because opinion-making intellectuals drew upon specific texts that shaped their understanding of who comprised the middle class and who did not. When leaders of Salvador Allende's socialist coalition increasingly iden-tified "middle class" with conservative business interests, party militants abandoned the middle class in their propaganda, their electoral strategies, and their platforms. The choice had fateful consequences.

Perhaps the greatest irony of all is that the worldwide diffusion of U.S. social science research, including research on the middle class by authors like those in part I of this book, contributed quite directly to the kinds of political discourses and controversies that Silva and others have described. Ideas have few borders, and in Latin America ideas from wealthy English- and French-speaking countries often come with a certain prestige. If Wahr-man is right, it is easy to imagine that when Johnson, Pike, Whiteford, and Wagley debated the characteristics of the Latin American middle class, they may have played a crucial role in creating the class that they believed they were only describing. Or, alternatively, Latin Americans may have imported from abroad the imagined picture of a "normal" Western middle class, with characteristics that they did not recognize in themselves. Failing to find in real life the middle class that inhabited their fantasies, they came to the mistaken conclusion that Latin America had no middle class, or that its middle class was uniquely weak, or that the class was disappearing.

CONCLUSION

When writers in the 1950s and 1960s debated the impact that a growing, confident middle class would have on Latin American society and politics, they understood that important changes were occurring in the region, and they asked most of the right questions. In many cases, however, they brought to the debate a tendency to treat the middle class as if it were a fixed thing with certain innate characteristics. There are notable exceptions to this rule, and Whiteford is one of those exceptions, but on balance participants in the debate paid too little attention to the politics of class labeling and the com-plexities of identity-making.

The contributors to part II of this book try to combat the temptation to essentialize. For them, class (and especially *middle* class) is not a scientific categorization based on a set of measurable criteria. Instead, the contributors find "class" both in the ways people feel and experience socioeconomic inequality in their everyday lives and in the ways people think and talk about class. That it is both things at once, a lived reality and a politicized discourse, makes class difficult to get a handle on. But that is what makes class so rich and so worthy of study. Looking at the Latin American middle class in this way encourages the student to listen to the voices of millions of ordinary people in the region's past and present, people whose voices deserve to be heard. If this book succeeds, it should also help the student to understand why "the middle class" is always changing, rising, falling, emerging, disappearing, and why Latin America's future will likely always be tied, in some complicated way, to the future of its middle class.

NOTES

1. "Gini Coefficient," in "Economics A-Z," *The Economist* (www.economist.com/research/Economics); Paul Gootenberg and Luis Reygadas, eds., *Indelible Inequalities in Latin America: Insights from History, Politics, and Culture* (Durham: Duke University Press, 2010), 3–5; Terry Lynn Karl, "The Vicious Cycle of Inequality in Latin America," in *What Justice? Whose Justice? Fighting for Fairness in Latin America*, ed. Susan Eckstein and Timothy Wickham-Crowley (Berkeley: University of California Press), 133. James K. Galbraith, "A Perfect Crime: Inequality in the Age of Globalization," *Daedalus* 131 (Winter 2002): 11–25.

2. Note the number of books with the words "decline" or "extinction" and "middle class" in the title, for example, Rami Schwartz and Salomón Barbaz Lapidus, *El ocaso de la clase media* (Mexico: Grupo Editorial Planeta, 1994); Francisco López Cámara, *Apogeo y extinción de la clase media mexicana* (Cuernavaca: UNAM, 1990).

3. On Argentina, the selection by Rodolfo Barros in this volume; Ezequiel Adamovsky, *Historia de la clase media argentina: Apogeo y decadencia de una illusion, 1919–2003* (Buenos Aires: Planeta, 2009); Alberto Minujin and Eduardo Anguita, *La clase media, seducida y abandonada* (Buenos Aires: Edhasa, 2004). On Venezuela and Ecuador (as well as the Philippines), see Celso M. Villegas, "Ascetic, Ambivalent, or Ascendant? Revolution 'from the Middle' and Middle-Class Formation in the Philippines, Venezuela, and Ecuador," paper written for the XXVI Congress of the Latin American Studies Association, Rio de Janeiro, 11 June 2009.

4. On the class structure and underdevelopment: Fernando Henrique Cardoso and Enzo Faletto, *Dependency and Development in Latin America* (1971). Ian Roxborough, "Unity and Diversity in Latin American History," *Journal of Latin American Studies* 16:1 (May 1984), esp. 16–22, critiques; also Diane E. Davis, *Discipline and Development: Middle Classes and Prosperity in East Asia and Latin America* (Cambridge, 2004). On class and democracy, Dietrich Rueschemeyer, Evelyne Huber Stephens, and John D. Stephens, *Capitalist Development and Democracy* (Cambridge: Polity Press, 1992), esp. chaps. 3 and 5. On state incorporation, David Collier and Ruth Berins Collier, *Shaping the Political Arena: Critical Junctures, the Labor Movement, and Regime Dynamics in Latin America* (Princeton: Princeton University Press, 1991).

5. For one effort to define the middle class in Mexico around the year 2000, see Dennis Gilbert, "'Magicians': The Response of Mexican Middle-Class Households to Economic Crisis," *Journal of Latin American Anthropology* 10:1 (April 2005), 129–33. Using a methodology that only highlights the complexity of the task, Gilbert comes up with a middle class comprising 18.2 percent of Mexican families.

6. Patrick Barr-Melej in *Reforming Chile: Cultural Politics, Nationalism, and the Rise of the Middle Class* (Chapel Hill: University of North Carolina Press, 2001) explores how a class might be defined according to its ideas, values, and political loyalties.

7. Íñigo L. García-Bryce, *Crafting the Republic: Lima's Artisans and Nation Building in Peru, 1821-1879* (Albuquerque: University of New Mexico Press, 2004), esp. 13–14, 118–25.

8. George Reid Andrews, *Blacks and Whites in São Paulo, Brazil, 1888–1988* (Madison: University of Wisconsin Press, 1991), chap. 6; Edward E. Telles, *Race in Another America: The Significance of Skin Color in Brazil* (Princeton: Princeton University Press, 2004), 99–101, 212–13.

9. On Cuzco, Marisol de la Cadena, *Indigenous Mestizos: the Politics of Race and Culture in Cuzco, Peru, 1919–1991* (Durham: Duke University Press, 2000). On Lima, D. S. Parker, *The Idea of the Middle Class: White-Collar Workers and Peruvian Society, 1900–1950* (University Park: Penn State University Press, 1998), 26, 126.

10. "Thus it is manifest that the best political community is formed by citizens of the middle class, and that those states are likely to be well-administered in which the middle class is large, and stronger if possible than both the other classes . . . for the addition of the middle class turns the scale, and prevents either of the extremes from being dominant" (Aristotle, *Politics*, book IV, parts 11 and 12, trans. Benjamin Jowett, The Internet Classics Archive [http://classics.mit.edu/Aristotle/politics.4.four.html]). Ezequiel Adamovsky in "Aristotle, Diderot, Liberalism and the idea of "Middle Class": A Comparison of Two Contexts of Emergence of a Metaphorical Formation," *History of Political Thought* 26:2 (2005): 303–33, critically analyzes the political function of this idea of a "golden mean."

11. Whether or not "bourgeoisie" and "middle class" should be used as synonyms, as they often are, opens up a debate that cannot be pursued here. Elsewhere in this introduction I take up the question of how scholars of Latin America have interpreted the concept of the "bourgeois revolution."

12. Brian P. Owensby selection in this volume; see also his *Intimate Ironies: Modernity and the Making of Middle-Class Lives in Brazil* (Stanford: Stanford University Press, 1999); David Watenpaugh, *Being Modern in the Middle East: Revolution, Nationalism, Colonialism, and the Arab Middle Class* (Princeton: Princeton University Press, 2006); Mark Liechty, *Suitably Modern*: Middle-Class Culture in a New Consumer Society (Princeton: Princeton University Press, 2002).

13. See the selection in this volume by William E. French and his book, *A Peaceful and Working People: Manners, Morals, and Class Formation in Porfirian Mexico* (Albuquerque: University of New Mexico Press, 1996). See also Leonore Davidoff and Catherine Hall, *Family Fortunes: Men and Women of the English Middle Class* (London: Hutchinson, 1987), esp. the prologue and part 1. Julio Moreno, in *Yankee Don't Go Home! Mexican Nationalism, American Business Culture, and the Shaping of Modern Mexico, 1920–1950* (Chapel Hill: University of North Carolina Press, 2003), chap. 7, sees a tension within the middle class between those who embraced ideals of modernity and capitalist consumerism and "anti-modernists" who decried the loss of traditional values.

14. Typical of the genre are Tad Szulc, *Twilight of the Tyrants* (New York: Henry Holt, 1959), esp. 3–4; Charles O. Porter and Robert J. Alexander, *The Struggle for Democracy in Latin America* (New York: Macmillan, 1961).

15. Milton S. Eisenhower, *The Wine is Bitter: The United States and Latin America* (Garden City, NY: Doubleday, 1963), xi.

16. Steven C. Rabe, *The Most Dangerous Area in the World: John F. Kennedy Confronts Communist Revolution in Latin America* (Chapel Hill: University of North Carolina Press, 1999), chap. 7; Jerome Levinson and Juan de Onís, "The Alliance That Lost Its Way: A Critical Report on the Alliance for Progress," in *Neighborly Adversaries: Readings in U.S.-Latin American Relations*, ed. Michael La Rosa and Frank O. Mora (Lanham, MD: Rowman and Littlefield Publishers, 2007), 179–91. Charles Kimber Pearce, in *Rostow, Kennedy, and the Rhetoric of Foreign Aid* (East Lansing: Michigan State University Press, 2001), traces the interplay between academic theorizing and public policy-making in the creation of the Alliance. Víctor Alba, in *Alliance without Allies: The Mythology of Progress in Latin America*, trans. John Pearson (New York: Praeger, 1965), attacks the Alliance's presuppositions.

17. Michael F. Jiménez, "The Elision of the Middle Classes and Beyond: History, Politics, and Development Studies in Latin America's 'Short Twentieth Century,'" in *Colonial Lega-*

20   *David S. Parker*

cies: The Problem of Persistence in Latin American History, ed. Jeremy Adelman (New York: Routledge, 1999), 211, 217.

18. Theo R. Crevenna, "La clase media en la América Latina," *Revista Mexicana de Sociología* 10, no. 2 (May–Aug. 1948): 281–82; Harold E. Davis, Review of "Materiales para el estudio de la clase media en la América Latina," *Hispanic American Historical Review* 32, no. 3 (Aug. 1952): 381–82.

19. Theo R. Crevenna, ed., *Materiales para el estudio de la clase media en la América Latina,* 6 vols. (Washington: Publicaciones de la Oficina de Ciencias Sociales, Pan American Union, 1950–52).

20. B. R. Wilson, Review of "*Materiales para el estudio de la clase media en la América Latina,*" *British Journal of Sociology* 2, no. 4 (Dec. 1951): 375–76.

21. John J. Johnson, *Political Change in Latin America: the Emergence of the Middle Sectors* (Stanford: Stanford University Press, 1958).

22. Johnson, in *Political Change,* viii–ix and 3–4, explains his rationale for avoiding the term "middle class."

23. The contributors to this volume also share no consensus on terminology. As readers will note, some talk about "class," others prefer "classes," while still others join Johnson in using terms like "sectors." In several cases the writers are simply echoing the words that appear most often in original documents from the era they study. In other cases their choice reflects deliberate analytical objectives.

24. Bert F. Hoselitz, "Economic Growth in Latin America," *First International Conference of Economic History, Stockholm, August 1960* (Paris: Mouton and Co., 1960).

25. John J. Johnson, ed., *The Role of the Military in Underdeveloped Countries* (Princeton: Princeton University Press, 1962), v; John J. Johnson, *The Military and Society in Latin America* (Stanford: Stanford University Press, 1964), 254. Edwin Lieuwen, in *Arms and Politics and Latin America* (New York: Praeger, 1961) and *Generals vs. Presidents: Neo-Militarism in Latin America* (New York: Praeger, 1964), covers similar analytical ground, but his conclusions are more critical of the military.

26. Samuel P. Huntington coined the term "breakthrough coups" to describe these anti-oligarchic interventions led by officers of middle-sector origins and/or sympathies (Huntington, *Political Order in Changing Societies* [New Haven and London: Yale University Press, 1968], 198–223).

27. Thomas C. Wright, in *Latin America in the Era of the Cuban Revolution,* 2nd ed. (Westport, CT: Praeger, 2001), surveys both the revolutionary impulse and counterrevolutionary responses.

28. To Johnson's credit, *Political Change in Latin America* was not over-optimistic about the middle sectors' commitment to democratic institutions, a point well made in Jiménez, "Elision of the Middle Classes," 212. Nevertheless, though Johnson's generally upbeat thesis was tempered by caution, the polarization of the late 1960s was so intense that he received heated criticism, even from some of his own graduate students.

29. James Petras, "The Middle Class in Latin America," in *Politics and Social Structure in Latin America* (New York: Monthly Review Press, 1970), 37–53; Maurice Zeitlin, *The Civil Wars in Chile (or the Bourgeois Revolutions That Never Were)* (Princeton: Princeton University Press, 1984); James Petras and Maurice Zeitlin, eds., *Latin America: Reform or Revolution?* (New York: Fawcett, 1968); James Cockcroft, Andre Gunder Frank, and Dale L. Johnson, *Dependence and Underdevelopment: Latin America's Political Economy* (Garden City, NY: Doubleday, 1972), esp. 106–11, 121–37, 342–44, 373–82.

30. Petras, "The Middle Class in Latin America," 37–53.

31. Lieuwen, *Arms and Politics in Latin America,* esp. 59–66.

32. Nun's argument went through a series of refinements over several years: see his "A Latin American Phenomenon: The Middle Class Military Coup," in *Trends in Social Science Research in Latin American Studies* (Mar. 1965), 55–99; "The Middle-Class Military Coup," in *The Politics of Conformity in Latin America,* ed. Claudio Véliz (London: Oxford University Press, 1967), 66–118; "The Middle-Class Military Coup in Latin America," in Petras and Zeitlin, *Latin America: Reform or Revolution?* 145–85; *Latin America: The Hegemonic Crisis and the Military Coup* (Berkeley and Los Angeles: Monthly Review Press/Institute of Interna-

tional Studies, 1969). The preceding paragraph is a summary based primarily on the 1967 version.

33. In one of his most often quoted passages, Thompson writes in *The Making of the English Working Class* (New York: Vintage Books, 1966), 9, "class happens when some men, as a result of common experiences (inherited or shared), feel and articulate the identity of their interests as between themselves, and as against other men whose interests are different from (and usually opposed to) theirs. The class experience is largely determined by the productive relations into which men are born—or enter involuntarily. Class-consciousness is the way in which these experiences are handled in cultural terms: embodied in traditions, value-systems, ideas, and institutional forms."

34. Gareth Stedman Jones, *Languages of Class: Studies in English Working Class History, 1832–1982* (Cambridge: Cambridge University Press, 1983); also Joan Wallach Scott, "The Evidence of Experience," *Critical Inquiry* 17 (Summer 1991): 793–97; William H. Sewell Jr., *Work and Revolution in France: the Language of Labor from the Old Regime to 1848* (Cambridge: Cambridge University Press, 1980). For a synopsis of the debates, two useful sources are Patrick Joyce, ed., *Class* (Oxford: Oxford University Press, 1995), and Ronald Grigor Suny, "Back and Beyond: Reversing the Cultural Turn?" *American Historical Review* 107:5 (Dec. 2002): 1476–99.

35. For an overview of the enormous body of "revisionist" literature in French history, see Sarah Maza, *The Myth of the French Bourgeoisie: An Essay on the Social Imaginary 1750–1850* (Cambridge: Harvard University Press, 2003); William Reddy, *Money and Liberty in Modern Europe: A Critique of Historical Understanding* (Cambridge: Cambridge University Press, 1987), chap. 1; David A. Bell, "Class, Consciousness, and the Fall of the Bourgeois Revolution," *Critical Inquiry* 2–3 (2004): 323–51.

36. Simon Gunn, "The Failure of the Victorian Middle Class: A Critique," in *The Culture of Capital: Art, Power, and the Nineteenth-Century Middle Class*, ed. Janet Wolff and John Seed, 18–19 (Manchester: Manchester University Press, 1988), citing in particular the early 1960s works of Perry Anderson and Tom Nairn.

37. Dipesh Chakrabarty, *Provincializing Europe: Postcolonial Thought and Historical Difference* (Princeton: Princeton University Press, 2000), criticizes the way that Western social science implicitly and often unthinkingly sets the European experience as the standard against which the histories of all other places are measured. Far too much scholarly writing about non-European regions of the world falls into the trap of trying to explain how and why those countries somehow took a "wrong" turn. Chakrabarty cites the concept of the "bourgeois revolution" as a specific example. See also Chakrabarty's "Postcoloniality and the Artifice of History: Who Speaks for 'Indian' Pasts?" *Representations* 37 (Winter 1992): 1–26 (esp. pp. 3–5).

38. Surveys tend to range between 40–50 percent at the low end and 80 percent at the high end, depending upon how the question is asked and the possible answers respondents were given to choose from. See Robert E. Weir, *Class in America: An Encyclopedia*, vol. 3, *Q-Z* (Westport, CT: Greenwood Publishing Group, 2007), 845–46.

39. Penelope J. Corfield, ed., *Language, History, and Class* (Oxford: Basil Blackwell, 1991), esp. Corfield's introduction and the selection by Keith Wrightson.

40. A good primer on discourse-centered approaches to Latin American history is Erik Kristofer Ching, Christina Buckley, and Angelica Lozano-Alonso, eds., *Reframing Latin America: A Cultural Theory Reading of the Nineteenth and Twentieth Centuries* (Austin: University of Texas Press, 2007).

41. Dale L. Johnson, ed., *Middle Classes in Dependent Countries* (Beverly Hills and London: Sage, 1985), chaps. 1, 6, 8.

42. Alberto Minujin, "Squeezed: The Middle Class in Latin America," *Environment and Urbanization* 7:2 (October 1995): 153–65; Minujin and Anguieta, *La clase media: seducida y abandonada*; Larissa Lominitz and Ana Melnick, *Chile's Middle Class: A Struggle for Survival in the Face of Neoliberalism*, trans. Jeanne Grant (Boulder: Lynne Rienner, 1991); Dennis Gilbert, "Magicians"; Dennis Gilbert, *Mexico's Middle Class in the Neoliberal Era* (Tucson: University of Arizona Press, 2007); Maureen O'Dougherty, *Consumption Intensified: The Politics of Middle-Class Daily Life in Brazil* (Durham: Duke University Press, 2002), especially

chaps. 1–2; Louise E. Walker, *Waking from the Dream: Mexico's Middle Classes after 1968* (Stanford: Stanford University Press, 2013).

43. Ana Wortman, *Pensar las clases medias: consumos culturales y estilos urbanos en la Argentina de los noventa* (Buenos Aires: La crujía, 2003); Maristella Svampa, *La brecha urbana: countries y barrios privados* (Buenos Aires: Capital Intelectual, 2004); Cecilia Arizaga, *El mito de la comunidad en la ciudad mundializada: estilos de vida y nuevas clases medias en urbanizaciones cerradas* (Buenos Aires: El cielo por asalto, 2005).

44. Santiago Pedraglio, "Los Olivos: clase 'a medias,'" and Abelardo Sánchez León, "Los avatares de la clase media," in Guillermo Nugent et al., *Peru hoy: la clase media ¿existe?* (Lima: Desco, 2003). Also Gonzalo Portocarrero, ed., *Las clases medias: entre la pretensión y la incertidumbre* (Lima: SUR/Oxfam, 1998).

45. On the "middle-class poor," see David S. Parker, Los pobres de la clase media: estilo de vida, consumo e identidad en una ciudad tradicional," in *Mundos Interiores: Lima 1850–1950*, ed. H. Aldo Panfichi and S. Felipe Portocarrero (Lima: CIUP, 1995), 161–65.

46. O'Dougherty, *Consumption Intensified*, chaps. 2–4.

47. Studies that touch on education and the middle class include Soledad Loayza, *Clases medias y política en México: la querella escolar, 1959–1963* (Mexico City: El Colegio de México, 1988), esp. 31–39; Alan Angell, "Classroom Maoists: The Politics of Peruvian Schoolteachers under Military Government," *Bulletin of Latin American Research* 1:2 (May 1982): 1–20; William F. Whyte, "High Level Manpower in Peru," in *Manpower and Education: Country Studies*, ed. F. Harbison and C. Myers (New York: McGraw-Hill, 1964), 37–72.

48. See Oscar Lewis, "The Castro Family," in *Five Families: Mexican Case Studies in the Culture of Poverty* (New York: Basic Books, 1959); and Gabriel Careaga, *Mitos y fantasías de la clase media en México* (Mexico City: Ediciones Océano, 1985), esp. 184–86, on corruption and the bureaucratic mentality. Also Arturo Jauretche, *El medio pelo en la sociedad argentina* (Buenos Aires: Corregidor, 1996), chap. 12 (first edition 1966).

49. P. N. Furbank, *Unholy Pleasure, or the Idea of Social Class* (Oxford: Oxford University Press, 1985), chap. 1.

I

The Debates, 1947–1968

Chapter One

Middle Groups in National Politics in Latin America

John J. Johnson

In this Hispanic American Historical Review *article, published in 1957, John J. Johnson had not yet coined his famous phrase "middle sectors," using "middle groups" instead. But the argument is the same: that the twentieth-century rise of "new" middle groups in commerce and industry had enabled the "traditional" middle sectors (liberal professionals, clergy, military officers, and bureaucrats) to break free from their former political dependence on the old elites. In those countries where the now-allied middle groups also won the electoral support of urban laborers, "one political era ended and another began." In power, governments representing middle-sector interests promoted policies of state-led industrialization, economic and cultural nationalism, public education, and "New Deal" style social legislation. In predicting the future of middle-group politics, Johnson believed that the most likely trend would be toward pragmatic reformism, although he also noted a less than firm commitment to democracy.*

This has been a century of profound changes in Latin America. One of the most significant developments has been the union of important segments of the traditional middle groups of society with major elements of the new middle groups to form highly effective political amalgams. Since to date there has been a close correlation between the political power of the middle groups and their success or failure in winning the mass support of urban labor, they have ordinarily assiduously cultivated those elements. In their efforts to serve both the interests of their own membership and those upon whom they are dependent for popular support, the leaders of the middle groups have pursued tactics and objectives that have left sharp imprints on the internal and external policies of the republic affected. . . .

25

Those that are herein referred to as the traditional middle groups have existed in Latin America almost from the beginning of the colonial period. In general their members come from the ranks of the liberal professions, including the teaching corps, the bureaucracies, the clergy of the Catholic Church and the commissioned officer corps of the armed services. The composition and thinking of these elements have undergone constant modification in this century. . . . The bureaucracies, in particular, have experienced unusual numerical growth while vastly increasing their influence over society as the various states have expanded their responsibilities beyond the strictly political field. The traditional middle elements have in common a relatively high degree of education and a dependence upon intellectual skills for a livelihood.

The new elements in the amalgam evolved out of the upheavals incident to the transition from . . . quasi-feudal agricultural economies to . . . semi-capitalistic industrial economies—most evident today in Argentina, Brazil, Chile, Mexico, and Uruguay. It is from the experiences of those five republics that the examples used in this paper are drawn. Of the owners of urban-controlled capital all are herein considered to belong to the new middle groups except the top level in banking, industry, and commerce at the one extreme and at the other those whose businesses do not provide them with sufficient income to enjoy at least the material symbols of "middleness." Also belonging to the new middle groups are scientists, highly trained technicians, managers of business, and leading officials of organized labor. In Latin America the outward symbols of middleness include living in a "middle class" section of town, enjoying water and indoor sanitary facilities, electricity and at least a few electric appliances; dressing as other members of the middle groups dress; being able to "spare" children so that they may attend school, preferably a private school; and ordinarily, having one or more servants. It is becoming increasingly acceptable for the lady of the house and even daughters to find outside employment in order to maintain family "status."

A significant characteristic common to the new middle groups is their close relationship to commerce and industry. Financially, educationally, culturally, and in certain instances racially and spiritually, they are highly heterogeneous.

In turn the traditional and new middle groups have at least three significant characteristics in common. (1) They are overwhelmingly urban. (2) They are dependents in that they are, in the vast majority, subject to wage worker contracts or draw salaries. (3) They lack, or at least in the past have lacked, the capabilities to take independent political action and consequently are tempted to seek support wherever they can find it.

The entrance of the middle groups into the political arena in Latin America coincided with the first strong stirrings for freedom on the part of the

Iberian colonials. The traditional middle groups were largely responsible for initiating and keeping alive the struggles for independence. Then as assurances of independence multiplied, there emerged a contest for control of the former colonies. In this contest the middle groups soon succumbed to the strength, based upon force and violence, of a trilogy composed of the elites of the land, church, and military. The political supremacy of the trilogy was seldom challenged during the next half-century or more. Under it the traditional middle groups lived a secondary existence as junior partners in an alliance in which the dominant element was strongly committed to the status quo.

The middle groups were offered few opportunities to strengthen any claim that they might have to the political leadership to which they aspired. Any increase in their numbers was rather closely correlated with overall population growth. They did not improve their economic status vis-à-vis the elite groups. The selling price of their skills did not rise, as the supply of those skills kept pace or possibly outran the demand. They were discouraged by their training and temperament from entering any new fields of economic endeavor. They did not increase their responsibilities in their chosen fields since top levels in the bureaucracies, the Church hierarchy and the officer corps of the armed forces ordinarily were reserved for the members of the elite. They had not become social reformers. When they thought of the lower social groups at all, they thought of them as abstractions or in terms of the few individuals they personally knew and helped. A vast inferiority complex which kept them intellectually dependent upon Europe prevented them from evolving an original and at the same time distinctive Latin American insight.

Then, as the nineteenth century drew to a close, there began to take place transformations which the traditional middle groups were able to exploit to their political advantage.

Streams of foreign capital, technicians and immigrant laborers which had begun in mid-century became torrents after 1885. In certain instances, notably in Argentina and Brazil, the agricultural frontiers were pushed out and a shift to large scale commercial farming was made. But it was the impact of foreign capital and "know-how" upon commercial and industrial activities . . . in . . . cities that most markedly affected politics. Urban areas began to feel the growing pains from which they continue to suffer. Cities that formerly . . . served essentially as administrative and cultural centers, and as such were basically consumers of wealth, acquired a new economic function in society.

Economic change and the rise of cities gave birth to two socioeconomic elements—the middle groups of commerce and industry and an industrial proletariat. These new socio-economic components were to become the important twentieth century additions to the Latin American political complex. The one group represented for Latin America a new and dynamic type of wealth and influence—the other a potential broad base for political action. They offered the traditional middle groups politically articulate alternatives to the oligarchies.

The new middle groups, like the traditional middle elements, were more inclined to look to modern, industrial Europe than were the members of the elite. They were willing to pay a higher price for support than were the oligarchies. The owners of commerce and industry and their scientists and managers on the one hand and the professionals, bureaucrats, teachers, and artists on the other had a common objective in modifying the political tactics of the elites.

Urban laborers soon proved themselves a different type from the rural peasants. A large percentage made themselves sufficiently literate to claim the voting privilege. They displayed an intractability and militancy hitherto dormant among the working groups.

As long as the traditional middle groups viewed themselves as essentially defenders of the status quo, the aggressiveness of the urban workers was one thing. It was quite another when representatives of the old and new groups joined forces with the objective of challenging the continued political domination of the elite. The urban workers had not approached the point of independent decision making, and hence could be manipulated. Their militancy complemented the dependence of the middle groups upon the written and spoken word.

When the traditional middle groups cast in their lot with the new urban elements one political era ended and another began. During the one that was closed, those trained in the liberal professions had served as the "watchdogs of the aristocracy." The new era—the current one—got under way when the "watchdogs" and untried new middle groups began to give direction to the politically immature urban laborer. Important sectors of Latin America were about to become vast laboratories for political, social, and economic experimentation with a major objective being to find the formula for attaining and retaining power. Modified versions of socialism, [M]arxism, and fascism would at one time or another threaten to overwhelm the values and institutions that Latin America earlier inherited or borrowed from Western Europe as well as certain ones with indigenous roots.

In Latin America the urban middle groups supported by urban labor won their first clear-cut victory in Uruguay. This success was achieved between 1903, when José Batlle y Ordóñez was first elected to the presidency, and 1915 when he completed his second term. Since 1915 the political leadership in Uruguay consistently has come from the urban middle groups of the south while the political influence on the national scene of the landholders of the livestock-producing north has been progressively weakened.

Hipólito Irigoyen's election in 1916 was the first triumph in a presidential contest in Argentina of a candidate both of the middle groups and appealing to urban labor. The middle groups remained in control for the succeeding decade and a half. They proved to be middle-of-the-roaders. They avoided drastic solutions to vital national problems. They held out some hope to each social group, but never quite trusted the industrial laborer, whose gains in many respects lagged behind those of his contemporaries in Chile, Uruguay, and Mexico. By the late 1920s the political leaders from the middle groups had become more accepted than respected by those upon whom they depended for popular support. When the depression struck, they were easily toppled by the old elites. Then in 1943 the urban groups—this time under the leadership of representatives of middle elements in the armed forces—took over and dominated the political scene at least until late September of 1955 when Juan Domingo Perón was ousted.

In Chile, political leaders from the middle groups first gained supremacy on the national level when Arturo Alessandri was elected to the presidency in 1920. Thereafter the members of the middle groups, backed by urban labor, more or less steadily increased their ability to name high public officials, until by 1952 they could, as they actually did, divide their forces in a presidential election and still retain control of the country.

In Mexico the first decisive victory of the urban middle groups came in 1940 with the election of Manuel Ávila Camacho. In and out of control of the highly unstable situation existing between 1911 and 1916, they were accepted as part of the revolution by the early 1920s. Once accepted, they struggled to reorient the revolution in the face of a constant threat of being submerged by the forces of agrarian radicalism. Under Ávila Camacho and later under Miguel Alemán and Adolfo Ruíz Cortines, the urban groups have raced to create an industrial economy capable of absorbing an ever-expanding labor supply before the laborers themselves erupt against the immediate price to them of greater industrialization. Politically the reorientation of the revolution meant a shift from left of center to right of center and then a settling back toward dead center. The remarkable phenomenon of Mexico making these political adjustments without serious infraction of its political stability can, it seems, be explained only in terms of the steadying influence of its middle groups.

In Brazil the urban middle groups won their first presidential victory in 1945. However, for fifteen years prior to that time, the social and economic programs of the Getulio Vargas regime, in broad outline, were designed to appeal to those social components which give the leadership from the middle groups its popular base. Since the middle groups' original triumph at the polls, the heat of political conflict generated by Vargas and those who inherited his mantle has made political alignments largely meaningless. Nevertheless, the preeminence of the political leadership from the middle groups has been clearly discernible during the past half-decade. The middle groups joined with labor to elect Vargas in 1950. When, forced to operate within a constitutional strait jacket, Vargas failed to produce the magic touch that he at times appeared to possess as dictator (1930–1945), the middle groups, if not labor, approved the action of the military which led to his suicide. Juscelino Kubitschek was elected to the Brazilian presidency in October 1955, with strong middle group backing.

The growing influence of the urban middle groups in the twentieth century has produced a new set of national concerns in which essentially socioeconomic issues have supplanted basically politico-religious ones. This shift of emphasis has in turn spawned new political requirements, tactics, and objectives.

There have been changes in what constitutes an individual's political assets. The advantages of an urban, commercial, industrial orientation have increased. The elevation of the life-long public servant, Adolfo Ruíz Cortines, to the rank of first citizen of Mexico suggests that the benefits of bureaucratic background to the office seeker are also on the increase. Of course a single swallow does not make a summer. However, it would be in line with the political mentality of large numbers of individuals belonging to the middle groups to favor the manipulatable type of chief executive, as represented by Ruíz Cortines, over the decisive men of action that historically have occupied the center of the stage in Latin American politics.

The techniques and appeals of the new political leadership are in strong contrast with those employed by the representatives of the ruling elites in an earlier era. The new type office seeker has made electioneering a part of every major campaign. His simple and direct appeals are aimed at the formerly forgotten masses. He speaks in terms of larger loaves of bread and shoes for unshod feet. His predecessors made capital of defending individualism; but the politician from the middle groups ordinarily today goes to great pains to place society above the individual, to make himself a spokesman of the masses. He emphasizes social justice rather than legal justice, social equality rather than political equality, the right to wealth over the right to vote. He favors a "Vital State" that makes economic problems the fundamental political problem. He speaks of the "nation for its nationals." His is economic nationalism—the nationalism that has come to express the thinking of so many people impatient for more rapid material progress. His economic nationalism is in marked contrast with cultural nationalism, which in its beginnings over a half century ago was bandied about by intellectuals more as a form of mental exercise than as a club with which to bludgeon political opponents. He writes constitutions that reflect the new social and economic requirements of society, constitutions which contrast sharply with earlier ones that were often little more than political treatises.

In office, the representatives of the new amalgam have ranged the political spectrum. They have, as in Uruguay, made respect for democratic processes and the dignity of the individual within the greater social complex not only a political but a moral obligation. In Mexico the new groups took over and perpetuated a political party which through control of the nation's electoral machinery has monopolized power for a quarter of a century. In Argentina, under Perón, they successfully adapted fascist and communist methods to the Argentine scene to make a mockery of representative government. These are but examples. Tentatively the feeling is that those who speak for the middle groups ordinarily view representative government and political democracy as luxuries which can readily be priced out of the ideological market.

To date public officials from the middle groups have relied heavily upon the sponsorship of advanced social legislation to win popular support. In fact much of the social legislation to come out of Latin America has been so impregnated with political propaganda that the separation of the social and political aspects are practically impossible. So long as those sectors of the economy required to finance social legislation remained primarily in foreign hands, the politician could hope to derive advantage by simultaneously offering himself as a friend of the working man and an enemy of foreign domination. Now that politically articulate native capitalists are being called upon to carry a growing share of the costs of social welfare, the demands have become incessant that the politicians, in effect, tell the working man that he cannot expect the same consideration when he fights domestic interests as when he served as the protagonist against "foreign rapacity." It may be that the survival of the middle groups in their presently strong political position is dependent upon their success in moderating labor-capital differences that in the past they were influential in bringing to the surface for purposes of political exploitation.

It appears certain that for some time a large majority of individuals belonging to the middle groups have given top priority to economic emancipation from more highly developed areas of the world. Governments representing the urban groups have seized upon this desire to enter the commercial and industrial fields. When domestic private capital has been lacking, the State has among other things used its power to encourage industrialization by providing credits, making direct investments and guaranteeing loans. These measures have often been taken at the price of budgetary deficits and a highly important, but as yet undetermined, price to agriculture.

In the field of international relations the representatives of governments dominated by the middle groups have been faced with seriously conflicting sets of interests. In essence their problem has been to reconcile a desire for the prestige they associate with decision making on the international level with an ardent nationalism which demands that acute internal social and economic problems be placed above the more remote problems of living together as a community of nations. To the extent to which these governments share in the responsibilities of carrying out international policies they have helped to formulate, they seek to do so in such a way as to leave no doubt of their independence of action.

Examples drawn from the above discussion could be used, as similar ones have been from time to time, to establish the inability of the new amalgam to rule effectively. The unwillingness of the middle groups to circumscribe their activities in the name of ideology could be employed to support the contention that they are today as lacking in political maturity as they were a quarter of a century ago. The tactics of their representatives, including the liberal use of demagoguery, could be utilized to indicate a strong current of political opportunism among them. Their approaches to economic problems could be employed in labeling the middle groups as champions of statism as the surest means of satisfying an aspiration to manage the wheels of industry and commerce which their own economic status prevents them from owning. The legislation which they have sponsored in the name of the public good could be construed as designed to delay solutions to basic social conflicts. Their deviations from the majority Western position could be employed in charging them with the lack of a high sense of international responsibility.

But there is another side to the coin. Even during periods of most rampant radicalism the middle groups have contained elements that have exercised a restraining influence along lines prescribed by what they have considered traditional to Latin America. The most urgent searches for solutions during the last quarter century were not permitted to alter basically the political framework within which the various republics operate. Throughout, the leadership of the middle groups continued to pay its respects to political democracy which generation after generation of Latin Americans have held to be their objective. The tendency for national government under the leadership of the middle groups to usurp power from the states and municipalities is not a new one. The general practice, under the leadership of the middle groups, for ultimate and final authority to reside in the executive branch of government is as old as is republican Latin America. The middle groups *can* probably be credited with speeding up the process of broadening the base of the political pyramid. It may be that their share in the broadening of the political base, with all that is implied in such a phenomenon, will prove to be the greatest single impact the middle groups have had to date upon the Latin American way of life.

It is perhaps too early to say just how bold the middle groups have been in the economic field. There are strong suggestions, however, that they have been less daring than they themselves have at times claimed and their opponents have charged. Certainly it can justifiably be asked if the threat to accepted concepts of private ownership of property and of private enterprise have been any greater in Latin America than in a number of the more mature nations of the western world. The middle groups' view of land ownership can hardly be termed radical. In Uruguay, Chile, Brazil, and Argentina, official representatives of the middle groups have largely avoided making decisions which would noticeably affect the pattern of land ownership. Even in Mexico, the middle groups have dared to meet the agrarian problem by placing the emphasis more upon scientific use of land already in production and bringing new areas under cultivation than upon the subdivision of the remaining extralegal holdings.

Contrary to what those who view attacks upon foreign capital as attacks upon private capital in general would sometimes have us believe, regimes under the leadership of the middle groups have left an important segment of commerce and industry open to individual initiative. The very rapidly expanding wholesale and retail trades have continued to be almost a complete monopoly of private enterprise, as has the highly speculative building trade. Favorable legislation has made the manufacturing industries generally profitable to private ventures. In the transportation field in particular, governments controlled by middle groups have invited private competition with public operated enterprises. More great fortunes are presently being accumulated in industry and commerce than ever before in the history of the republics.

The Catholic Church seemingly has been little affected adversely by the increased participation of the urban middle groups in the affairs of state. The view of the middle groups has been in broad outline a continuation of the one taken by the so-called anti-clericals during the nineteenth century, namely to restrict the church as completely as possible to the spiritual field. Recent developments in Mexico and Argentina strongly suggest that the Catholic Church has firm friends within the middle group leadership as it traditionally has had. The same may be said of Colombia.

Although there has been cause for misgivings over the conduct of the new governments in the United Nations, the record shows that they have been strongly oriented toward the Western bloc. They have disagreed with the United States on the extent of the threat of international communism. They have on occasion supported the Arab-Asiatic bloc on colonial issues to the embarrassment of the major Western powers. But their overall voting and abstention from voting leave little doubt where they stand.

Tentatively then it would appear that those governments dominated by the new amalgams have not hesitated to employ novel and unorthodox maneuvers to obtain and retain power. Also, it would appear that representatives of the middle groups have been less moderate while seeking office than when charged with the national welfare. If they have not always been as others would have them be, neither have they been guilty of some of the more damning charges that have been hurled at them.

In conclusion and with no desire to suggest that the pressure to seek radical solutions has passed, it should be observed that recently the forces of moderation within the middle groups have gained adherents from among those who out of economic self-interest or through loss of faith in simple

John J. Johnson

answers to complex questions have come to prefer more orthodox approaches. When and where this has occurred—during 1955 Argentina and Brazil would seem to offer the best examples—the moderates have worked to slow down the rate of change generated by their predecessors.

The temper of current thinking suggests that the middle groups are approaching the day when they will have to reexamine their political arrangements. They would seem to have a choice of several alternatives. They might achieve a degree of unity which, given their appreciable numerical growth in recent years, would give them considerable independent strength and hence freedom for political action. Or they might favor abating welfare policies dear to the working elements and seek alignments with those who have come to control wealth. Or, finally, they might reaffirm their political cooperation with the working elements. The latter alternative will be particularly attractive. There are still many unfulfilled demands of the expanding and articulate working elements. There are still many belonging to the middle groups who believe it is possible to telescope social and economic processes. But whatever the course of the middle groups, they have become an active force in the political process and will continue to affect meaningfully the development of Latin America.

NOTE

This chapter was previously published in the *Hispanic American Historical Review* 37, no. 3 (Aug. 1957): 313–29.

Chapter Two

Aspects of Class Relations in Chile, 1850–1960

Fredrick B. Pike

Fredrick B. Pike's historical analysis of the relationship between upper, middle, and lower classes in Chile is an implicit critique of Johnson. Writing in 1963, Pike notes Chile's historical fusion of urban and rural elites, as well as the openness of those elites to new blood. Both trends, he believes, diminished conflict between the "oligarchy" and the urban middle groups. He argues that the more significant social gulf was that separating this open, hybrid elite from workers and the poor, whom elites and middle groups alike continue to view with a mixture of arrogant disdain, racism, and fear. Drawing primarily on Chilean essayists and social commentators from the late nineteenth and early twentieth centuries, Pike depicts a middle class that attempts to emulate upper-class lifestyles and values, that consumes beyond its means, that sees itself as "white," that supports the political status quo, and that lacks any distinct class consciousness of its own. See Pablo Silva's critical and historiographical discussion of Pike later in this volume.

Between 1830 and the outbreak of the War of the Pacific in 1879, Chile made remarkable progress in establishing political stability and devising smoothly functioning politico-economic institutions. Still, many Chilean observers remained highly critical of their country's accomplishments. Of all the analysts of the contemporary scene, perhaps the most brilliant was Miguel Cruchaga Montt, economist of the laissez-faire school and professor of economics at the University of Chile. A prolific author, Cruchaga published his major work in 1878, *Estudio sobre la organización económica y la hacienda pública de Chile*,[1] which contains one of the first criticisms of the Chilean middle class to appear in non-fiction writing.

Examining his country's past, Cruchaga concluded that colonial practices had bequeathed a legacy that impeded economic progress. Cruchaga felt

Chile's only hope for development and progress lay in giving the lower classes some share in society. Education might encourage the masses not only to lead better moral lives but equip them to produce and therefore to earn enough to enjoy adequate material comfort. Education might also instill in the middle class respect for the virtues of work, efficiency, and frugality. Once these goals were achieved, Cruchaga hoped the Chilean upper classes would abandon their inordinate devotion to economic activity and leave the nation's material development to the middle class. The upper classes could then, by turning to pursuits of mind and soul, produce a Chilean culture.

Subsequent developments in the nineteenth century prevented realization of the division of labor between middle and upper classes urged by Cruchaga. Instead, the trend toward the creation of a middle-class, upper-class amalgam gained momentum. . . . By the 1850s a new class, its wealth based on commerce, industry, banking, and above all on mining, was coming to occupy positions of social and political importance formerly reserved to landowners who could trace their lineage back to colonial times. . . . By the mid-nineteenth century, [Chile] was revealing a remarkable tolerance for allowing entry of new blood into the ranks of the social elite. Even more striking, by the latter part of the century the upper class was studded with the names of foreigners whose grandfathers had arrived in the country only around the time of independence. From the United Kingdom had come settlers with the names of Ross, Edwards, Lyon, Walker, MacClure, Garland, MacIver, Jackson, Brown, Price, Phillips, Waddington, Blest, Simpson, Eastman, Budge, Page, and others; from France came the Cousiño, Subercaseaux, and Rogers families; while from Slavic and German areas had come the Piwonkas and the Königs. A survey of Chilean biographical encyclopedias, or membership lists for such elite organizations as the Club de la Unión, or of the roll of the stock-market founders,[2] and a scanning of prominent names in diplomacy, politics, and the fine arts will reveal the prominence that these names have enjoyed from the mid-to-late nineteenth century to the present time. A conspicuous factor in this development was the "well-known preference" of Chilean ruling classes for marrying their children to financially successful immigrants and their descendants.[3]

. . . The social and political merging of middle and upper groups produced a cross-pollenization between apparently opposed political philosophies. Championed largely by middle groups, nineteenth--century liberalism in Chile taught that poverty was something of a disgrace, but that the humble man could and should rise and thereby gain honorable status and the power of self-protection. The upper groups, on the other hand, generally advanced the conservative belief that poverty was no disgrace but rather the estate richest in the means of salvation, and that lower groups should not aspire to political articulateness or to a status of comfort that they themselves could safeguard and augment. To gain even the tolerance of the advocates of the liberal philosophy, the masses had to attain precisely what the conservatives were dedicated to prevent them from attaining: self-improvement, self-assertiveness, and a rise in social status. Through the years, beginning in the latter nineteenth century, the social and political contact between middle and upper groups led to a mingling of their philosophical principles. Liberals, at least those who became successful, were enticed by the practical convenience of the concept of a providentially ordained stratified society. They came to question the perfectibility of the lower class, and thus grew increasingly indifferent to supplying its members with opportunities to advance. Conservatives, influenced by secular, material standards, questioned the feasibility of supplying paternalistic protection to groups that appeared to lack economic virtues and the capitalist mentality. Middle and upper groups tended therefore to join in a disparaging attitude toward the lower mass.

This disparaging attitude contributed significantly to the neglect shown by the ruling class to the social problem that began to manifest itself during the parliamentary period, 1892–1920. Other factors also contributed to the indifference with which urban middle and upper groups regarded a growing urban proletariat. Between 1892 and 1920 the Chilean population increased by only one-half million, rising from 3.3 to 3.8 million.[4] Yet, the demographic shift underway was startling. The urban population, only 27 percent of the total in 1875, had risen to over 43 percent in 1902.[5] From 1885 to 1895, the population of Santiago went up over 30 percent, and by 1907 had increased an additional 22 percent. During the same two periods the population of Antofagasta rose 58 percent and 73 percent, of Iquique 76 percent and 16 percent, of Concepción 50 percent and 27 percent, and of Valparaíso 15 percent and 24 percent.[6]

In short, the period from 1885 to 1907 witnessed the most dramatic population shift in Chile's history. The *inquilinos* or serfs who had previously labored on the vast estates of southern Chile and the central valley flocked in unprecedented numbers to northern and central towns. In their migration, the rural masses passed directly from a manorial situation—in which they had been cared for paternalistically, had never learned to protect themselves in a competitive society, and had almost never acquired education—into the modern conditions of semi-industrial urban life. In the rural setting they had at least possessed sufficient skill to be useful to their *patrones*. In the cities they had no skills to offer. They comprised a vast pool of untrained, largely unproductive, brute labor. The rising industrial and commercial capitalists would have been more than human if they had not exploited the new urban masses. And even as the element of *noblesse oblige* disappeared from the employer-employee relationship when the rural masses crowded into the city, so also the bonds between the *patrón* and the *inquilinos* who remained on the agricultural estates were weakened as the landowners began to maintain their principal residences in Concepción, Santiago, or Paris. Under these conditions, human labor fell increasingly into disrepute. . . .

Socially, the important feature of Chile's move to the cities was the manner in which a landed aristocracy either became, or merged with, an urban upper or middle class earlier and more completely than elsewhere in Latin America. A strictly landowning aristocracy dwindled in importance as absentee owners, continuing the process initiated in the middle of the nineteenth century, invested in urban pursuits and married into the new-money classes of the mushrooming cities. In addition, the urban rich found continuing opportunities to gain the distinction of rural landownership, especially when many older families of social prominence lost their fortunes in the 1907 stock-market crash and were forced to sell their lands.[7] By the turn-of-the-century period, then, urban and rural interests were crossed and crisscrossed to such a degree as to make the distinction often meaningless.

From these conditions resulted a close union between new, urban--middle and old, rural-upper classes. A hybrid aristocracy, together with urban middle-class supporters, came into being, and neither aristocrats nor middle sectors were under pressure to minister to the needs of the lower classes. The urban nouveaux riches, both upper and middle class, found it totally unnecessary to enlist the aid of the city proletariat in a struggle with the old order, for they had already joined or were in the process of joining the old order. Nor were the landowners willing, as occasionally they have been in Peru and other countries, to support modest reforms of strictly urban application. In Chile, urban and rural interests were becoming too intertwined to permit landowners to pursue this policy. Similarly, because of interlocking features, urban interests were unwilling to press for rural reforms. Thus, upper and middle classes, old and new or potential aristocrats, rural and urban sectors united in regarding the lower classes, wherever found, as fair prey.[8]

. . . The alliance of middle and upper groups in what came to assume characteristics of a class war against the lower mass has continued through the years. Chile's urban middle sectors have largely persisted in manifesting indifference to the social problem. At the same time they have dedicated themselves to the defense of traditional, upper-class value judgments.[9] The readily observable traits of the middle class have led to the introduction into the Chilean vocabulary of the word *siútico*. Such a person is a middle-class individual who emulates the aristocracy and its usages and hopes to be taken for one of its members.[10] It is generally agreed that Chile's middle class abounds in *siúticos*.

Because of their desire to assume upper-class attitudes, middle groups have developed very little consciousness of themselves as members of a distinct class. It is extremely difficult to detect opinions, customs, and value judgments in Chile that are demonstrably middle class. Almost the only clear middle-class trait has been the tendency to shun the lower mass and to embrace the aristocracy. . . . It is also revealing that the first attempt to mold the middle class into a cohesive, articulate group, leading in 1919 to the formation of the *Federación de la Clase Media*, produced a platform which, although containing a mild warning to the oligarchy to refrain from some of its more notorious abuses, said absolutely nothing about aiding the lower classes.[11] A decade later, Santiago Macchiavello speculated that Chile's main ills had stemmed from exploitation of the lower by the middle class, and from the attempt by members of the latter to pose as aristocrats and therefore to shun all useful and productive work.[12] In the early 1930s, when Chile was suffering from the effects of the depression, *El Mercurio* noted approvingly that in these times of crisis, the Chilean middle class had once again demonstrated its customary responsibility by siding with the upper classes in the attempt to cope with economic disruption.[13]

Journalist Jorge Gustavo Silva observed in 1930 that "in whatever profession they enter, middle-class elements seek to obscure their humble origins and to convert themselves, even at the risk of appearing ridiculous, into aristocrats and oligarchs."[14] A much more scathing attack against the middle class was delivered by Gabriela Mistral. The great poetess charged it with having turned viciously upon the manual laborers and with having failed to contribute to balanced national development.[15] She noted also the revulsion felt by novelist Pedro Prado for the middle class because of the manner in which it had harassed the humble people.[16] Distinguished author Domingo Melfi suggested in 1948 that the plot situation which had most intrigued Chilean novelists in the twentieth century was the rise of a middle-class hero into the aristocracy, either by the acquisition of wealth or by a judicious marriage. To Melfi, this indicated the lack of middle-class consciousness.[17] Other journalists and critics, as Raúl Silva Castro, Manuel Rojas, and Hernán Díaz Arrieta (pseud., Alone), have agreed that middle and upper-class authors alike have tended to ignore in their fiction the theme of Chile's social problem and the plight of the masses.[18]

Raúl Alarcón Pino, author of the principal—but nonetheless superficial—university dissertation that has been written on the Chilean middle class, notes that the main vice of this social sector is its adoration of the aristocracy's way of life.[19] Alarcón Pino asserts that the Chilean middle class has remained steadfastly unconvinced that it has any common purpose with the lower classes.[20] Much the same message is conveyed by Francisco Pinto Salvatierra, who argues that the overriding cause of Chilean stagnation, which allegedly threatens to become retrogression, is the total indifference of the middle class to the mounting social and economic problems of the masses.[21]

As much as any single Chilean writer and intellectual, Julio Vega has studied the role of the middle class. Vega has concluded that in Chile there is no artisan tradition. The artisan's chief desire is that his son should enter one of the professions that is recognized as the province of the upper classes. [22] Members of the lower middle class, Vega observed, will spend most of their income on clothes and housing, trying to present an upper-class façade. The result is that not enough of the budget is allocated for food, and consequently some middle-class members are actually more undernourished than the lower classes. [23]

An observer of the social scene in 1951, Julio Heise González, offered assurances that the middle class had begun finally to develop a class consciousness, to emancipate itself from prejudice, to withdraw from the traditional aristocracy, and to approach the proletariat. Two pages later in the same work he seemed to contradict himself when he stated that members of the middle class were perpetuating their poverty by their conspicuous consumption, apparently in the desire to create the impression that they belonged to a higher social level than actually they did. [24]

The number of authors who have commented upon the middle-class betrayal and exploitation of the manual laborers is imposing. Because of their number and their close agreement, their charges cannot be lightly dismissed. This writer's own observations and conversations in Chile have confirmed, moreover, that the country is still to a large degree characterized by a close association between upper and middle groups which works to the disadvantage of the lower mass. . . .

Probably the attitudes of Chile's middle class have produced an important superficial advantage for the country. Because this group has in its political, social, and economic thinking so closely reflected the attitudes of the aristocracy, there has been almost no disruption as middle sectors have won increasing power in Chilean politics. This has contributed notably to Chilean stability. The role assumed by middle sectors may also have contributed to economic and social stagnation.

Obviously, not all middle-class members uphold aristocratic values. As of 1960 there were many signs that middle groups might be seeking an alliance with the lower classes and not, as in the past, simply trying to play the game of political opportunism. Stung by inflation and with their hopes for expanding opportunities frustrated by Chile's lack of real growth, some middle-class supporters of the Christian Democrat Party, of the activist wing of the Radical Party, and of the FRAP (an alliance of socialists and communists) seemed intent upon siding with the lower mass in a genuine attempt to alter the traditional socio-political structure. Some of the young members of the Conservative Party seemed also to fit into this category. This was a relatively new development in Chilean politics, one that could in the years ahead prove to be of great significance.

There are still many obstacles to cooperation between middle groups and the lower masses. One of these is the educational structure. Since early in this century Chilean educators and intellectuals have pointed out the inadequacy and outmoded orientation of national education. In 1910 Alejandro Venegas in *Sinceridad*[25] charged that education in Chile produced stuffy sycophants of the aristocracy, utterly devoid of interest in the common good, and unable to contribute to the vitally needed economic progress of their country. *El Mercurio* in 1916 observed: "We have among us thousands of university graduates who are true monuments of uselessness, and at the same time a living indictment of our national educational system."[26]

More recently, criticisms of a similar nature have been made. Many of these are well summarized in the writings of Amanda Labarca, who for longer than she might care to recall has been one of Chile's outstanding *pensadores*, feminists, and educators. Possessing faith in the ultimate role of the middle class in moving Chile ahead, Labarca feels that a superannuated educational system has unduly delayed this class in fulfilling its destiny.[27] Coming to the heart of the problem, another writer-educator urged in 1950 that education begin to emancipate itself from the social prejudices which led 99 percent of those entering the *liceo* to want to be professionals, so as to gain access to the world of the aristocracy. Educators, it was further alleged, had passively permitted the continuing neglect of those studies that would be genuinely useful in developing the country.[28]

Chilean education has continued to be characterized by its lack of attention to technical training and by its emphasis on the philosophical approach. This has not only slowed the rate of economic progress, but has meant that the typical middle-class product of the national educational system—which is largely controlled by middle-class, Radical- Party bureaucrats—has been taught to think like an aristocrat of a past century and to disdain manual labor and those who perform it.

Contributing also to a gulf between middle and lower groups are racial considerations. The majority of Chile's lower classes display recognizable Indian features, often manifest in some degree of skin-darkness. On the other hand, the great majority of the middle and practically the entirety of the upper classes do not clearly exhibit physical characteristics attributable to Indian blood. This fact has exercised profound effects upon the nation's social structure.

Racist interpretations are commonplace in Chile. Early in the twentieth century Nicolás Palacios, in a very popular book, *La raza chilena* (1911), suggested that Chilean superiority over other Latin American populations stemmed largely from the predominance of Basque, or actually Gothic, blood. In later times one of the most convinced of Chile's many racists has been the distinguished and prolific historian Francisco Antonio Encina, who basically repeats the Palacios assertions about the superiority of Gothic blood.[29] Marxian-socialist author Julio César Jobet appeared to be largely justified when he accused Encina in 1949 of believing in the racist theories of Joseph Arthur de Gobineau and Houston Stewart Chamberlain.[30] Similar charges could be leveled against such Chilean *pensadores* as the extremely active Carlos Keller, the late Alberto Edwards Vives, and a multitude of lesser writers, especially those active in neofascist and *hispanista* movements.

If Chilean superiority is regarded as the consequence of Basque or Gothic blood, what place is left for the Indian and those who share his blood? It is not necessary to search far in Chilean literature for the answer, for anti-Indian writings are vast in number. A random sampling illustrates the broad aspects of the prejudice that is an important national characteristic. One writer asserted that the reason for high infant mortality is the stupidity and proneness toward uncleanliness and drunkenness which Indian blood inevitably produced in the lower classes;[31] another stated that the mental inferiority of the Araucanians is recognized by almost all Chileans;[32] while from still a different source came the pronouncement that the racial superiority of the white upper classes made unavoidable the exploitation of the inferior, mixed-blood, lower classes.[33] A prominent army general contended that Indians are lazy, dirty, irresponsible, and that southern Chile was doomed unless Indian influence was eradicated by European immigration.[34] A noted intellectual was even more pessimistic, observing that because Chilean lower classes in general had a certain proportion of Indian blood, national progress was unlikely unless a veritable flood of white immigration descended upon the entire country.[35] Echoing this pessimistic tone, another writer suggested that the Indian mentality, which could not advance beyond concepts of subsistence production, was responsible for Chile's problems.[36] On the other hand, there have been many writers who although defending the Indian have sadly noted the prevailing tendency to hold aborigines and those sharing their blood in contempt,[37] and to consider the Indians and mixed-bloods as an impediment to national progress.[38]

The anti-Indian prejudice may explain why the visitor to Chile is assured over and over again, "We have no Indians, and therefore no Indian problem, here." The typical Chilean attitude was expressed once by Deputy Ricasio Retamales who during congressional debates interjected: "What, are there still Indians in Chile? I think not."[39] For a Chilean who is proudly nationalistic and optimistic about the progress potential of his country, and who is at the same time convinced of the inferiority of Indians and mestizos, it is convenient to forget the overwhelming evidence of Indian blood among the lower classes and the fact that, as Benjamín Subercaseaux has observed, the Chilean lower class is distinguished primarily by its color.[40] It is possible that the cruel treatment of the mixed-blood lower classes has stemmed from the fact that upper and middle sectors would really be happier if somehow the reminder of Indian inheritance in Chile could be stamped out.

The factor of Indian blood has contributed in telling manner to the traditional middle-class rejection of the lower mass. Priding itself on its whiteness, the middle class to a large extent has believed in the inferiority of Indians and mixed bloods. Clinging to the aristocracy, it has erected a psychological barrier between itself and at least one-third of the population. To a subtler, but to just as deep-rooted an extent as in Peru, Ecuador, Bolivia, and Guatemala, the Indian problem, or a variant of it, is involved in Chile's social and economic ills.   *Prediction*

. . . If Chile's ruling class, made up of an amalgam of upper and middle sectors, does not accommodate itself to new forces, it may be swept away. Despite their many human shortcomings and failures, the ruling classes of Chile have demonstrated wisdom, talent, and responsibility in degree sufficient to compile a proud political tradition for their country. An established aristocracy learned in the nineteenth century how to accommodate to new forces. If this success is not repeated in the present century, then the ruling group instead of assimilating will likely be replaced by men who initially at least may possess less ability and whose exercise of power will not necessarily bring greater integrity or balance to national administration.

NOTES

This chapter was previously published in the *Hispanic American Historical Review* 43, no. 1 (Feb. 1963): 14–33.

1. A second edition of the work was published in Madrid in 1929.
2. Luis Escobar Cerda, in *El mercado de valores* (1959), reveals the prevalence of first- and second-generation Chileans among the founders of the stock market.
3. Julio Heise González, *La constitución de 1925 y las nuevas tendencias político-sociales* (1950), 154.
4. Oficina Central de Estadística, *Sinopsis estadística y jeográfica de Chile en 1891* (1892); Dirección General de Estadística, X *censo de la población efectuado el 27 de noviembre de 1930* (1935), vol. 3, xix.
5. *Memoria presentada al Supremo Gobierno por la Comisión Central de Censo* (1910), 1262. P. León Alterman, "El movimiento demográfico en Chile" (thesis, 1946); Alfredo Rodríguez, *Los movimientos de población* (1900); Armando Vergara, *La población en Chile* (1900). Julio César Jobet, "Movimiento social obrero," in Universidad de Chile, *Desarrollo de Chile en la primera mitad del siglo XX* (1953), vol. 1, esp. 66 ff.
6. Dirección General de Estadística, *X censo*, vol. 2, 167.
7. Humberto Fuenzalida Villegas, "La conquista del territorio y la utilización durante la primera mitad del siglo xx," *Desarrollo*, vol. 1, 11–34.
8. Jorge Ahumada, *En vez de la miseria* (1958), 53; Alberto Edwards Vives and Eduardo Frei, *Historia de los partidos politicos chilenos* (1949), 145–63.
9. When aristocrat Luis Orrego Luco published his powerful novel *Casa grande* (1910), in which he attacked the vices of the oligarchy, it was primarily middle-class writers who rallied to the defense of their allegedly affronted brethren. See Domingo Melfi, "La novela *Casa grande y* la transformación de la sociedad chilena," *Anales de la Universidad de Chile* 111, nos. 69–72 (1948).
10. Ricardo Valdés, " Sobre el siútico criollo," *Pacífico Magazine*, January 1919.
11. El Diario Ilustrado, 19 May 1919.
12. Macchiavello, *Política económica nacional* (1929).
13. *El Mercurio,* 1 April 1932.
14. Silva, *Nuestra evolución político-social, 1900–1930* (1930), 100.

15. Mistral, *Recados contando a Chile* (1957), 92–93.

16. Mistral, *Recados*, 99.

17. Melfi, "La novela Casa grande."

18. *La Nación*, 28 November 1930.

19. Alarcón Pino, "La clase media en Chile" (thesis, 1947), 95.

20. Ibid., 98–99.

21. Pinto Salvatierra, *La clase media y socialismo* (1941), 9.

22. Vega, "La clase media en Chile," in *Materiales para el estudio de la clase media en la américa latina* (Washington, 1950), 80.

23. Vega, "La clase media en Chile," 87.

24. Heise González, *La constitución de 1925*, 159, 161.

25. Dr. J. Valdés Canje (pseudonym), *Sinceridad: Chile íntimo en 1910.*

26. *El Mercurio*, 10 February 1916.

27. Amanda Labarca, *Bases para una política educacional* (Buenos Aires, 1944); *Historia de la enseñanza en Chile* (1939); *Realidades y problemas de nuestra enseñanza* (1953).

28. Vega, "La clase media en Chile."

29. Francisco Encina, *Historia de Chile desde la prehistoria hasta 1891* (1943), esp. vol. 3, chaps. 3–5.

30. Jobet, "Notas sobre la historiografía," in Ricardo Donoso et al., *Historiografía chilena* (1949), 354–55.

31. León Alterman P., *El movimiento demográfico en Chile* (1946), 60.

32. Enrique L. Marshall, "Los araucanos ante el derecho penal" (thesis, 1917), 41.

33. E. Maguire Ibar, *Formación racial chilena* (1949), 13, 64.

34. Arturo Ahumada, quoted in *El Mercurio*, 4 March 1928.

35. Onofre Lindsay, *El problema fundamental: la repoblación de Chile y los estados unidos de Sudamérica* (1925), 38.

36. Francisco Javier Díaz Salazar, "La influencia racial en la actividad económica de los indígenas chilenos" (thesis, 1940), 13.

37. Humberto Gacitúa Vergara, "Estudio social y consideraciones legales del problema indígena en Chile" (thesis, 1916), 4.

38. José Inalaf Navarro, "Rol económico, social, y político del indígena en Chile" (thesis, 1945), 9.

39. Cámara de Diputados, *Boletín de sesiones extraordinarias, 1929*, Sesión 15, November 20.

40. Subercaseaux, "La super gente bien," *Zig Zag*, 27 March 1954, 51.

Chapter Three

Community Pillars: The Middle Class

Andrew H. Whiteford

Anthropologist Andrew Whiteford's study of middle-class lifestyles is the product of fieldwork carried out in Querétaro, Mexico, and Popayán, Colombia, between 1950 and 1957. Using interviews, questionnaires, and participant observation, Whiteford examined how ordinary people in each city talked about themselves and their neighbors as members of one class or another, and what they believed determined the class to which one belonged. Whiteford found that informants in Querétaro distinguished between three different types of middle-class people: the clase media acomodada *(comfortable middle class), the* clase media sin dinero *(middle class without money), and the* clase media sin cultura *(middle class without culture/education). In an attempt to give those phrases some social science precision, Whiteford translates them as "Upper Middle," "Middle Middle," and "Lower Middle Class." In the process he almost hides his most important insight: that Queretanos distinguished people on several different hierarchical scales, including wealth and occupation but also education, lifestyle, manners, and culture. The citizens of more isolated Popayán had a simpler set of class categories that reflected their city's more limited social mobility and the weight of tradition. Middle-class behavior and aspirations in Popayán tended to follow the lead of the upper class.*

THE SEARCH FOR THE MIDDLE CLASS

The study of the Middle Class in Latin America is an exploration into unknown territory. It is a territory which has been mapped from the air, and through which casual observers have passed hurriedly, but it has almost never been examined at close range. And yet many articles have been written about the Middle Class during the past decade, for there is a growing recognition among social scientists and others that an understanding of this social segment is essential to our understanding of the contemporary society of Latin America.

The major result of the many articles and essays about the Middle Class seems to have been the demonstration of a conviction that such a social phenomenon does indeed exist in Latin America. Such an unspectacular conclusion would hardly appear worthy of mention except that it succeeded in giving quietus to the widespread belief that a "real Middle Class" existed only in the industrialized countries of Northern Europe and North America, and the social structure of Latin America consisted of a clear dichotomy, with the aristocracy at the top and the working people at the bottom—perhaps with a thin line of socially unclassifiable merchants between them.

MIDDLE CLASS RANGE AND DIVERSIONS

As times changed, as revolutions toppled the mighty and raised the lowly, different kinds of people graced the ranks of the Middle Class. Rude soldiers and uneducated but clever peons seized their opportunities and, with newly acquired properties and wealth, established themselves as solid members of the Middle Class. Others, who were still cleverer or had even more opportunities, simply passed through the middle class on their way to an Upper Class mode of life. Still others arrived in the Middle Class from the opposite direction as their fortunes dwindled, their properties were sold or confiscated, and their society disappeared. Some of these former aristocrats lost their pride with their possessions, and Queretanos tell of a scion of one of the wealthy old families who now sells pigs in the market, but a much greater number of the old aristocracy who remained in the community clung tenaciously to the manners, interests, and refinements of their former status.

These various elements contributed to the Middle Class of Querétaro to make it what it was in the middle of the twentieth century. This does not mean that it consisted simply of a loose amalgam of ambitious Lower Class people and declining members of the Upper Class. It was not merely an undefined area between the extremes of the society, but actually possessed in itself a reality which gave its members a sense of identification and position. Its members interacted with each other, conscious of the social position which they shared and proud of the characteristics which distinguished them from the other classes:

> Speaking in general terms, you don't find professional people in the Upper Class. This is true, I feel, because the members of the aristocratic class feel that they are above everybody else, either because they have a lot of money or because they have blue blood. Their sons don't have any motivation. They don't see any reason for having culture or getting an education. This is how the Middle Class is primarily distinguished from the Upper Class.

This type of evaluation was expressed frequently by members of the Middle Class, emphasizing their self-identification as the pillars of culture and learning in the community. Another example:

> The people of the *Clase Media Acomodada* (Upper Middle) are refined. They use the best language, they are interested in music, art, history, and literature. This isn't the case at all in the Upper Class. I think this is the same as in the United States or in any part of the world. The Upper Class people have everything they want. They have arrived at a high position and they have no desire to progress or to improve themselves in the least. That's why they don't act any better. It's human nature I guess.

. . . Those members of the Middle Class who expressed such low regard for the intellectual and cultural level of the Upper Class were looking first at some of the aristocratic *hacendados* who devoted themselves to the operations of their estates and manifested little interest in higher degrees or local cultural events, and second at the successful businessmen who had attained sufficient wealth to indulge in an ostentatiously impressive style of living without benefit of much education and without much concern for events beyond their own affairs.

. . . Distinctions within the Middle Class were commonly recognized in Querétaro as were the various terms most frequently used to designate them. The *clase media acomodada* (the comfortable Middle Class) included lawyers, doctors, engineers, merchants who owned good businesses, bank managers, and some moderately wealthy farmers. Economically these were families which enjoyed an income between 3,000 and 5,000 pesos each month. (At the exchange rate of 12.50 pesos to one dollar, 1,000 pesos equaled 80 dollars). Some might have had a little less and some might have had more, but it was used to provide a mode of life which was comfortable but which did not include the luxuries enjoyed by members of the Upper Class. Education was regarded as important by these families and most of the men in this class had attended a university and sent their sons to such private secondary schools as the Instituto Queretano instead of to the public schools provided by the government. Characteristically these families owned their homes, possessed a car of some sort and dressed well—cleanly and neatly, with taste but without ostentation. Their homes were well furnished, they ate a sufficiency and variety, most of them owned such luxuries as refrigerators, radios, phonographs and even television sets. The sons entered their fathers' businesses or studied for the professions, and the daughters helped their mothers in the home or attended the commercial institute in order to become secretaries in their relatives' offices, or in one of the new industrial concerns. Every family had at least one maid and the people were, as one informant said "generally intelligent, industrious, moral, and progressive."

The same informants described the *clase media pobre* (the poor Middle Class) as characterized by a lack of money and culture. These families had an income of only 400 to 1,000 pesos each month, which made it impossible for them to own their homes, to possess and maintain a car, or to send their children to the better schools. As a result of the poorer education which they received, they spoke poor Spanish with a great deal of slang and exhibited little interest in the more "refined" aspects of life. In this class the men worked as employees in banks and offices, owned small businesses, held minor positions in the government, or taught in the public schools. Many of the women worked as clerks or stenographers before they were married.

Two views were expressed toward the *clase media pobre*. Some Queretanos saw it as consisting of solid members of the Middle Class whose interests, ideals, and ambitions were fundamentally similar to those of the *clase media acomodada* and who were restricted only by a lack of means from becoming identified with it. In other words, they saw every member of the *clase media pobre* striving conscientiously, within the limits of his financial, personal and political resources, to become an accepted member of the *clase media acomodada*. The other view was that there was a cultural discontinuity between these two social divisions and, while the *clase media acomodada* was oriented toward upward progress, culture and the wider world, the *clase media pobre* was static and stagnant, interested only in pleasure and a few material comforts, uninterested in culture or self-improvement, and basically concerned only with the immediate locale and with its own differentiation from the Lower Class. According to this view, the lack of money was less important in defining the *clase media pobre* than the absence of a particular attitude and system of values. Some of these families possessed an adequate income but it was used "improperly." Instead of emulating the pattern of the *clase media acomodada* and investing their money in education, a home, and a bank account, they "threw it around" on fancy clothes, fiestas, trips to the capital, and such material prestige items as cars and television sets. Such an approach to life was regarded by the members of the *clase media acomodada* as the result of a lack of education and culture, and indicative that those who enjoyed it were more closely related to the Lower Class than to the Middle Class.

This confusion regarding the *clase media pobre* was clarified by a slightly different description of the Middle Class which was given to us by other informants. This classification conceived of three divisions: the *clase media acomodada* (comfortable middle class), *clase media sin dinero* (middle class without money), and the *clase media sin cultura* (middle class without culture). The first category was identical with that previously described under the same name, a circumstance which indicates that this group was broadly agreed upon by many Queretanos and was considered to be the Upper Middle Class. The *clase media sin dinero* was regarded as including those families which, in spite of their meager incomes, strove to maintain a respectable Middle Class style of life: dressing carefully, maintaining good manners, valuing things of culture and the intellect within their means, and exerting themselves to procure an education for their children. This was the "white-collar class" of Querétaro and included public schoolteachers, many merchants with small businesses, and the growing number of clerks and accountants who worked in the banks, the offices of local industries, and the various agencies of the municipal, state, and federal governments. It might be called the Middle Middle Class. Families in this division were oriented toward the top of the social structure. They emulated the Upper Middle Class as much as their generally inadequate incomes of 500 to 1,000 pesos a month would permit, and they lived in constant fear of losing their identification and declining into the Lower Class. The designation *sin dinero* expressed the most significant and most compelling single factor in their lives.

The division called *clase media sin cultura* included those families whose incomes were roughly the same as the *clase media sin dinero*, or Middle Middle Class, but who did not suffer as much from their deficiencies because they used their money for different ends. This group, which might be called Lower Middle Class, was less anxious to enjoy Upper Middle Class standards of propriety and refinement, largely because it did not discern them. These more subtle aspects of living escaped them because they were never intimately exposed to them. But they did respond to the obvious value of material possessions. Their level of education was generally considerably lower than for the men of the Middle Middle Class. A few of them were lower-level government clerks, but the majority of them were skilled workers or artisans: watchmakers, postal employees, midwives, typesetters, electricians, printers, cabinetmakers, and mechanics or otherwise skilled workers on the railroad or in one of the new industries such as the Singer Sewing Machine plant. As owners of commercial enterprises of various sizes extended throughout the complete social range, there were also owners or operators of small stores who were included in this category.

On the basis of our interviews and observations, this three-part division of the Middle Class agreed most closely with the actuality of the situation and provided the most assistance in understanding the society. In material possessions and income the Lower Middle Class sometimes exceeded the Middle Middle, but its mode of life was further from that of the Upper Middle Class and it was almost always ranked lower on the social scale. It is true, as has been suggested, that there was a cultural discontinuity between the Middle Middle and the Lower Middle Class, and in some communities the latter division might have been excluded from the Middle Class completely. I have chosen to consider it a part of our Middle Class because I believe that our data show it to have been classified here by most Queretanos, and its inclusion was one of the factors which tended to give the city its strong Middle

Class flavor. The people in this category considered themselves to be Middle Class and pointed with considerable pride to the things which they possessed and to the ways in which their way of life was distinct from that of the Lower Class. They knew the differences well because many of them had only recently come from there.

—⋘〰⋙—

COMPARISON WITH THE MIDDLE CLASS IN POPAYÁN

In Querétaro the borderline between the Middle Class and Upper Class was more difficult to define than the one which distinguished the Middle Class from the Lower Class. In Popayán the reverse was true. The possession of money was important to social status in Querétaro because the importance of noble or aristocratic antecedents had lost all social significance for the majority of the population. With the acquisition of sufficient wealth, a family could move from the Middle Class into the Lower Upper Class without difficulty and without question. In Popayán this was almost impossible without extraordinary accomplishments and/or marriage into one of the old families, an event which would in effect legitimize the heirs.

The occupations of the Middle Class in Querétaro and Popayán were basically the same. In Popayán a much greater proportion of the professional men belonged to the Upper Class because of the insistence of the aristocratic families that their sons receive a university degree. The lawyers, doctors, and engineers who were members of the Middle Class were classified here, not because they were necessarily less successful than the professionals of the Upper Class, but because they had come from different family backgrounds and had no claims to aristocratic lineage. They were respected, and sometimes rich, members of the Upper Middle Class, and few of them questioned their position in the social hierarchy. Other members of the Upper Middle Class in Popayán were the well-to-do owners of dry-goods stores, hardware stores, small ranches and coffee plantations, bank managers, and a considerable number of higher-ranking officials in the government of the department. This was very similar to Querétaro.

In both cities the most common designation for those who were typical of the Middle Class was the word *empleado*, which simply meant anyone who worked for someone else, but more specifically, referred to white-collar workers in offices and banks. In Popayán these were commonly people who were improving their position in the society and were on their way up in the social scale. In Querétaro many of the office and teaching personnel were educated individuals whose families had been impoverished by the effects of land reforms; others were their first-generation descendants who had not yet

been able to recoup their wealth or social position. They continued to depre-
cate manual labor and increasingly esteem education as one of the acceptable
means for improving their condition. Because both cities were administrative
centers, there was a larger number of empleados in governmental positions
than would otherwise have been true, but they still did not constitute a large
part of the population.

From the top to the bottom of the middle class the society of Popayán was
an almost unbroken continuum marked by decline in income, subsistence
level, housing, education, and social status. There was no distinct Middle
Middle Class division such as existed in Querétaro. The Lower Middle Class
in Popayán consisted largely of master craftsmen who owned their own
businesses and employed other workers while they continued to work at their
trade themselves: tailors, bakers, electricians, mechanics, masons, small merchants, and schoolteachers. Even the most exceptionally successful . . . rarely
attained anything like the wealth which was apparently possible in Querétaro. As a result they lived very modest lives with none of the material possessions of their Mexican counterparts and at a level parallel to, or slightly
below, that of the *empleados* of the Middle Middle Class in Querétaro. They
were even more strikingly different from the Queretanos in their attitudes and
values.

Material goods were scarcer in Popayán and more difficult to obtain
because of the city's isolated location. A successful *ebanista*, a cabinetmak-
er, might use his increased income to buy a house in a slightly better neighborhood, and to improve the quantity and quality of his family's dress and
diet, but it is unlikely that he would even aspire to such a thing as an automobile or a television set. He might buy his son a bicycle, he might purchase a
sewing machine for his wife, but more than likely he would use [his income]
to keep his sons in school until they had finished the *liceo*, or high school,
and, if possible, he would try to send at least one of them through the
university.

Throughout the society of Popayán there was a particularly strong emphasis upon the value of education and the importance of good appearance and
proper behavior. Many members of the Middle Class extended themselves so
far to achieve these all-important ends that they impoverished themselves
and sacrificed their physical well-being. It was sometimes necessary to
skimp on food in order to keep a son in school, for, although tuition was
determined on the basis of the family's income and was usually no great
burden, he had to be provided with books, with a dark suit and white shirts,
and probably with such prestige items as a Parker fountain pen and a fancy
cigarette lighter, to make him acceptable to his fellow students. The rest of
the family also had to be dressed properly in order not to disgrace him, and
the public occasions of fifteenth birthday, saints' days, and first communions

had to be properly observed with gifts and a fiesta, even if the family starved for a month and the father was forced to borrow from a moneylender.

The sons might surreptitiously help their father at his work, but an effort was usually made to hide or disguise the working source of the family income. When the family had committed itself to a program of improvement through education, the young men and, to some extent, the rest of the family tried to behave like gentry. This meant wearing a suit, being rigorously clean and properly behaved, and eschewing physical work of any kind in public, even if it only involved carrying a small parcel through the streets. Daughters were even more jealously guarded here than among the Middle Class in Querétaro. The entire picture was one of rigidity and conservatism, of a pattern so demanding that social acceptance meant constant restriction and sacrifice.

—*♫♪♫*—

Another significant difference between the Middle Classes of Popayán and Querétaro was the kind of self-identification which their members possessed. The Middle Class of Popayán was just as real as it was in the Mexican city, but it seemed to me to be referred to less frequently. This is a completely subjective statement and would be almost impossible to qualify, but it did appear that the term *clase media* or its equivalent appeared in interviews and conversations very commonly in Querétaro. The Middle Class was much more numerous there, and a greater number of people voluntarily identified themselves with it. Even more impressive than the numbers was the pride with which such identification seemed to be made, and the frequency of expressions of superiority, not only toward the Lower Class but particularly toward the Upper Class. This . . . should be contrasted with Popayán, where such attitudes were either largely lacking or else did not come to our attention. In both cities some antagonism toward the members of the Upper Class was expressed and we were told in both Popayán and Querétaro that they were self-centered and arrogant, contributing nothing to the welfare and development of the city and concerned only with their own affairs and the furtherance of their own private interests. It was only in Querétaro, however, that they were also accused of being ignorant, uneducated, and uncultured. The typical Middle Class Queretano's assurance that he was representative of the finest, most progressive, and most substantial element of his society probably reflected the vigor of the growing Mexican Middle Class and appeared to be almost absent in Popayán.

In the Colombian city the Upper Class still controlled the power, set the pace, and established the standards. To a much greater degree than in Querétaro they were accepted and emulated by the Middle Class. As a result, the characteristic tone of the Middle Class was cautious, conservative, and rigid.

With the emphasis upon ascribed rather than achieved status, the society enjoyed the advantages of stability, but the members of the Middle Class were committed to a system in which they could attain only a limited degree of success. In Querétaro the Middle Class was in the process of developing standards of its own within which success might be achieved on its own terms.

NOTE

This chapter was previously published as, Andrew H. Whiteford, *Two Cities of Latin America: A Comparative Description of Social Classes* (Garden City, NY: Anchor Books, 1964), 94, 98–100, 101, 102–6, 124–127, 134–35.

Chapter Four

The Budget

Mario Benedetti

"El Presupuesto" ("The Budget"), written in 1947 by Uruguayan author Mario Benedetti, remains one of Latin America's best-loved short stories and has been reprinted many times in several languages. It portrays the monotonous yet precarious life of a low-level government clerk in Montevideo, the most white collar of all Latin American cities. Benedetti allows the reader to empathize with his underpaid and mostly powerless middle-class hero, while at the same time delivering biting satire on government disorganization, bureaucratic inefficiency, the arrogant obliviousness of ministers and other high functionaries, and, perhaps above all else, the sheer absurdity of office life.

In our office, the same budget had been in operation since the 1920s, that is, since a time when most of us were struggling with geography and fractions. Our Chief, however, remembered the great event, and sometimes, when there wasn't so much work, he would sit down familiarly on one of our desks, and there, with his legs dangling, and immaculate white socks showing below his trousers, he would tell us, with all his old feeling and with his usual 598 words, of that distant and splendid day when his Chief—he was Head Clerk then—had patted him on the shoulder and said: "My boy, we're having a new budget," with the broad and satisfied smile of a man who had already worked out how many new shirts he will be able to buy with the increase.

A new budget is the supreme ambition of a government office. We knew that other departments with bigger staffs than ours had been given new budgets every two or three years. We observed them from our own little administrative island with the same hopeless resignation that Robinson Crusoe felt as he watched ships passing across the horizon, knowing that it was as useless to make signals as to feel envy. Neither our envy nor our signals would have done much good; since even at the best of times we never had a

55

staff of more than nine, it was only logical that nobody should bother about so small an office.

As we knew that nothing and nobody in the world would improve our salaries, we limited our hopes to a progressive reduction of expenses, and by means of a quite elementary cooperative system we had gone a good way toward achieving this. I paid for the *yerba mate*, for example; the Head Assistant, the afternoon tea; the Second Assistant, the sugar; the Head Clerk, the toast; the Second Clerk, the butter. The two typists were excused contributions, but the Chief, since he earned a bit more, paid for the newspaper that we all read.

Our private entertainments had also been reduced to a minimum. We went to the cinema once a month, taking good care that everyone would see different films, so that by talking about them all in the office afterwards we could keep abreast of all the new pictures. We had encouraged the adoption of games of mental concentration, like checkers and chess, which cost little and helped pass the time without too much yawning. We played between five and six o'clock, when it was unlikely that any new files would arrive, because the notice in the counter window said that after five no further "business" would be accepted. We had read it so often that in the end we didn't know who had invented it, nor even exactly what the idea of "business" was related to. Sometimes someone would come and ask for the number of his "business." We would give him the number of his file, and he would go away satisfied. So "business" could be files, for instance.

Really our life there wasn't a bad one. From time to time the Chief would think himself obliged to explain to us the advantages of working in public administration as compared with commerce—though some of us thought that by now it was a bit late for him to take any other view.

One of his arguments was security. The security of not getting the sack. For this to happen, there had to be a meeting of Senators, and we know that the Senators hardly managed to meet even when they had business with a Minister. So in this respect the Chief was right. We had Security. Naturally there was also the other kind of security, the security of knowing that we should never have a pay increase that would permit us to buy a new overcoat cash down. But the Chief, who couldn't buy one either, considered that this wasn't the moment to start criticizing his job or ours. And—as always—he was right.

This settled, almost absolute, peace that weighed down on our office, leaving us resigned to our little destinies and somewhat sluggish on account of not losing any sleep, was shattered one day by some news brought by the Second Clerk. He was the nephew of a Head Clerk in the Ministry, and it turned out that this uncle (speaking properly and without disrespect) had learnt that there was talk of a new budget for our office. As we didn't know at first what person or persons had been talking about our budget, we smiled with that particularly luxurious irony that we reserved for certain occasions, as if the Second Clerk were a bit mad, or as if we realized that he thought we were a bit stupid. But when he added that, according to the uncle, the person who had talked had been the Secretary himself, that is, the *alma parens* of the Ministry, we suddenly felt that something was already changing in our seventy-peso lives, as if some invisible hand had at last tightened the screw that had been slack, as if we had had all our conformity and all our resignation knocked out of us.

In my own case, the first thing that it occurred to me to think and say was "fountain pen." Until that moment I hadn't known I wanted to buy a fountain pen. As soon as the Second Clerk's news opened up that enormous future that any possibility, however small, reveals, I at once dragged up from some unknown basement of my desires a black fountain pen with a silver cap, and my name engraved on it. Goodness only knows at what period in my life the desire had taken root in me.

Besides, I saw and heard the Head Assistant talking about a bicycle, I saw the Chief absently contemplating the broken heels of his shoes, and one of the typists looking with affectionate contempt at the handbag she had been using for the last five years. I also saw and heard how we all immediately began to discuss our various plans, not really bothering about what the others were saying, but just needing to find an outlet for so many repressed and unsuspected dreams. I also saw and heard how we all decided to celebrate the good news by paying out of the reserve fund for a special afternoon of cookies.

This—the cookies—was the first step. Then followed the pair of shoes that the Chief bought himself. After the Chief's shoes, my pen, to be paid for in ten installments. After my pen, the Second Clerk's overcoat, the Head Typist's handbag, the Head Assistant's bicycle. A month and a half later we were all in debt and full of anxiety.

The Second Clerk had brought more news. First of all, that the business of the new budget was pending consideration by the Secretariat of the Ministry. Then it turned out that this wasn't so. It wasn't with the Secretariat. It was with the Accounting Department. But the Chief of Accounting was ill, and his views had to be consulted. We all worried about the health of this Chief, though all we knew about him was that his name was Eugenio and that he was going to study our new budget. We would even have liked to receive a daily bulletin about his health. But we only had a right to the depressing news that came from our Second Clerk's uncle. The Chief of Accounting continued to get worse. We lived through so long a sadness on account of this official's illness that on the day he died we felt, like the relatives of someone suffering from acute asthma, a kind of relief that we wouldn't have to worry about him anymore. Indeed, we became selfishly happy, because his death meant the possibility that they would fill the empty post and appoint a new Chief who would at last study our budget.

Four months after Don Eugenio's death they appointed a new Chief of Accounting. That afternoon we suspended the chess-game, the *mate*, and the administrative processes. The Chief started to hum an aria from "Aida," and the rest of us—because of this and everything else—grew so nervous that we had to go out for a while to look at shop-windows. There was a shock waiting for us when we got back. The uncle revealed that our budget had never been pending consideration by Accounting. That had been a mistake. In fact it had never left the Secretariat. This meant a considerable darkening of our horizons. If the budget had been with Accounting, we shouldn't have been alarmed. After all, we knew it hadn't been studied until then because of the Chief's illness. But if during all this time it had really been in the Secretariat, whose Secretary, its head, enjoyed perfect health, the delay was not due to anything and could well turn into a delay without end.

At this point the critical stage in our misgivings began. On arrival in the mornings we would exchange the usual looks of unhopeful interrogation. At first we still asked: "Has anyone heard anything?" Then we changed to saying simply: "Well?" and finally just to asking with raised eyebrows. Nobody knew anything. If anyone did know anything, it was that the budget was still being considered by the Secretariat.

Eight months after we had had the original news, my fountain pen had already not been working for two. The Head Assistant had cracked a rib thanks to the bicycle. A pawnbroker was the present owner of the books that the Second Assistant had bought; the Head Clerk's watch was losing a quarter of an hour a day; the Chief's shoes had twice needed replacement soles (the first time sewn on, the second time just tacked on), and the lapels of the Second Clerk's overcoat were worn out and curled up.

Once we heard that the Minister had asked about the budget. A week later the Secretariat had sent him a report. We wanted to know what the report said, but the uncle couldn't find out, because it was "strictly confidential." We thought this downright stupid; in our office, all the files that had cards attached to the top corner saying "very urgent," "for special attention," or "strictly reserved," were treated exactly like the rest. But apparently in the Ministry they did not hold the same point of view.

On another occasion we learnt that the Minister had talked to the Secretary about the budget. Since they don't attach special cards to conversations, the uncle was able to discover and to let us know that the Minister was in agreement. With what or with whom was he in agreement? When the uncle tried to find this out, the Minister was no longer in agreement. Whereupon, without further explanation, we understood that it was with us that he had been in agreement before.

On yet another occasion we learnt that the budget had been revised. It was going to be dealt with at next Friday's session, but fourteen Fridays after that next one the budget still hadn't been dealt with. We began to keep our eye on the date of the next session, and every Saturday we would say to each other: "Ah well, now it won't be till next Friday. We'll see what happens then." Friday would come and nothing would happen. And on the Saturday we would say: "Ah well, now it won't be till next Friday. We'll see what happens then." And nothing happened. Absolutely nothing at all ever happened, ever.

By now I was too deeply in debt to remain impassive; the fountain pen had ruined my economic rhythm, and since then I hadn't been able to recover my balance. It was because of this that it occurred to me that we might go and see the Minister.

We spent several afternoons rehearsing the interview. The Head Clerk played the Minister, and the Chief, who had been unanimously appointed to speak on behalf of all of us, presented our petition to him. When we were satisfied with the rehearsals, we requested an interview at the Ministry and were given an appointment for Thursday. So on Thursday we left one of the typists and the porter in the office, and the rest of us went to speak to the Minister. Speaking to the Minister isn't the same as speaking to anyone else. To speak to the Minister you have to wait two and a half hours, and it sometimes happens, as in fact happened in our case, that even after these two and a half hours you still can't speak to the Minister. We only got into the presence of the Secretary, who took note of the Chief's words—said much worse than in the worst of the rehearsals, where no one had stammered—and came back with the Minister's reply, that our budget would be dealt with in the following day's session.

As we were leaving the Ministry—relatively satisfied—a car pulled up at the door and we saw the Minister get out of it.

It seemed strange to us that the Secretary should have brought us the Minister's personal reply when the Minister wasn't there. But really it was as well to have a little confidence, and we all agreed with satisfaction and relief when the Chief suggested that the Secretary must surely have consulted the Minister by telephone.

The next day at five o'clock in the afternoon we were all pretty nervous. Five o'clock in the afternoon was the time we had been told we could ask what had happened. We hadn't done much work; we were too uneasy for things to turn out right. Nobody said anything. The Chief wasn't even humming his aria. We let six minutes of strict abstinence go by. Then the Chief dialed the number that we all knew by heart, and asked to speak to the Secretary. The conversation didn't last long. Between the Chief's intermittent "Yes," "Ah, yes," "Yes, I see," we could hear the indistinct croaking of the other voice. When the Chief hung up the receiver we all knew the answer.

It was only to confirm it that we paid attention. "It seems that they didn't have time today. But the Minister says that the budget will be dealt with without fail at next Friday's session."

NOTE

This chapter was previously published as, Mario Benedetti, "The Budget," Gerald Brown, trans., in *Spanish Short Stories 1/Cuentos Hispánicos 1*, ed. Jean Franco (London: Penguin Books, 1966), 27–41. Minor translation revisions by David S. Parker.

Chapter Five

Middle-Class Rebels

Francisco López Cámara

Mexican sociologist Francisco López Cámara wrote this essay in 1967, one year before a student movement exploded across Mexico City. Through the summer of 1968 middle-class students took to the streets to protest the authoritarianism of Mexico's one-party state; this movement ended in tragedy in October when government forces opened fire on a peaceful student demonstration at Tlatelolco. López Cámara foreshadows events by describing a growing rupture in Mexican society and politics, which he attributes to structural shifts in the economy that narrowed the job opportunities for middle-class students and betrayed their aspirations. He worries that the crisis of the middle class will lead young people down one of two paths: to embrace radical leftist ideologies in the wake of the Cuban Revolution or to embrace irrational rebellion—to become "rebels without a cause."

The issue of our day is *youth*. . . . The new generation appears to be building their own world, abandoning old ways of life, even conspiring against them. Youth protest manifests itself in the rejection of traditional mores, habits, ideas, and institutions. . . . On the one hand, young people today embody an energy that seems poorly channeled, expressed in the irrational acts of the "rebel without a cause": troubling, impetuous, violent. On the other hand, today's youth gravitate to "causes" and organized political action. Perhaps there is not that much distance between the rebel without a cause and the ultra-theoretical extremist who seeks, through violence, to bring about radical political change in one blow: both involve a symbolic protest against a society that they deem foreign and restrictive. . . .

This phenomenon is not just a characteristic of youth; . . . it has much to do with today's social and historical context. . . . These diverse forms of protest and rebellion result, in large part, from young people having a vision of the future that does not seem to hold any place for them. . . . It would be absurd to deny that Mexico has developed considerably in recent decades, but development produces new contradictions. The demands of the emerging middle classes increasingly outstrip their real possibilities: despite the growing number and variety of occupations, they inevitably run into barriers. The middle class, by its very nature, always seeks to climb the social ladder, and its aspirations are at their most intense in those moments when the country is least able to satisfy them. As in other poor countries, cities grow rapidly without a matching expansion of opportunities. The middle class, fruit of this process of urbanization, has but two paths open to them: education and politics. . . .

The fact is that the youth who are recruited into higher education or into politics tend to be middle class. In both spheres, the room for newcomers is shrinking. With only a few exceptions, education no longer guarantees social mobility. Modern employment structures have less need for traditional liberal professionals. Yet the middle class, clinging to an obsolete ideal, cannot imagine any other kind of education, and universities, responding to those expectations, do not change their curriculum. As a result, even in the best of cases, all that educated middle-class youths can do is to swell the ranks of the state bureaucracy.

In politics we can already begin to see a clash of generations. The problem is not just that there is no room for new blood, though that is part of it. There is equally a divergence of political ideas and methods. A greater social consciousness, the diffusion of information, and the broadening of those sectors of the population who pay attention to political matters, have given rise to new concerns, . . . new ideologies, [and] new forms of collective action that challenge the "rules" laid down by previous generations.

If it seems that today's youth are irrational or embrace extremist ideologies, the explanation lies in the convulsive instability of the middle classes. . . . Lacking a coherent political project consistent with their own class situation, young people easily latch onto movements of other classes or channel their concerns into seemingly irrational acts of violence. . . . It is impossible to understand these problems if one attributes everything to permissive parenting or failures of moral education. Remember that what today's youth are rebelling *against*, in large part, is the very system that their parents want to impose on them: a system that makes less and less sense as it becomes increasingly obsolete. . . . Working in large productive organizations—the fruits of industrialization and the technification of modern work—has suffocated many of the traditional "liberal" aspirations characteristic of the middle classes. Feeling trapped with ever-shrinking horizons, the middle class rebels.

Middle-class youth, the most restless sector of today's generation, thus see their upward mobility blocked. . . . The old liberal professions are shrinking. . . . Those lawyers, doctors, and architects who still practice their professions independently owe their good fortune, to a large degree, to family support and connections, not to expanding professional opportunities. Because of this, our educational system is plagued by a contradiction: universities open their doors to youth with the promise of [a degree that will allow them to practice] a liberal profession . . . likely knowing that employment opportunities within these professions are every day more scarce. Yet just as the career prospects of independent professionals are narrowing, the number of aspirants is growing out of control, a product of expanding university enrolments.

Students end up feeling defrauded. What is the point of their effort? . . . Only a wealthy minority see education as an end in itself; for everyone else, it continues to be thought of as an "instrument" of upward mobility, a road to a better income and higher family standing. [But when mobility becomes the exception rather than the rule], fear of failure leads young people into a veiled protest against the ideology of their parents—which they blame for leading them down this misguided path—or to the open renunciation of their educational institutions, which they blame for not preparing them adequately for futures as professionals.

The nation's political tensions are also an outgrowth of the concerns of youth. For young people without prior political loyalties, all issues and conflicts are viewed through an ideological lens, and they feel that their education entitles them to have a significant voice. . . . They demand change, the reform of existing conditions, the elimination of obstacles that hold their generation back. Reformist tendencies turn easily into demands for revolution: they want to change the entire system, convinced that the creation of a new order of things is always the responsibility of the younger generation. The spirit of innovation begets organized rebellion. If today's world belongs to the old people, it is up to youth to build a world of their own.

NOTE

This chapter was previously published as, Francisco López Cámara, "Los rebeldes de la clase media," in *El desafío de la clase media* (Mexico City: Editorial Joaquín Mortiz, 1971), 90–91, 94–96, 97, 98, 100–102. Translated by Louise E. Walker and David S. Parker, edited by David S. Parker.

Chapter Six

The Dilemma of the Latin American Middle Class

Charles Wagley

This 1968 version of an essay originally drafted in 1964 contained several major revisions, reflecting the author's need to account more fully for middle-class complicity in the 1964 military coup in Brazil, the country he knew best. The article offers a portrait of a middle class caught between its desire to create a more modern, democratic society and its fear that change will not end up being in its best interest. Like Pike, Wagley doubted the longevity of any political alliance between the middle class and the working class, noting that the "middle class becomes jittery in face of rapid change and the increased power of the urban and rural masses." Focusing on Brazil, he argued that the middle class's search for stability translated into acquiescence and even out-right support for military rule.

The nineteenth-century concept of Latin American class structure no longer is valid. Latin American nations are not composed nowadays of a landed gentry versus a mass of illiterate peons, mestizos, Indians, colonos, share-croppers, or squatters. Most Latin American nations are today infinitely more complex in social structure. Whether it is the result of industrialization, the growth of great cities, mechanization of agriculture, or other processes of modernization, new social groups have appeared, and there has been a funda-mental realignment of social classes.

In the last generation or so, a new sector of industrialists and businessmen has appeared in such countries as Mexico, Venezuela, Colombia, Peru, Chile, Argentina, Uruguay, and Brazil. In most countries they are today more im-portant in the national power structure than the traditional landholding and rural-based elite. Likewise, with the growth of industry a significant urban working class has appeared. And, also, most Latin American cities contain a large mass of mainly rural migrants who inhabit the *barriadas, favelas, invasões,* or *callampas*—the enormous shantytowns. In the rural areas there is an enlarged rural proletariat—the wage workers on the large mechanized plantations—producing sugar, coffee, bananas, cacao, cotton, and other commercial crops. Finally there is a new Latin American middle class that has come to have an increasing voice in the life of many nations. It is the purpose of this paper to identify this new middle class and to point out some of its real problems. It is my thesis that this sector of the Latin American population is caught up in a dilemma between its liberal democratic ideals and the realities involved in the extension of liberal democracy—between a desire to extend the benefits of modern technology to the whole body politic and the terrible cost of doing so.

The presence of a middle class patterned on the model of those which exist in western Europe and the United States has been doubted or denied by many analysts of Latin American society. Most observers agree on the rapid increase both numerically and strategically of a "middle group," a "middle mass," a "middle sector," a "middle strata," or another term that dodges the word "class." It is pointed out, however, that this sector in Latin American societies is heterogeneous in origin. Some of the members of this "class" derive from the old elite who have declined economically from the position once held by their ancestors. Others are of middle class origin; still others are immigrants or children of immigrants. A few have lower class origins. Economically they range from wealthy businessmen to small shopkeepers and, in terms of education, from highly trained technicians and professors with PhD degrees to people who have not completed primary school. It is also pointed out that these middle groups lack a class consciousness and a class ideology. These people are apt to model themselves in social behavior and cultural values after the old aristocracy. They place great value on a white-collar occupation, even though it may pay less than skilled manual labor; they value classical literary education over technical and scientific training; they tend toward conspicuous consumption and even ostentation. These middle groups from this point might best be viewed as marginal to an enlarged upper class.

This view of the Latin American middle groups was certainly true in the nineteenth and early twentieth centuries, and it may still be true in many Latin American countries. Yet it seems to me that we should recognize that in certain Latin American countries such as Argentina, Chile, Uruguay, Brazil, Mexico, and Venezuela, a middle class of sizeable proportions now exists with a distinctive way of life and its own self-identity as well as an objective middle position in the economic structure of the nation. Its emergence as a rather large and distinctive group is recent and is part of the massive social and political change in process in most of Latin America.

WHO IS MIDDLE CLASS IN LATIN AMERICA?

Who are these people who I believe belong to a middle class rather than to an amorphous "middle mass" or "middle sector"? Several writers dubious of the existence of a Latin American middle class speak of an upper and lower middle sector or class. The upper middle class consists of people of some wealth—businessmen, managers, high level and successful professionals, and high level bureaucrats and politicians. They are not quite wealthy enough to belong to the new upper class; they lack the family background of the traditional elite. In fact, they may be immigrants or the children of immigrants. But this is the group, in my opinion, which shares the aristocratic values of the upper class. These people can afford to join the same clubs and to send their children to the same schools as those attended by the children of the upper class. They are upwardly mobile and ambitious. The successful sons of this "upper middle sector" often marry into elite families. They are, in a sense, a recognizable group—a marginal sector of the upper class.

It is those people who can be classed in the lower "middle sectors" or strata who are a new phenomenon in Latin American society and who have the characteristics of a middle class that sets them off from the elite. It is this group that I shall speak of as the middle class in the pages that follow.

Members of the middle class share a series of common qualities. First, they have white-collar occupations, but not the most lucrative or prestigious ones. They are small businessmen, professionals of various sorts (dentists, pharmacists, not-so-successful lawyers, physicians, engineers, and the like). Above all they are salaried workers—employees of banks and business firms, teachers in primary and secondary schools, and government employees. Artisans and other skilled workers, even though they earn more money than many of the middle class, are considered lower class. In fact the middle class is poorly paid—although when the average income is compared to the average income of the lower classes, they are wealthy. . . .

Second, the middle class is overwhelmingly urban because this class is, in a sense, the result of industrial and commercial development. Few small farmers, except perhaps in southern Brazil, Antioquia (Colombia), and Costa Rica, could be counted members of the middle class. But in all small towns there is a local elite—government employees, storekeepers, clergy, and others who are "white collar"—who, from a national perspective, can be considered members of the middle class. Even the middle class living in small towns has an urban ethos—it is turned away from the rural zone toward the city in its thinking.[1]

Third, members of the Latin American middle class are literate. Their education may range from a few years of primary school to a university degree. This means several things. They value education for their children and believe strongly in universal public education. They are also consumers of newspapers and magazines including such foreign imports as *Life en Español* and *Seleciones* (*Reader's Digest*). Because the electoral laws of most Latin American nations require literacy, only the middle and upper classes vote. The middle class is well aware of political events and problems, although it may not altogether understand them.

Fourth, the Latin American middle class is traditionalistic and nationalistic. While the lower class shares almost vicariously in national traditions, this middle class is anxious to live them out. While the upper class (and the upper-middle class) have cosmopolitan tastes and manners (that is, French and North American), members of the middle class attempt to retain Latin American tastes and manners of behavior—they express "*Mexicanidad*," the *Gaucho* spirit of Argentina and Uruguay; the *Bandeirante* spirit of São Paulo (Brazil); and other forms of creolisms throughout the continent. In terms of ideal patterns of behavior they value large kinship groups (*parentela*), respect for the obligations and rights of their *compadres*, a dual role for the sexes (*machismo* for males and virginity before marriage for girls), and other traditional Latin American ideal patterns today often honored in the breach.

THE MIDDLE CLASS AND NATIONALISM

The middle class is not only nationalistic but its members have a most vociferous voice. The elite (and upper-middle class) are likely to be cosmopolitan; the lower class is likely to be relatively unaware of nationalistic symbols. The middle class is fully cognizant of all the stereotypes and symbols of nationalism. Their nationalism tends to have a negative aspect. A great Mexican historian has described Latin American nationalism: "It was seldom born or suckled by faith in its own values, but was born, grew, and flourished as a reaction of protest, suspicion, and even hatred and contempt for the wrongs done by foreign individuals, companies, and governments."[2] This nationalism, he adds, "in the last twenty years reached incredible extremes of emotion and irrationality."

In the past, Great Britain, France, and Germany as well as the United States were the butts of this suspicion and hatred, but today the United States is the principal scapegoat. Hundreds of thousands of the Latin American middle class may study English in binational centers sponsored by the United States government; they may also be eager to study in colleges and universities in the United States; they may be addicts of North American music, movies, and novels (in translation); but they are anti-American. They believe that United States corporations plot to exploit their countries' raw materials. They point out penetration of American firms into commerce and industry. They distrust, with some reason, the foreign policy of the United States government. They fear intervention, and they point out that U.S. foreign aid comes with strings attached.[3]

Yet there is also a positive side of this Latin American nationalism which is again expressed most articulately by the middle class. A generation or so ago, the Latin American upper class and the small peripheral middle class looked to Europe, sometimes to the United States, for almost all they admired. They were ashamed of the non-European aspects of their own national cultures. For example, Mexico rejected the Indian and the mestizo. Today these sectors of the Mexican population stand as symbols of the Mexican Revolution. Twenty years ago a Guatemalan lady of the upper or middle class would not have been "caught dead" in a dress made of local fabric with an Indian design; today, "Indian inspired" fabrics made in Guatemala are a source of national pride. Brazil has gone through a veritable about-face in this regard in the last twenty years. Before, the middle class was ashamed of life in the backlands and of its African heritage. Nowadays, books, music, and movies such as *Black Orpheus* (a story of the *favelas*) and *The Man Who Fulfilled His Vows* (a story of religious fanaticism in the backlands and of the African candomblé ceremonies of Bahia) are exported with pride. This positive aspect of nationalism has given the middle class a pride in itself, a self-respect, and the courage to value its own national traditions. . . .

THE MIDDLE CLASS DILEMMA

This Latin American middle class finds itself in an economic, political, and social dilemma. The realities of present day Latin American society run contrary to the needs, the aspirations, and the ideology of this new social group. Although it holds many traditional values, the new middle class has modern needs and aspirations. But it is still living in a society in transition from a rural agrarian semi-feudal and personalistic social system to an urban, industrial, impersonal social system.

Middle class people in Latin America are consumers. They are accustomed to adequate housing. Since they work in offices, classrooms, stores, and other public places in a white--collar capacity, they need to dress well. They want television sets, electric refrigerators, washing machines, and other accoutrements of the modern world. They would like to have an automobile if that were possible. But the realities of their economic situation are otherwise. Manufactured goods are expensive in any terms—because even if not imported, they are produced by a protected national industry. Rents, clothes, medicines, and even food are expensive for the poorly paid middle class. . . . Furthermore, inflation is constant, sometimes rampant, in countries with a significant middle class. The middle class lives on fixed income, almost always salaries, which lag behind the rising cost of living and are adjusted slowly in face of inflation. Middle class people are often heavily in debt.

There is only one answer to the economic dilemma of the Latin American middle class, namely, to make more money. Thus Latin American middle class men—teachers, poorly paid professionals, government employees, and others—"moonlight," holding down several jobs. It is common for a government employee to work also in a private firm. Obviously he neglects his relatively secure government job. It is common for professors in universities to teach in more than one faculty and for secondary school teachers to teach their subject in several schools. Furthermore, the budget of most middle class families in Latin America can only be balanced if there are several wage-earners contributing; thus, sons and daughters work while still studying, and it is more and more common for the wife to work.

The middle classes are also frustrated by the lack of public services in the cities in which they typically live. Public services have not been able to keep pace with the extremely rapid growth of cities; in some cases, they have actually deteriorated. The middle class spends endless hours waiting for infrequent and poor public transportation. They bear the lack of water and lack of telephones with amazing patience but also with irritation. Public services, until recently, were foreign owned. Nationalists were certain that foreign transportation and utility companies were extracting tremendous loot from their countries, and in many cases this was probably so. Such corporations were not allowed to increase their rates and in turn they refused to improve facilities, expecting that they would be expropriated. By now most of them have been nationalized. But compensation to these foreign companies put a heavy weight on countries which are short in foreign exchange. And, once nationalized, the public transportation and utilities were in poor condition. Water supply systems, sewers, roads, telephone systems, public transportation, and the other public services—which the middle class needs more than any other sector of the Latin American population—call for heavy capital expenditures. If this is to be done, then taxes must be increased. Neither the Latin American elite nor the middle class is accustomed to paying heavy direct taxes, but they are now learning. Increased taxes are an added burden to a middle class which hardly lives within its income. (I might add that this is not a distinctive Latin American phenomenon.)

As it is with public facilities, so it is with education. The Latin American middle class, as we have said, places a high value on education, and they want public schools for their children. They are no longer satisfied with just the primary education to which many of the present-day adults were limited, and their children crowd into secondary schools and universities. Public primary schools are crowded; public secondary schools are too few in many cities. So the middle class must take on the extra cost of private secondary schools. They are willing to make sacrifices to allow their children to attend the university. Yet even though universities are almost free, most university students, especially those from the middle class, work as they study.

The dilemma of the Latin American middle class is not only material and economic. They are faced with ideological and cultural conflicts as well. They are traditionalists, but they are also liberal democrats, and they believe that equality of opportunity should be extended to the mass of people in their countries. Their children may be university students who vibrate with nationalism and with the ideal of equal opportunity for all. Yet, given the relatively underdeveloped economy of their nations, to provide the same conditions of life for the mass of people which the middle class itself struggles to maintain might well destroy their relatively favored position. They may not be overtly aware of this dilemma, but it lies ominously in the background.

A single example of what I mean will have to suffice. As stated several times, the Latin American middle class believes strongly in the extension of free public education to the entire population. In most Latin American countries, this is an ideal far from realized. It is estimated that in 1950, 49 percent of the population of Latin America over fifteen years of age had never attended school or had dropped out before completing one year.[4] The educational institutions of most countries were originally established for the elite— a very small proportion of the total population. The educational system inherited from the past provides a poor basis for the building of a system making education available to all. Then too, the well-known population explosion which in a generation or so more than doubled the number of Latin Americans (even greater in the school population) does not make the task easier. To make universal education a reality, a massive undertaking—of training teachers, building schools, and reorganizing the curricula—would be necessary. This would call for a financial outlay by the governments far beyond that now made for education. In the process, the quality of the existing schools would certainly deteriorate. If a rich nation such as the United States has such problems in racial integration of its schools, one can only imagine the problems most Latin American nations would face in assimilating the entire mass of people into its educational institutions. Although this is the stated ideal of the Latin American middle class, it has to settle for less.

Furthermore, the Latin American middle class equivocates in its liberal democratic views. It favors universal suffrage and freely elected governments. Literacy is a qualification for voting in most of Latin America, thereby automatically disfranchising a large sector of most national populations. Although several writers have spoken of some sort of middle-class alliance with the workers, the facts do not seem to support this theory. It may be true that for a time the Argentine middle class sided with Peron and the *descamisados* against the oligarchy, or that the Brazilian middle class supported Vargas and his Brazilian Labor Party (PTB). But, at the time, the middle class felt that it was in control. They did not cogitate turning over the dominant political power to the workers. And the so-called alliance ended when the working groups took, or seemed to take, control.

The middle class has a real political dilemma. Middle class people are energetically interested in politics. They know and appreciate the power of government. In fact, a large percentage of them owe their very class position to the expansion of government bureaucracy. They believe in honesty and morality in politics and in government. They are perforce adherents of statism, for they are not convinced that capitalism and free enterprise will lead to social and economic development of their countries as it seems to have in the United States. But with few exceptions . . . there are no political parties that clearly represent their interests. . . . With their dependence on the state, the Latin American middle class becomes jittery in face of rapid change and the increased power of the urban and rural masses. Faced with a crisis, the middle class acquiesces; it remains passive before a military coup that guarantees stability, or it actively supports a political party or a coalition of parties aimed at stability rather than abrupt change. There is no guarantee at all that the development of a strong middle class in Latin America will lead to the strengthening of democratic institutions.

THE CASE OF THE BRAZILIAN MIDDLE CLASS

Perhaps I may illustrate the economic, social, and political dilemma of the middle class by the case of the Brazilian middle class—a group about which I have had considerable knowledge. The Brazilian middle class is not numerically the strongest in Latin America in relation to the total population of the country. But, since World War II, it has gained remarkably in numerical strength and in self-identity, especially in south Brazil—in Rio de Janeiro, São Paulo, Belo Horizonte, Porto Alegre, and other rapidly growing cities. The Brazilian middle class has suffered, perhaps more intensely than their counterparts in other countries, all the ills we have described: lack of public facilities, crowded schools, and low salaries that do not keep up with rampant inflation. Furthermore, Brazil has suffered a series of political crises since 1954 when the ex-dictator and then elected president, Getulio Vargas, committed suicide. In 1961 there was the dramatic resignation of President Jânio Quadros, a man who seemed to have a basis of political support and whose political symbol "the broom that swept the house clean" was pleasing to middle class morality. Then, the elected vice president, João Goulart, was allowed by the Army to assume the presidency only after a constitutional amendment establishing a parliamentary form of government was passed. This was done to curb Goulart's power. A plebiscite in 1963 returned the country to a presidential form of government restoring most of the executive powers.

The year 1963 and the first months of 1964 were marked with continual crisis in Brazil. In 1963 a series of strikes upset transportation and industrial production. Inflation continued at an increased rate. The cost of living is said to have increased 80 percent in 1963.

In the first three months of 1964, it almost seemed that Brazil was in a state of chaos. The *cruzeiro* dropped in value from 600 to the dollar in January to 1,360 in March. A new round of strikes broke out among the dock workers, the bank employees, the transportation workers, and others. President Goulart seemed to be seeking his support from labor, the peasants, and the students. He announced a series of "basic reforms"—including a land reform bill authorizing the federal government to expropriate unused lands along highways, railroads, and waterways. He signed a bill lowering the rates on rent control. He was said to favor granting legality to the Brazilian Communist Party, and there were discussions about the feasibility of recognition of Communist China. Goulart also announced that he was in favor of amending the Constitution of 1946 to grant suffrage to illiterates and to allow military personnel to run for elective office by placing themselves on inactive status. (Several noncommissioned officers had petitioned for this right.) There was a round of increases for labor but little help for the low-level white-collar worker. The middle class suffered, and they were frightened.

There was a strong reaction from the middle class (and the upper class). *O Estado de São Paulo* and *O Globo,* conservative papers of wide circulation, warned of "socialist" and "communist" policies of Goulart's government. Carlos Lacerda, the governor of Guanabara State in which Rio de Janeiro is situated and a critic of almost all federal regimes, fanned the flames by spectacular speeches over television lasting for hours. Anti-communist groups called for demonstrations in the streets to protest against the leftist trends of the Goulart government. In March of 1964 an estimated 500,000 people in São Paulo took part in a "God and Family" protest. Stories of the influence of China, Russia, and Cuba among the peasants in north Brazil were rife. It was rumored that Goulart planned to declare himself a dictator of the left. The middle class (and certain elements of the upper class) were in near panic.

The result is well known. Set off by a "sit down strike" or "mutiny" among 1,425 enlisted men and noncommissioned officers which Goulart supported on March 31, 1964, the Brazilian Army took over the national government of Brazil within twenty-four hours. There was almost no resistance. Reportedly over 7,000 people were arrested in a few days following the take-over, including important legislators and officials. On the evening of the coup, tons of paper was thrown from the windows of apartment houses and office buildings—obviously by people of the middle class. White candles of victory were lighted in middle-class apartment windows in Rio de Janeiro. And a march of protest similar to that which was carried out in São

Paulo became a march of victory a day or so later. Evidently the middle class was pleased; it was relieved to have the military in charge.

In the first months after the March 31 "revolution," the middle class seemed to give its support despite the numerous actions contrary to middle class liberal democratic ideology. On April 9, 1966, the military command proclaimed the first Institutional Act (two more followed) decreeing that "the victorious revolution dictates juridical powers without being limited in this right by the norms existing prior to its victory." On April 11, 1966, contrary to the existing Constitution, Marshal Humberto Castelo Branco was elected by the Chamber of Deputies as president of Brazil to serve until January 1966 (later extended one year). In the first two months, some 400 people lost their political rights, among them three ex-presidents and six state governors. These governors, fifty-five federal legislators, public officials, labor leaders, and others were included among those who lost the right to vote, to run for public office, or to hold government jobs. Despite the trappings of a Congress and Senate, a civilian ministry, and an "elected" president, this was clearly government by the military.

The new government seriously attempted to curb inflation with only moderate success. In 1965 it allowed three state elections; anti-government candidates won in the two important states of Minas Gerais and Guanabara. This indication of loss of support, particularly in states with an articulate middle class, led the government to tighten control. Political parties were abolished and a "Pro-Revolutionary" coalition was formed. (As yet there is no true opposition coalition.) It was decreed that the forthcoming election for presidency and state governments would be indirect by the legislation. This was followed by further *cassoc õ es* (cancellations) of political rights seemingly to guarantee the election of government candidates. A "revolutionary" General, Costa e Silva, who was Minister of War, announced his candidacy for president, and he was elected virtually without opposition. It looks as if the Brazilian government will be dominated by the military for many years to come.[5] If this should happen, then the middle class will have made a bad bargain. As a result of its basic economic, social, and political dilemma, the Brazilian middle class opted for stability over change.

CONCLUSION

What happened in Brazil . . . is not a unique phenomenon in Latin America. In its essential features, it has happened again and again—in Argentina, Colombia, Ecuador, the Dominican Republic, Peru, and Venezuela. After initial support of a military regime which promised stability, the middle class found itself prisoner of a quasi-authoritarian state. And in Cuba, what seemed to begin as a middle-class revolution against the dictator became a communist revolution that has driven most of the middle class into exile. In all of these situations, the middle class might have been the crucial element for social and political change. It was not so; rather it faltered and acquiesced in favor of the status quo.

The Latin American middle class must solve its dilemma. It must decide to promote social and economic change and to build a society in its own image, no matter what the cost. And it will be a costly and difficult task to extend education, health, food, public services, and the right to vote to the mass of people. The middle class will itself suffer in the process. But the alternatives are to live in a nation policed by the military or face a left-wing authoritarian regime which would aim at its destruction. The question for the next generation in Latin America is whether or not the middle class is willing to pay the price of a peaceful revolution.

NOTES

This chapter was originally published as chapter 7 of Charles Wagley's *The Latin American Tradition: Essays on the Unity and the Diversity of Latin American Culture* (New York: Columbia University Press, 1968), 194–212.

1. Marvin Harris, *Town and Country in Brazil* (New York: Columbia University Press, 1956), 279ff.

2. Daniel Cosio Villegas, "Nationalism and Development," in *Latin America: Evolution or Explosion*, ed. Mildred Adams (New York: Dodd Mead, 1963), 122.

3. One of the most widely circulated and cited books in Latin America in the last few years was John Gerassi's *The Great Fear* (1963), which is a rather shrill exposé of U.S. intrigue in Latin America.

4. W. Stanley Rycroft and Myrtle M. Clemen, *A Factual Study of Latin America* (New York: Office of Research, United Presbyterian Church), 146.

5. Editor's note: Military rule ended in 1985.

II

New Histories

Chapter Seven

Moralizing the Masses

William E. French

In this study of the mining town of Parral, Chihuahua, during the Porfiriato
*(the 1876–1910 regime of Mexican dictator Porfirio Díaz), William French
examines elite and middle-class efforts to impose increasingly rigid standards
of moral behavior upon a recalcitrant working class. Inspired by European
and U.S. scholarship on so-called bourgeois culture, French provides a portrait of a middle class that defined itself not by income or occupation but by
lifestyle and the values of domesticity, sobriety, efficiency, and self-discipline.
French's middle class (or* sociedad culta, *as they called themselves) became
missionaries for a "civilizing process" that they saw as essential to the triumph of modern capitalism. On this issue, French sees no significant distinction between the attitudes of Parral's "middle" and "upper" classes.*

—————

The last year, or a little more, has witnessed a wonderful decrease in intemper-
ance among the people in this state, and especially so among the laboring
classes. . . . The credit for this change is wholly due to Governor Enrique C.
Creel. . . . The result has been the cleaning out of the cheap dives which were
frequented by the laboring classes, and, as a consequence, the great lessening
of drunkenness.

Chihuahua Enterprise, 1907

During the Porfiriato, a nascent middle class sought to enlist the state in the
task of implanting the ethic of modern capitalism. The numerous references
to vice in middle-class discourse reveal its central role in this struggle over
values. The Mexican bourgeoisie hoped to eradicate vice and inculcate values of thrift, sobriety, hygiene, and punctuality in succeeding generations of
workers through state regulation of alcohol, prostitution, gambling, vagrancy, and public space. In short, members of so-called respectable society,

79

known as *sociedad culta*, subscribed to a developmentalist ideology in hopes of turning a new, and feared, floating population of rural and urban workers into patriotic citizens and peaceful, hardworking, and suitably motivated workers.[1]

In adopting an ideology stressing development and moral reform, middle-class Mexicans were adhering to a well-established pattern. In the first half of the nineteenth century, French industrialists also condemned activities and attitudes that distracted workers from work and family. They hoped to transform workers' morality by instilling selective middle-class values: "from being ignorant the worker was to become educated; from improvident, economical; from apathetic, ambitious; from drunk, sober; from a philanderer, a devoted family man."[2] Industrialists asserted their right to supervise this metamorphosis because they believed that they already possessed the necessary virtues. Similarly, in the United States at the beginning of the twentieth century, Ford personnel managers attempted to inculcate middle-class values of the nuclear family, cleanliness in personal and domestic life, thrift, sobriety, traditional morality, family-centered recreation and entertainment, and, most of all, hard work in their workforce.[3]

Studies such as these point out that the values of what it means to be a patriotic citizen and a good worker must be inculcated, often in the face of a great deal of intransigence. As Corrigan and Sayer have shown in their work on England, capitalism necessitates the construction of an entire social, economic, and cultural edifice—a Great Arch. According to these authors, the construction of this arch is intimately linked to state formation, a process of cultural revolution by which means rulers moralize, normalize, and create individuals out of workers and build the cultural frame through which they claim their right to rule. Their work is premised upon Weber's insight that capitalism requires a specific and practical ethos.[4]

In Mexico, developmentalist beliefs provided an ideological underpinning for capitalism, as Protestantism had done elsewhere. According to Weber, the asceticism associated with the Protestant religion, leading to the disciplined and methodical organization of conduct, was an important factor motivating and legitimating continuous, rational economic enterprise.[5] Among the Mexican middle class, adherence to "American" values of hard work, thrift, hygiene, entrepreneurialism, and moral reform served the same purpose.[6] In addition, morality, served as a symbolic shorthand around which concepts of citizenship, work, and race were clustered, allowing members of *sociedad culta* to mark off the respectable from the dangerous lower classes while, at the same time, providing themselves with a means of class and self-identification.

A HISTORY OF MORAL REFORM

Attempts to impose moral reform and inculcate developmentalist values in Mexico occurred long before Porfirio Díaz became president. In the seventeenth century, mine owners hoped to discipline workers by bringing priests to their mines. A century later, viceroys attempted, although with little success, to stop mine workers, whom they regarded as insolent, lazy, rebellious, and vice-ridden, from drinking, gambling, frequenting taverns, and assembling in cemeteries.[7] These actions formed part of a more general campaign against popular culture carried out by the Bourbons in the final decades of colonial rule. Bourbon reformers waged a struggle that took place on many fronts, including the cleaning, beautification, and rationalization of city streets and buildings; reform of bullfighting, the theater, and other popular pastimes and celebrations; an attack on drinking, gambling, and vice; and a campaign against religious "superstition." Such measures served both to educate the lower orders in the new values of the bourgeoisie and to provide them with a means of self- and class definition.[8]

Elites in newly independent Mexico continued to champion moral reform. As early as the 1820s, the liberal intelligentsia envisioned the creation of a homogenized modern society "dressed in European clothes and generally scrubbed and tidied up," in which the lower classes would be symbolically whitened through education, the influence of the press, and civilizing literature.[9] Municipal authorities in towns outside the nation's capital implemented measures designed to achieve these and related goals, a process of putting the basic principles of the Enlightenment into effect; they mandated that homeowners number their houses, build indoor toilets, regularly sweep the street and sidewalk in front of their properties, and remove all garbage. In addition, new regulations governed street entertainment and the sale of alcohol. By enacting these measures, authorities desired to ensure decency, a characteristic sign of a people governed by reason and amenable to it.[10]

During the Porfiriato, the emergence of a new and dangerous class, no longer under the sway of traditional authority, prompted northern Mexicans to emphasize moral reform. Especially after the turn of the century, middle-class Mexicans in Chihuahua perceived their society to be convulsed in social crisis. While they touted railroads as the primary example of Porfirian progress, they were appalled by the growing army of beggars, drifters, and workers who rode the rails into Chihuahua's cities and mining towns. Increased incidence of criminality was one sign of the supposed breakdown of order; idleness was another. Middle-class Chihuahuans described their state as inundated with a plague of men, women, and children all supposedly sustaining idle lives by begging in the streets. Idleness itself was a symptom of moral and social crisis, with criminal behavior never more than a temptation away. Beggars, vendors, unemployed workers, and unskilled laborers shared one common characteristic: transience. All new arrivals, working or idle, unknown by the community and lacking permanent residences, were outsiders—people without a stake in the community. Many considered their presence a negative consequence of Porfirian growth and a threat to social stability.[11]

Middle-class Chihuahuans quickly condemned the behavior of this transient population. The municipal president of the mining town of Villa Escobedo reported frequent scandals in which drunken workers shot off their pistols at night. Paydays became occasions for egregious drinking and gambling. In San Francisco del Oro, another mining municipality, prohibition of liquor sales forced workers to journey to Santa Bárbara to purchase large quantities of mescal liquor. They then frustrated local officials by drinking and stirring up scandals (singing loudly, shooting off guns, disturbing neighbors) inside their own homes. In the isolated railroad construction camps of the district, workers celebrated paydays with alcohol, horse racing, and cockfighting; on one occasion in 1904, the chief of public security arrived during a drinking spree and threw thirty-six workers into jail.[12]

The boom-and-bust nature of the mining economy added to the sense of a population in flux. Between 1895 and 1909 . . . Parral's population first expanded from 11,250 to 17,000, then contracted to less than 9,000. Similar dramatic fluctuations took place in Santa Bárbara and Villa Escobedo. Moreover, many migrants were simply passing through Chihuahua on their way to higher paying railroad and mining jobs in the United States. Forced off the land, searching for work, or supplementing agricultural income with wage labor in railroad and mining camps, these migrants swelled the *población flotante*.[13]

In addition to disparaging the floating population, the Chihuahuan middle class drew sharp boundaries between itself and the working class. Middle-class Chihuahuans were the literate, educated, propertied, and self-proclaimed respectable members of society. Teachers, journalists, and government officials, as well as merchants, shopkeepers, mine owners, and *rancheros*, fit into this category. In Hidalgo District, the Stallforth family was representative of the new middle class. Owners of a local mine, the Stallforths sponsored the building of an industrial school for young women. Also representative was Pedro Alvarado: his family connections and access to credit enabled him to persevere through bad economic times before his Palmilla mine turned into a bonanza. Local officials such as Manuel G. Martínez and Agustín Páez were also members of the Chihuahuan middle class; they attempted to carry out moral reform in Hidalgo District's municipalities. By 1910, this literate middle class made up some 8 percent of Mexico's total population; in Chihuahua, its numbers had greatly expanded during the economic boom that had taken place in the early years of the twentieth century.[14]

Still, in the opinion of many members of *sociedad culta*, some workers might qualify as morally acceptable. For example, Rodolfo Valles, the *jefe político* in Hidalgo District, distinguished between the underclass and the working class. He condemned unwalled and undeveloped city lots as a threat to public health and security and as unworthy of the culture and beauty of Parral. Although owned by the Parral's well-to-do, these lots provided safe haven for criminals and those addicted to vice. Valles specifically excluded lands owned by the working class from condemnation, stressing instead workers' commitment to improving their properties and aiding in the city's expansion.[15] On another occasion, *El Hijo del Parral* dismissed speculation about the town's impending collapse when a downturn in the mining economy prompted workers to leave the district for railroad construction jobs in a neighboring state. As far as the paper was concerned, this exodus of workers had little significance because they were not true members of the community but merely part of the floating population carried along by the changing economic tides of late Porfirian Mexico: their arrival and departure coincided with that of the trains.[16] By means of the criteria of vice and transience, middle-class Chihuahuans clarified, in their own minds, the relationship between the dangerous and the respectable poor. Those who adopted middle-class values and lived permanently in their communities might quality as members of the respectable working class.

Despite distinguishing between workers and the floating, vice-ridden population, many were troubled by the working class itself. Those in the middle class conceived of class boundaries in cultural terms, referring to themselves as members of cultured or refined society (*sociedad culta*) and to workers as representatives of the lowest orders (*gente baja*). One contributor to *El Correo*, for example, conceded that society accorded artisans derogatory and contemptuous treatment. This he blamed on the underdeveloped culture of workers, asking, "Will the working class be the only class that remains stationary and segregates itself from the rest?"[17] Other correspondents noted the weak sense of duty and patriotism among the working class. They appeared astonished that workers labored only in order to eat, not to improve themselves; working-class Mexicans did not seem to regard work as the means of obtaining independence, prosperity, or happiness. According to members of refined society, workers lacked civilization, justice, liberty, and a sense of duty: rather than ennobled, workers felt oppressed and enslaved by work.[18] As far as middle-class Chihuahuans were concerned, workers failed to measure up to the behavioral standards needed for inclusion in refined society; they refused to share in Mexico's progress.

The belief that one could obtain perfection through work formed part of a package of values promoted by adherents to the doctrine of what can be called social Catholicism. Indeed, *El Correo*, the reformers' forum, was an avowedly pro-Catholic publication. After 1891, with the publication and dissemination in Mexico of the Rerum Novarum proclamation, and especially in the final decade of Porfirian rule, social Catholics were preoccupied with what they referred to as the "social problem" or "corruption of the masses." They pointed to high levels of alcohol consumption, the common practice of cohabitation instead of marriage, the increase in prostitution, and the proliferation of illegal activities as evidence of the failure of progress in the moral and spiritual realm. In four national Catholic congresses held between 1900 and 1909, delegates considered, among other issues, measures to free workers from the grasp of vice, especially alcohol, and ways to ensure jobs that would pay a living wage to all workers. They also stressed the dignity of women and the sanctity of marriage, home, children, and family.[19] Yet this preoccupation with the perceived moral decadence of Porfirian society was not a uniquely social Catholic phenomenon. Nationally, the press of every ideological stripe lamented that material progress had not been accompanied by intellectual and moral advances. In Chihuahua, the liberal press, although it often identified the Catholic Church as an obstacle to Mexican development, echoed the views of its Catholic colleague.[20] When it came to moral reform and the role of women, middle-class Catholics and liberals had more in common with each other than with their co-religionists among the *gente baja*.

THE VILE TRINITY OF VICE

Members of *sociedad culta* lamented the effects on Mexican workers of alcohol, which they considered to be one of the greatest evils to afflict humanity. In their opinion, alcohol promoted worker absenteeism and poor work habits, and led to a loss of what they referred to as "productive wealth." What good is a drunk at work? asked *El Hijo del Parral*. He spends most of his energy in the *cantina* rather than in the shop; even worse, once he turns up at work he sleeps on the job or stops the rest of the workers from doing theirs. By behaving like this the worker fails to fulfill his obligations, dishonors his trade, and discredits his workplace.[21] Another newspaper lamented that alcohol filled city jails with criminals and converted men's hands into instruments of brutality and crime rather than making them apt for useful duties and work.[22] This was a common refrain. Middle-class Chihuahuans, bemoaning alcohol's effect on contemporary public order, demanded restricted hours of *cantina* operation—especially Sunday afternoon closing—to prevent drunken scandals and crime. Similar concern with crime led officials in Mexico City to make concerted efforts to enforce *pulquería* regulations there.[23] Common, too, was the preoccupation with utility. Porfirians of the *sociedad culta* measured themselves and their countrymen with the yardstick of usefulness to family and society. In their view, "useful" meant "working": by contrast, idlers, slackers, and the unemployed were the greatest social villains.

While, in the short term, drinking threatened to turn potentially productive workers into men useless to society or, worse still, criminals, its long-term consequences promised to be even more devastating. *El Correo*, claiming that its conclusions had been well proven by Charles Darwin, chronicled the generational effects of alcohol abuse: drunkenness and alcoholism predominated in the first generation, followed, in the second, by manic excesses and paralysis; hypochondriachal tendencies, suicidal ideas, and homicidal inclinations appeared in the third; finally, in the fourth generation, stupidity, idiotism, and the extinction of the "race" took place.[24] In accordance with the neo-Lamarckian assumptions of Latin American public health and medical practitioners (in which acquired characteristics could be passed on), alcohol, long viewed as a moral evil, also became an "enemy of the race." Not only was it thought to lead to crime, juvenile delinquency, prostitution, and mental illness, alcohol was also a "racial poison," portending permanent, hereditary degeneration capable of affecting entire populations.[25] Fear of racial degeneracy led middle-class Chihuahuans to demand strict compliance with regulations prohibiting minors from entering *cantinas* or consuming alcohol, and parents and governmental officials were expected to set a proper example for Chihuahua's youth.

Racial degeneration promised political consequences. Instead of citizens imbued with patriotism and free will, subsequent generations might end up as a "shapeless," "rotten," "decayed," and "repulsive" mass. Such a population would find it impossible to stand up to oppressive despotism and tyranny at home or protect Mexico's sovereignty against a foreign aggressor. In short, deformed future generations would be incapable of complying with the obligations of citizenship.[26] For many members of *sociedad culta*, then, campaigning against alcohol became a patriotic duty that rose above politics or religion. At stake were both the future of the country and the liberty of man.

Drunkenness also announced the end of virtue—liberty's natural ally. As they located virtue in the household and family, middle-class Chihuahuans sought to form a working-class home where all the proper values could be passed on to future generations. As one paper explained, in the house of the honest and intelligent worker, a sanctuary of noble affections and purest enjoyment, children grew up docile, hard-working, and patriotic, while the wife concerned herself with the care of her husband. Such families did not contract debts or commit shameful acts; they lived without remorse, avoiding crime and poverty. Rather than spending money frivolously, they saved their paycheck. By turning to alcohol and forgetting his duties to family and nation, the non-virtuous worker lost domestic peace, injuring man, family, and nation in the process. The newspaper concluded by stating that the best legacy a worker could leave his children was the example of his virtues:

these children would be honorable, hardworking, and active citizens.[27] In short, drunkenness led to family breakdown with society suffering the consequences.

It was, in part, the link between drinking and prostitution that caused moral reformers to turn their attention to the latter "vice." Bent on reducing drunkenness by limiting alcohol's accessibility, middle-class Chihuahuans began to criticize its sale and consumption in licensed brothels. For them, the union of alcohol and prostitution represented both a corruption of public morals and a source of criminality.[28] Because "enlightened" Chihuahuans considered public morality and good customs to be essential for order and the achievement of a cultured society, they demanded the prohibition of the sale of alcohol in brothels. Once they had accomplished this end (a new "tolerance regulation" was made law in Chihuahua City in the fall of 1903), members of *sociedad culta* campaigned for this prohibition's strict enforcement.[29]

Prostitution posed additional threats to morality and good customs. When petitioning city officials for the removal of prostitutes from their neighborhood, for example, five residents in Parral stressed that the immoral behavior of prostitutes negated the moral example they provided for their own children.[30] In another instance, *El Hijo del Parral* worried that the continual rubbing of shoulders between "ostentatious and luxuriously dressed fast women" (*mujeres alegres*) and those who lived by means of honest work might entice young women down the slippery slide into prostitution. In the event of such an occurrence, returning to honest life and moral living was deemed impossible, even if so desired, once the first peso changed hands. The newspaper concluded that prostitution was a cancer attacking the moral basis upon which society rested. Rehearsing many of the same arguments used against alcohol, *El Hijo* lamented that youths who frequented brothels were likely to become men useless to themselves and society.[31] Also as in the case of alcohol, brothels promised to lead to the progressive degeneracy of the Mexican "race" by facilitating the spread of venereal disease and the corruption of minors.

Perhaps of greater significance for so-called respectable Chihuahuans was that the location of brothels, especially those in the center of the city, allowed prostitutes to blend in and "confuse" themselves with honorable folk. They resented that prostitutes would attempt to make themselves equal to honorable people, and to solve this problem, they attempted physically to separate the categories of people they distinguished in Porfirian society. The desire to preserve social distinctions was often reflected in the very regulations governing brothels: prostitutes were required to be of the same social class as their clientele.[32] Such social segregation promised an orderly society in which everyone knew, and kept to, their place.

Reform-minded Chihuahuans, then, did not object principally to the existence of brothels or prostitutes (indeed, for many, they were seen as a social necessity), but rather to their visibility and location. In the struggle to control public space, they coveted the city center for themselves and attempted to banish prostitutes to isolated neighborhoods. Lamenting the newly established presence of an immoral lodging house, residents of one Parral neighborhood campaigned to have its resident thrown out of the city, "as is done in all cultured societies."[33] Shortly after the turn of the century, municipal officials in Chihuahua City proposed to locate all brothels in one neighborhood at what was then the outskirts of the city. Although supportive of the scheme in theory, *El Correo*—whose editor, Silvestre Terrazas, had identified the isolation of all prostitutes in remote neighborhoods as one of the most needed of all moral reforms—advocated a longer-term approach to the problems posed by prostitution. The newspaper concluded that, given the city's incessant growth and progress, this measure would merely postpone dealing with the problem. In its place, it proposed that city officials designate a yet more remote neighborhood—characterized by cheap land and no hope of increased population—in which to locate all brothels. It suggested that the new barrio be called "El Puerto de Cochinos."[34]

Middle-class Chihuahuans regarded gambling as the third component of the vile trinity of vice. For them, it was impossible to be both a gambler and an honorable man. As well as a social "cancer," gambling was described as a "gangrene of the social organism," which promoted the characteristics of avarice, jealously, vengeance, depravity, and the loss of shame and riches and led to robbery, jail, the *presidio*, and even the scaffold.[35] Upon entering a gambling den, men trampled on their duties as fathers and husbands, sacrificing all they had at the altar of this vice. Much like alcohol and prostitution, gambling undermined cultured society to the detriment of individual, family, and nation, and led eventually to the destruction of the family and the moral death of society.

As gambling represented wealth acquired through the ruin of other families or, perhaps worse, wealth that did not result from hard work, it was particularly repugnant to those who desired to inculcate the capitalist work ethic. Most middle-class commentators asserted that gamblers damaged society by robbing industry, commerce, and agriculture of hours that could have been spent working. In Parral, for example, *El Hijo* juxtaposed gamblers with hard workers: what was needed was working men for Parral's mines, not gamblers, whom it characterized as idlers and slackers.[36]

Some reversed the causal relationship between vice and idleness, blaming the latter for increasing alcoholism, prostitution, and gambling. The mother of gambling is vagrancy, and the love of acquiring money without work the father, concluded *El Correo*.[37] Middle-class Chihuahuans invoked familiar themes to condemn idleness, citing loss of honor and virtue; the ruin of families, future generations and the nation; and fear of increased crime. To begin with, slackers failed in their duty to family and nation; deprived of work's moralizing effect, they ended up as depraved, parasitic beings without shame or knowledge of human dignity. Moral reformers described idlers as a useless horde dedicated to robbery, deception, fraud, and swindling—to everything, in fact, except work, which would take from them a good part of their sweet leisure hours. Idleness also threatened Mexico's future by corrupting young people. In an initiative presented to the city council in Chihuahua, for example, one official urged action against the growing number of shoeshine boys on the city's principal streets. This rabble, as he described it, which was composed of young boys, had abandoned home and shop, becoming parasites who used shoe-shining as a pretext to wander freely, living a life of idleness. These children were a threat not only to passersby (thus invoking the fear of increased crime) but also to the country's future, as they were the men of tomorrow.

While others focused on the effect of vice on work habits, these moral reformers, viewing work as a virtue in its own right, stressed its reformative power: "To work is to live," stated *El Hijo.* "Man, family and society develop and progress through work. . . . [Work] increases inventions, improves customs, conserves health, combats vice, provides riches, and maintains independence and liberty."[38] Rather than scorn the gambler and other "degraded" beings, *El Correo*—viewing work as essential to the process of moral and physical redemption—implored its readers to help in the task of regeneration. Moreover, according to the newspaper, the gambling problem was not an inherent evil but a matter of interpretation: the gambler simply had to be made to understand that honest poverty was more worthy than wrongly acquired wealth.[39] For one contributor to *El Correo*, however, work alone was not sufficient to cure slackers. Like many nineteenth-century Mexican liberals imbued with utilitarian ideals, he believed that regeneration could only take place in the workshops of the penitentiary.[40]

The association of idleness with vice led middle-class Chihuahuans to demand state action against vagrants and idle men. *El Correo* directly linked vagrancy to vice: "The house of the slacker is the brothel, the gambling den, and the *cantina.* There he lives, there he is, and there he will be found at all hours, idle and satisfied."[41] The newspaper also criticized men who set up crates on street corners to sell cheap merchandise instead of deigning to soil their hands with real work. Whereas these individuals were merely miserable, however, those in the first group, described as a stain on cultured society, were in need of state prosecution. During the last decade of Porfirian rule, middle-class Chihuahuans puzzled as to why there should be labor shortages in the face of a seeming abundance of "vagrants." Drawing on the 1871 criminal code—which defined a vagrant as someone lacking property and income, and having no legitimate impediment, not exercising any skill, craft, or honest profession in order to subsist—they demanded state intervention to put such individuals to work.[42]

State officials agreed. In 1904, Governor Terrazas, describing vagrancy as one of the most noxious social evils, encouraged *jefes políticos* energetically to pursue and punish vagrants in order to return them to activity and work. In this instance, the labor shortages paralyzing mines in the state prompted official action.[43] That same year, the governor, in a letter to the *jefe político* of Hidalgo District, praised local efforts at regulating those who were not dedicated to honest work. Correcting vagrancy, he maintained, allowed companies to count on the availability of more workers.[44] A few years later another governor, Enrique C. Creel, proposed that municipal lands on the north side of Ciudad Chihuahua be set aside for workers' permanent dwellings. The "Colonia de Obreros," as it was to be called, was to be "comfortable, pleasant, and sanitary"; to help ensure this, no *cantinas* were to be permitted.[45]

Distinguishing between vagrants and workers, however, posed somewhat of a problem for those in the middle class. Writing in *El Correo*, Francisco Díaz blamed the precarious situation of the majority of artisans and workers on their poor work habits. In his opinion, instead of being dedicated to work and family, artisans, in growing numbers, swarmed the streets like true layabouts without credit or resources, confusing themselves with beggars. Most Mondays, he continued, they deserted their shops to squander their weekly wages with friends and to indulge in the degrading vice of alcohol. Díaz blamed artisans for their own plight: when workshops had made advantageous offers to workers, provided that they complied with their obligations in a full and exact manner, they had refused. In his opinion, their precarious situation would remain unchanged until they modified their conduct, complied with their duties, and learned to keep their word. At present, however, artisans lived in humiliation, playing a role little honored in society, and they were unworthy of public appreciation or social esteem.[46] Another writer, in demanding legislation to discipline unreliable workers, declared it as absurd that the public's rights and interests should remain at the mercy of lazy, capricious workers. He called for corporal punishment and prison terms to instill proper work habits.[47] All in all, in the opinion of middle-class Chihuahuans, a problematic relationship existed between vagrancy, vice, and the working class. Workers, already extremely mobile, became vagrants if they refused to comport themselves according to the standards of *sociedad culta*.

While these writers blamed workers for creating social confusion by missing work and indulging in vice, others used the criterion of vice itself to distinguish between social groups. For them, indulgence in vice served to mark off the dangerous from the respectable working class. "We have a veritable army of slackers that lives on top of the working classes," maintained *El Hijo del Parral*. In its opinion, slackers represented not only a criminal threat to society but a heavy burden for the proletariat that sustained itself by hard work.[48] Others distinguished between frock-coated middle-class, and lower-class idlers, often reserving their harshest comments for middle-class slackers. *El Correo* contrasted "frock-coated *léperos*" with lower-class drunks. Although each group occupied distinct drinking venues, upper-class drinkers were the most arrogant and scandalous, and thus deserving of the heartiest condemnation because they bribed authorities to ignore *cantina* closing regulations. Reformers insisted that the authorities apply such regulations fairly.[49]

THE REGULATION OF VICE

Many members of *sociedad culta* recognized the impossibility of eliminating vice and called, instead, for its regulation—the next best option in the struggle to moralize the masses. While they strove to reduce the consumption of alcohol to as low a level as possible, they favored a different strategy with regard to prostitution: as a necessary evil, even a benefit to society, prostitution would be conducted under state auspices in well-defined, and properly invigilated, areas. As for gambling, *El Hijo*, in commenting on popular Christmas fairs, admitted its inevitability, particularly since, in its opinion, gambling was the sole purpose of such fairs. How much better it would be, the newspaper concluded, to reform the law in a liberal and honorable sense, for regulating games of chance, as the state regulated prostitution and liquor sales, rather than making them illegal, would give more dignity to authority.[50] In the opinion of moral reformers, the mere passage of legislation outlawing vice, with no possibility of enforcement, served only to mock authority. By contrast, they anticipated that the regulation of vice would bolster citizens' respect for government. Middle-class Chihuahuans expected state and municipal officials to enforce reasonable moralizing measures.

Although prostitution and alcohol regulations existed before the turn of the century, the legislation of morals began in earnest when Luis Terrazas returned to the governor's chair in 1903, a position he had not enjoyed since the 1880s.[51] Before handing Enrique C. Creel that same office the following year, Terrazas enacted measures to regulate alcohol, prostitution, and gambling. Although such policies are commonly associated with Creel, many were begun under Terrazas. According to *El Correo*, Terrazas, in addition to dominating Chihuahua's economy and acting as a regional strongman, presided over a "moral and moralizing administration."[52]

Moral reform was also a municipal concern. In May 1903, Silvestre Terrazas presented Chihuahua City councilors with an initiative against alcohol and prostitution. Along with encouraging healthy public recreations, the initiative mandated increased taxes on alcoholic beverages, rigorous limitation of new *cantina* openings, reduced hours of operation, and penalties for *cantineros* who continued to serve intoxicated clients. Terrazas also called for a commission to be appointed to study the best means of combating alcoholism and prostitution and to designate a neighborhood for the establishment of brothels. Using statistics drawn from the operation of the jail in Chihuahua City to bolster his case, he concluded that these measures—especially the closing of *cantinas* early on Sunday—would significantly reduce crime and aid in the struggle to impose new work habits. Moreover, according to Terrazas, employers could do their part to moralize the popular masses by changing pay days from Saturday to Monday or another day of the week and offering a weekly or monthly bonus to dutiful employees.[53] In June, the Interior Secretary called for municipal councils throughout the state to enact *cantina* reforms. He hoped to reduce criminality and remove the bad moral example corrupting Chihuahua's youth because he feared that future as well as formerly productive workers would be corrupted into becoming men useless to society.[54]

In July 1903, the state government approved *cantina* regulations submitted by Chihuahua City town councilors. Based on laws previously enacted in Mexico City, the new measure stipulated that liquor sales end at nine in the evening, Monday through Saturday, and that *cantinas* close at two in the afternoon on Sundays and during fiestas. It also required *jefes políticos* and *presidentes municipales* to license all establishments selling liquor, dividing such businesses into *cantinas*, on the one hand, and commercial outlets—such as cafes, candy shops, bakeries, restaurants, stores, and small shops—on the other. The measure distinguished between first class *cantinas*, which were to be located in a central zone, and those in a second class, which would be situated throughout the rest of the city. While both types were subject to periodic inspection and had to meet hygienic standards, first-class *cantinas* also had to be constructed for easy cleaning, have tables and chairs of solid construction that were easy to keep clean, use glasses that were crystal, and offer a sufficient number of spittoons. Whereas *jefes políticos* had formerly been able to grant special permission for extended hours of operation, this right now became the prerogative of the state executive. A final article prohibited people from remaining in *cantinas* after closing hours.[55]

At the same time, Governor Terrazas directed *jefes políticos* to prohibit gambling in their jurisdictions, even during the traditional fiestas celebrated by each *pueblo*. The following year, in citing gambling's role in making men lazy and dishonorable, he issued gambling regulations that defined permissible games. Henceforth, chess, bowling, billiards, cockfights, horse racing, bicycle racing, foot racing, raffles, lotteries, dominoes, checkers, *conquian*, *brisca*, *escarte*, *tresillo*, *Panguin gui*, common poker, paco, *pelota*, *tiro al blanco*, and whist were to be permitted. All other games were prohibited. Under the new measure, clubs, casinos, and gaming establishments required a written license from the *jefe político* or *presidente municipal*. Though games were not permitted in public plazas during fairs, gambling was limited to easily policed areas outside public view. Finally, the regulation prohibited gambling in brothels and ordered municipal and state employees to refrain from gambling.[56]

In September 1903, the state executive approved a Tolerance Regulation for Chihuahua City. The measure removed brothels from the city center, designating, as an alternative, three brothel zones, each with a different rate of taxation (those in the first zone were to be taxed at one hundred pesos per month). In addition to prohibiting gambling and liquor sales in brothels, the regulation required prostitutes to dress "properly" and not appear in the street in groups of more than two; it banned them from *cantinas*, billiard halls, restaurants, or cafes, and even from living in the first zone. Nor could they exhibit themselves from windows or balconies. Brothels could sport no external signs and were required to have opaque windows.[57] Such attempts to control public space and the bodies, even gestures, of prostitutes, were common in Chihuahua. By dividing brothels into classes, middle-class Chihuahuans hoped to keep social groups from mixing in these establishments. They also intended to remove the example of vice provided by the prostitute from what they perceived to be increasingly promiscuous and vice-ridden city streets.

Taking office in 1904, Governor Enrique C. Creel continued the campaign begun by Terrazas. Upon assuming office, Creel reorganized Chihuahua's districts and replaced elected *presidentes municipales* with appointed officials known as *jefes municipales*, a move designed to strengthen state government at the expense of the municipalities.[58] He envisioned governing through a new breed of local official who would serve as a moral example in each *municipio*, and to back up his commitment to alcohol and gambling regulation, Creel mandated that, henceforth, state and municipal employees would be fired for drunkenness. Early the following year, he reiterated his commitment to combat vice through the example of good government: state employees not contributing to the moralization of society faced dismissal—an order Creel reaffirmed in June of that year.[59]

Under Creel, state and municipal officials focused on two hotbeds of vice: the billiard hall and the *cantina*. Members of *sociedad culta* reserved their harshest criticism for "mixed" commercial establishments—those that sold alcohol along with other goods and services—including billiard halls, restaurants, and grocery stores. Although some were willing to accept billiards as a legitimate form of recreation, most believed that the sale of alcohol and the gambling that took place in most halls turned them into dens of vice. Such businesses, described by the press as loci of immorality, proved especially difficult to regulate. Gambling regulations were also flouted in Chihuahua's *cantinas*, much to the disgust of *El Correo*. In mid-1905, the newspaper applauded municipal officials for finally enforcing these ordinances.[60] The year before, the *jefe político* had affixed notices to the doors of the city's *cantinas*, reminding *cantineros* that regulations prohibited minors from being on the premises or alcohol from being sold to minors, police agents, or those already inebriated.[61]

In mid-1906, at Creel's insistence, legislators passed a new law against intoxicating liquors. The regulation demanded official authorization for the establishment of new cantinas and reserved all rights of vigilance and control for state government. The law divided merchants into two classes: those who contributed to social well-being and those who made money through immoral enterprises. While members of the first group were to enjoy constitutional guarantees, those in the second became subject to the full force of the new law. Creel believed the law to be so advanced that it would not be surpassed by future legislation.[62] *El Correo*, however, remained unconvinced. It hoped that the regulation would not run up against the indolence, if not the complicity, of certain authorities. Believing that some aspects of the law were outside state jurisdiction, even unconstitutional in its curtailment of individual rights, the newspaper nevertheless wished Creel well in his campaign against alcohol—the cancer of modern society, in its opinion.[63] Finally, Creel's regulation also called for the formation of societies to work with state government to promote popular temperance.

THE "BURNING MORALITY" IN HIDALGO DISTRICT

One moral reformer, in an address to the Anti-Alcoholic League, praised the recently passed *cantina* regulations and pointed to the "burning morality" alive in Chihuahuan society. He also pointed to other social advances—laws that would make education available to thousands of Indians in the mountains; laws that would benefit workers and encourage their honor, patriotism, and thrift; and the worthy example of women workers. Without an open war on alcoholism, he declared, all these initiatives would remain a chimera.[64] In implanting the ethic of capitalism, progress required the elimination of alcoholism.

This "burning morality" extended beyond the seat of state government to the districts, municipalities, and mining camps of the state. Between 1900 and 1910, local officials in Hidalgo District regulated gambling, brothels, fairs, circuses, leisure activities, and the sale and consumption of alcohol. Perhaps none did so more keenly than the *jefe municipal* of Santa Bárbara, one of the district's most important mining centers. Concerned that working people should know the arrival and departure hours for mine work, Agustín Páez appropriated 1,300 pesos from the municipal budget to purchase a four-sided public clock. Despite the scarcity of municipal funds, he ordered the clock to be sent from Mexico City and arranged for expert supervision of its shipment and installation. Páez, supported by mine company managers and the town's principal residents, undertook construction of a ten-meter clock tower on Chapultepec Hill, dominating the village.[65] There could be no more visible example of the desire to impose time discipline on Mexico's laboring classes.

In Valle de Zaragoza, another municipality in the district, the *presidente municipal* exhibited a similar commitment to the developmentalist ethos. After observing that textile workers from Bella Vista were forced to miss a day's work in order to appear before him to register civil acts such as births and marriages, he requested permission to perform these acts after working hours and during holidays, either in the registry office or in workers' homes. Not only would this save a day's pay for the worker, it would boost the income of factory owners by keeping the machines running. Believing himself to be possessed of the same spirit that moved state government to regulate vice, he further proposed to register sites where suspected clandestine liquor sales took place. Failing to catch red-handed those involved in these illegal transactions, he favored aggressive regulation of certain areas of the municipality on the basis of his suspicions.[66]

Municipal officials, advocating higher taxes and shorter stays for circuses, dramatic functions, operas, concerts, magicians, and somersaulters, drafted regulations for public amusements in 1903, prohibiting festivities that, in their opinion, corrupted good customs and attack morality, especially certain dances introduced from the United States.[67] In striving to create a refined society by imposing high standards of public morality, they also justified the need for these measures by pointing to the losses suffered by local merchants, the poverty in which the needy classes remained after the circus left town, and the damage incurred by local mining companies. With prolonged festive periods, they maintained, workers stayed awake and were unable to report to work at the proper hour. Recognizing that mining companies needed a regular supply of punctual laborers, they sought to foster reliable work habits through regulation of public amusements.

District officials also regulated gambling. In 1904, Governor Terrazas congratulated Rodolfo Valles, the *jefe político* in Hidalgo District, for his efforts at controlling gaming in district *cantinas*. The governor was applauding Valles' initiative that required *cantina* owners to apply for gaming permits—licenses granted only to those who ran games approved by the state.[68] In Santa Bárbara, the municipal chief lamented that the limited powers granted to him by law did not allow him to punish severely enough those caught indulging in games of chance. As a solution, he proposed that, upon discovering gambling, he close the establishment and remit to Parral those caught taking part. There, the *jefe político* himself might deal properly with the transgressors.[69]

Other officials in Hidalgo District were imbued with a similar commitment to moral reform. In April 1900, town councilors in Hidalgo del Parral attempted to control prostitution in their city by passing a Tolerance Regulation. They designated several city blocks as the area where brothels were to be located—called the *zona de tolerancia*—and prohibited prostitutes, who now had to be registered, from leaving the zone during hours specified by the act. A new municipal official, the *agente de sanidad*, was charged with recording and regulating the whereabouts of prostitutes, who were required to submit to weekly medical examinations, to dress and behave "decently," and refrain from encouraging business by standing in doorways, windows, and balconies, or through signs, signals, and words. Every brothel fell under the care and vigilance of a woman at least forty years old, this advanced age supposedly being sufficient guarantee against her participation in the trade itself.[70] The regulation, like those elsewhere in the country, was modeled on the French system, which rested on three goals: to create an enclosed milieu for prostitution invisible to women, children, and other members of society; to impose constant supervision of the authorities in such a location, the first tier of which was the matron running the brothel; and to prevent the mixing of age groups and classes in such establishments. In Parral, as in France, vice was meant to be concentrated in one spot and thus purged from the rest of the community.[71]

In June 1903, on his own initiative, the *presidente municipal* in Santa Bárbara established a well-defined brothel zone on the outskirts of town, giving resident prostitutes a week to leave their current lodgings and move to the area. This local official justified his action as the best means of imposing police vigilance in brothels and thus avoiding scandals, which was a very difficult task because prostitutes lived scattered throughout the town and along the street running to the train station. He asked the *jefe político* in Parral to approve his measure.[72]

Initially, regulations did not prevent the sale of alcohol in registered brothels. A 1902 register reveals the existence of four brothels in Parral housing some sixty-nine women, differentiated into first and second-class prostitutes, with the former paying three pesos per month in municipal taxes and the latter, two. Octaviana Ruíz, owner of the city's largest brothel, complained of excessive taxation: not only did she pay eight pesos each month in city taxes as well as taxes for weekly at-home medical examinations for every woman working for her, she faced an additional monthly levy of ten pesos because her brothel had also been classified as a *cantina*. This she bitterly denied, maintaining that she sold only soda water in her establishment.[73]

By mid-1903, *cantinas* and brothels could no longer legally coexist. Responding to demands of the local press, complaints of mine managers concerning working-class alcoholism, and the suggestion of state officials that municipalities enact their own alcohol reforms, the *jefe político* prohibited alcohol sales in brothels and ordered *cantinas* to close during specific hours.

On Sunday, *cantinas* located in neighborhoods were to close at two in the afternoon, while those in the center of town could remain open until four. The rest of the week, closing time was ten o'clock and midnight, respectively. "Mixed" commercial establishments were also to adhere to this schedule for alcohol sales, even if they remained open to sell other merchandise. Those violating the new regulation faced heavy fines and loss of their license.[74]

Other officials in municipalities under Parral's jurisdiction quickly followed suit. In Santa Bárbara, officials ordered *cantinas* to close at ten o'clock, except those situated in the city center, which could remain open until midnight. The *presidente municipal* in Huejotitan, blaming alcohol for the frequency of violent crime, issued regulations making merchants who sold alcohol responsible for preserving order in their establishments. Especially problematic were the groups of inebriated singers that caroused through the *pueblo* bothering peaceful citizens, exhibiting a lack of morals and civilization, and carrying on drunken scandals. According to this official, since workers, who made up the bulk of the population, were unable to attend to their tasks the day following drinking, all liquor outlets would henceforth close at eight o'clock.[75]

As an integral aspect of the 1903 reform drive, state officials ordered *jefes políticos* and *presidentes municipales* to submit crime statistics so that the effect of the new regulations on the crime rate could be measured. Less than a month after regulating liquor sales in his jurisdiction, the *presidente municipal* in Santa Bárbara reported magnificent results: whereas only ninety-two men had been arrested for crimes motivated by drunkenness since July 12 1903, the day the new measure went into effect, in an equivalent period before passage of the regulation 157 had been detained on similar charges.[76]

Dramatic changes were not so apparent in other jurisdictions, especially in municipalities dominated by agriculture rather than mining. In San Isidro de las Cuevas, for example, the *presidente municipal* noted no difference; all people in the community were docile, he explained, and had always been dedicated to their work. In Valle de Zaragoza, however, the absence of police and the alarm caused by the new regulations made compliance impossible. Because *cantina* owners refused to close, the *presidente municipal* found himself confronting a large number of drunken scandals. Maintaining that the layout of the town prevented proper police vigilance, he asked the *jefe político* for a corporal and two additional policemen to enable him to enforce the regulations.[77]

The *jefe político* had to rely on *presidentes municipales* to arrest and fine those indulging in alcohol-induced scandals and ensure that *cantinas* closed during restricted hours. Yet attempts to enforce the 1903 law in several municipalities met with the resistance of these very officials. Many supplemented a grocery or clothing business by selling liquor. To comply with the regulations, they were required to install blinds to prevent liquor sales from being observed from the street; they complained that not only would this prevent customers from seeing their goods, but more serious still was that no respectable woman or family would dare enter their premises once blinds separated the shop from the public view. Municipal officials in Balleza petitioned the *jefe político* to overlook this aspect of the reform.[78]

Local records reveal a new concern with regulating the sale and consumption of alcohol in Hidalgo District after 1903. After the passage of regulations governing *cantinas* in that year, the presence of the police became the most important criterion when officials made decisions regarding liquor sales and the establishment of new *cantinas*. Police vigilance became critical to reform, and its absence prompted *presidentes municipales* to prohibit the sale of alcohol, even in closed bottles, in stores removed from the main centers of population and in isolated *ranchos* and *pueblos* throughout the district. In Santa Bárbara, for example, the *presidente municipal* explained to an unsuccessful petitioner that liquor sales would no longer be permitted in company stores in areas without police supervision. In late 1903, this became policy for all mining companies operating within his jurisdiction.[79]

Police-imposed vigilance also became a prerequisite to obtaining approval for establishing new brothels, for permission to host fairs and circuses, and to run lotteries. Members of *sociedad culta* contrasted vigilance with clandestinity, and in the terminology of the day, unregistered prostitutes became clandestine as did liquor, its illegal sale, and the location of such transactions. Gambling and gambling dens fell into the same descriptive category. While historians have emphasized the police role in imposing order during the Porfiriato, they have not addressed its role in implementing and enforcing moral reform: police agencies were to keep watch over moral reform, combating clandestinity with their vigilance.[80]

In 1906 and 1907, alcohol regulation and enforcement acquired new momentum in Hidalgo District. Frustrated by their inability to control alcohol sales in "mixed" establishments, district officials closed such outlets in many areas of the district and imposed new closing regulations in those that remained open. In Parral, the police commander and the *jefe político* energetically enforced laws mandating Sunday drinking hours and closing times for *cantinas*. In January 1907, the *jefe político* introduced a new regulation governing the sale of intoxicating beverages, which reflected his concern with a new danger to public health posed by alcohol. Not only did alcohol promise the generational debilitation of the Mexican race; the poor quality of liquor and its adulteration at the hands of unscrupulous small vendors posed an immediate health hazard. In the mining areas, including Villa Escobedo and Santa Bárbara, local officials carried out measures to combat this menace.[81]

Despite this program of moral reform, a degree of hypocrisy characterizes the rhetoric and actions of moral reformers and state officials in Chihuahua who seemed more concerned with preserving the outward appearance of order than with actually changing behavior. As in Puritanism in seventeenth-century England, such hypocrisy derived from the reluctance of the multitude to accept discipline: those in *sociedad culta* could do little more than make men "visibly" rather than "truly" religious.[82] They advocated vigilance rather than the elimination of vice: the isolation, especially, of prostitutes in pre-scribed zones removed from city centers to where they could not rub shoulders with or provide a bad moral example for decent, honorable people; and opaque windows and Persian blinds to keep families safe from viewing corrupt interiors. Middle-class Chihuahuans stressed the outward appearance of conformity rather than the creation of true believers in the developmentalist ethos.

Increasingly, governmental officials became the targets of reformers' wrath as indulgence in vice seemed unabated in the state. In perceiving the police to be part of the problem rather than part of the solution, members of *sociedad culta* called for new standards in police recruitment and the establishment of a police training school to improve the quality and morality of policemen. They stressed that society did not need new regulations but rather proper enforcement of the existing morals laws. Despite state efforts to enforce higher standards for state and municipal employees—including threats to fire those who did not set a "moral example" for the masses—moral reformers lamented the duplicity of the police and governmental officials in vice.[83] They complained that political authorities were not active enough in imposing the new discipline, the new sense of the necessity of labor, upon the mass of the population. Disappointment in the slow pace of reform and outright governmental involvement in "immoral" acts turned many reformers against Terrazas-Creel rule.[84] Rather than less government, these Chihuahuans demanded more, better, and responsible government.[85]

CONCLUSION

Members of *sociedad culta* struggled to impose a new developmentalist ethos on the masses. They meant to create suitably motivated workers and patriotic citizens through state-enforced discipline, vigilance, supervision, and control. As vice jeopardized the inculcation of time discipline, habits of thrift and saving, and proper work patterns, all progress would be for naught without its regulation. Immorality posed even greater threats to Mexican society. Subscribing to a belief in racial and biological causation, middle-class Chihuahuans feared that uncontrolled alcoholism, prostitution, gambling, and vagrancy threatened the degeneration of the Mexican race. Although alcoholism and venereal disease represented the greatest evils, "degeneracy" could be moral as well as physical. Moreover, unregulated vice destroyed virtue, provided poor moral examples for the youth of Chihuahua, and created men useless to society. The struggle to impose morality thus transcended politics and the workplace to become a patriotic duty—at stake were the future of the country and the race itself.

In stressing the importance of moral reform and the preoccupation of middle-class Chihuahuans (including governmental authorities) with the inculcation of the developmentalist ideology, more than a simple functionalist model of social control is implied. Faced with a new, floating, and working population no longer subject to "traditional" rural authorities, members of *sociedad culta* contested for control of city space. They sought to differentiate between the dangerous and the respectable poor, and to distance themselves physically, by removing vice from city centers, and socially—as honorable members of society—from this new mass. Profession of a moral lifestyle reveals as much about their attempts at self- and class definition as it does the need for social control.

In their struggle to regenerate the Mexican masses, members of *sociedad culta* identified the stability of the family as vital to national progress. They expected discipline to begin in the family, and parents were asked to provide an example of high moral standards. In one sense, they envisioned governmental regulation as an extension of family control. As the family head provided discipline and the example of virtuous conduct, so must governmental authorities. As the formation and endurance of the working-class family became increasingly premised upon the male laboring for a wage, squandering of wages on vice threatened the family's destruction and, with it, a means of disciplining the masses. When middle-class Chihuahuans spoke of regenerating the lower classes, they not only meant regeneration from dishonorable to honorable and from useless to socially productive, they also hoped to build ideally happy homes out of the rubble of families fractured by vice.

NOTES

This chapter was previously published as chapter 3 of William E. French's *A Peaceful and Working People: Manners, Morals, and Class Formation in Porfirian Mexico* (Albuquerque: University of New Mexico Press, 1996).

1. Alan Knight uses the term *developmentalist ideology* to describe beliefs shared by respectable Porfirians, particularly an emphasis on time discipline, thrift, hard work, hygiene, and progress. See Knight, *The Mexican Revolution*, 2 vols. (Cambridge: Cambridge University Press, 1986), 1, 23–84. On the inculcation of work discipline, see Thompson, "Time, Work-Discipline, and Industrial Capitalism," *Past and Present* 38 (1967). For the case of the Mexican working class and time discipline, see Knight, "The Working Class and the Mexican Revolution, c. 1900–1920," *Journal of Latin American Studies* 16 (May 1984): 51–97. Also on developmentalist ideology in Latin America, see David McCreery, "'This Life of Misery and Shame': Female Prostitution in Guatemala City, 1880–1920," *Journal of Latin American Studies* 18, no. 2 (November 1986): 333–53.

2. Peter Stearns, *Paths to Authority: T he Middle Class and the Industrial Labor Force in France, 1820–48* (Urbana: University of Illinois Press, 1978), 150.

3. Stephen Meyer, *Five Dollar Day: Social Control in the Ford Motor Company, 1908–1921* (Albany: State University of New York Press, 1981), 151.

4. Philip Corrigan and Derek Sayer, *The Great Arch: English State Formation as Cultural Revolution* (Oxford: Basil Blackwell, 1985), 61, 117–19, 129, 132, 140, 155, 171, 184, and 200. For a discussion of the "Great Arch" in the Mexican context, see Alan Knight, "The Peculiarities of Mexican History: Mexico Compared to Latin America, 1821–1992," *Journal of Latin American Studies* 24 (Quincentenary Supplement 1992): 134–44.

5. Max Weber cited in Robert Moore, "History, Economics and Religion: A Review of 'The Max Weber Thesis,'" in *Max Weber and Modern Sociology*, ed. Arun Sahay (London: Routledge and Kegan Paul, 1971), 86.

6. Alan Knight discusses these "American" values in *The Mexican Revolution*, 1, 69. A recent work judges these values to be "negative." See Ramon Eduardo Ruiz, *The People of Sonora and Yankee Capitalists* (Tucson: University of Arizona Press, 1988), 20, 194–96.

7. Doris M. Ladd, *The Making of a Strike: Mexican Silver Workers' Struggles in Real del Monte, 1766–1775* (Lincoln: University of Nebraska Press, 1988), 43 and 74; Cheryl Martin, "Public Celebrations, Popular Culture and Labor Discipline in Eighteenth-Century Chihuahua," in *Rituals of Rule, Rituals of Resistance: Public Celebrations and Popular Culture in Mexico*, ed. William H. Beezley, Cheryl E. Martin, and William E. French (Wilmington, Delaware: Scholarly Resources, 1994).

8. Juan Pedro Viqueira Albán, *¿Relajados o reprimidos? Diversiones públicas y vida social en la ciudad de México durante el Siglo de las Luces* (Mexico City: Fondo de Cultura Económica, 1987). Moral reform in Bourbon New Spain is a subject with a growing historiography; for some recent works, see Pamela Voekel, "Peeing on the Palace: Bodily Resistance to Bourbon Reforms in Mexico," *Journal of Historical Sociology* 5, no. 2 (June 1992); and Susan Deans-Smith, "The Working Poor and the Eighteenth-Century Colonial State: Gender, Public Order and Work Discipline," in *Rituals of Rule, Rituals of Resistance*, ed. Beezley, Martin, and French, 47–75.

9. Jean Franco, *Plotting Women: Gender and Representation in Mexico* (New York: Columbia University Press, 1989), 79.

10. Anne Staples, "'Policia y buen gobierno': Nineteenth-Century Efforts to Regulate Public Behavior," in *Rituals of Rule, Rituals of Resistance*, ed. Beezley, Martin, and French, 115–26.

11. Officials and residents in Parral and smaller mining centers constantly referred to arriving workers and other newcomers as outsiders or unknown people (*gente desconocida*). For two examples, see Presidente municipal, Santa Bárbara, to jefe político, Distrito de Hidalgo, 25 Sept. 1903, AM, caja 1903I and 29 residents to the jefe político, Distrito de Hidalgo, 10 June 1903, AM, caja 1903M. Laurence Rohlfes maintains that during the final decade of Porfirian rule, residents of Mexico City also perceived an increasing "crime problem" in their city. See his "Police and Penal Correction in Mexico City, 1876–1911: A Study of Order and Progress in Porfirian Mexico" (PhD diss., Tulane University, 1983), 139.

12. Jefe de la Seguridad Pública, Los Azules, to jefe político, Hidalgo District, 21 June 1904, AM, caja 1904G; Presidente municipal, Santa Bárbara, to jefe político, 25 June 1904, AM, caja 1904O; Agustín Páez, jefe municipal, Santa Bárbara, to jefe político, 3 Oct. 1908, AM, caja 1908AA. For Villa Escobedo, see Presidente municipal, Villa Escobedo, to jefe político, 27 Sept. 1904, and 9 Nov. 1904, AM, caja 1904C. Reports from San Francisco del Oro in Presidente municipal, San Francisco del Oro, to jefe político, 13 Apr. 1906, AM, caja 1906C; Páez to jefe político, 2 Jan. 1911, AM, caja 1911B. On railroad workers, see J. J. Gutiérrez, presidente municipal, Santa Bárbara, to jefe político, 17 Dec. 1900, AM, caja 1900SUSY.

13. This phrase began to appear in Chihuahua newspapers and Hidalgo District reports soon after the turn of the century. For an early usage, see "El Ferro-Carril a Guanacevi. Emigración de trabajadores," *El Hijo del Parral*, 22 June 1902, 1, AM, caja 1902D.

14. This figure is from José Iturriaga as cited in Knight, *The Mexican Revolution*, vol. 1, 43. On the middle class and moral reform, see ibid., 63–68. On the middle class in Chihuahua, see Mark Wasserman, *Capitalists, Caciques, and Revolution: The Native Elite and Foreign Enter-*

prise in Chihuahua, Mexico, 1854–1911 (Chapel Hill: University of North Carolina Press, 1984), 95–97.

15. Rodolfo Valles, jefe político to C.C. Miembros de la Asamblea Municipal, Parral, 2 July 1906, AM, caja 1906N.

16. "El Ferro-Carril á Guanaceví. Emigración de trabajadores," *El Hijo del Parral*, 22 June 1902, 1, AM, caja 1902D.

17. "Como debe ser un obrero," *El Correo de Chihuahua*, 15 July 1904, 3,

18. "Las clases trabajadores: cooperación y ahorro," *La Nueva Era* (Santa Bárbara), 1 May 1904, 1, AM, caja 1904F. For an interesting discussion of the social divide between the "gente decente" and workers, also conceptualized in cultural terms and in a comparative context, that of Lima, see David S. Parker, "White-Collar Lima, 1910–1929: Commercial Employees and the Rise of the Peruvian Middle Class," chap. 8, this volume.

19. The material on social Catholicism is from Jorge Adame Goddard, *El pensamiento político y social de los católicos mexicanos, 1867–1914* (México: Universidad Nacional Autónoma de México, 1981), 117, 145–49, 190–91, 206, 219.

20. In Hidalgo district, liberal papers such as *El Hijo del Parral* and *La Nueva Era* devoted considerable attention to these issues. Goddard puts it as follows: "The theme of the 'corruption of the masses' was a topic treated constantly by Catholics and liberals" (*El pensamiento político*, 206; see also 114–15).

21. "La embriaguez," *El Hijo del Parral*, 29 April 1900, 1, AM, caja 1900.

22. "Desastrosos efectos de la embriaguez," *El Correo*, 14 March 1905, 1, reel 4.

23. Rohlfes, "Police and Penal Correction in Mexico City, 1876–1911," 139. In Chihuahua, governmental authorities and their respectable critics linked criminality with alcohol. For examples of this viewpoint, see J. Cortazar, Ramo de Gobernación, Estado de Chihuahua to Jefe Político, Hidalgo District, 16 June 1903, AM, caja 1903A and "Iniciativa contra el alcoholismo. . . ." *El Correo*, 2 May 1903, 2, reel 2. On the link between alcohol and crime in Mexico City, see Carlos Roumagnac, *Los criminales en México: Ensayo de psicología criminal* (México: Tipografía "El Fenix," 1904), esp. 47–53 and Miguel Macedo, *La criminalidad en México: Medios de combatirla* (México: Secretaría de Fomento, 1897), 31–32.

24. "México," *El Correo*, 7 Feb. 1903, 3, reel 2.

25. For a discussion of the impact of Lamarckianism in Latin America, alcohol's role as a racial poison, and race, see Nancy Leys Stepan, *"The Hour of Eugenics": Race, Gender and Nation in Latin America* (Ithaca: Cornell University Press, 1991), esp. 63–101.

26. Silvestre Terrazas, "El alcoholismo," *El Correo*, 11 June 1902, 1, reel 1; "Iniciativa contra el alcoholismo . . .," *El Correo*, 2 May 1903, 2, reel 2.

27. Alfonzo Cinelti, "El Trabajo," *El Hijo del Parral*, 9 Dec. 1900, 1, AM, caja 1902G. See also "La embriaguez," *El Hijo del Parral*, 29 April 1900, 1, AM, caja 1900.

28. For a discussion of prostitution's effect on corrupting public morals in Hidalgo District, see "La prostitución y los menores de edad," *El Hijo del Parral*, 2 Sept. 1900, 1, AM, caja 1902D.

29. *El Correo* constantly complained of alcohol sales in brothels. For one example, see "Ventas clandestinas," *El Correo*, 21 Jan. 1908, 1, reel 7.

30. Cinco vecinos al C.C. Presidente y Vocales del C. Ayuntamiento del Hidalgo del Parral, 21 July 1903, in Expediente que contiene negocios correspondientes al mes de julio, Año 1903, Parral, AM, caja 1903H.

31. "Necesidad de reglamentar la prostitución," *El Hijo del Parral*, 30 April 1899, 2, AM, caja 1900I. See also "Iniciativa contra el alcoholismo y la prostitución . . .," *El Correo*, 2 May 1903, 2, reel 2.

32. See the discussion of brothel regulations in Mexico City and a short summary of regulation in Mexico in Sergio González Rodríguez, *Los bajos fondos: El antro, la bohemia y el café* (México: Cal y Arena, 1989), 32, 34, and 61–68.

33. "A través del Estado: Parral," *El Correo*, 8 July 1902, 2, reel 1.

34. "A dónde podrian ser trasladadas," *El Correo*, 17 Dec. 1907, 1, reel 6.

35. Originally published in *El Hijo del Parral* and reprinted as "A través del Estado: Parral," *El Correo*, 29 Aug. 1902, 1, reel 1.

36. Ibid.

37. "El juego," *El Correo*, 21 June 1905, 2, reel 4.

38. "El juego," *El Hijo del Parral*, 15 June 1902, 1, AM, caja 1902D.

39. J. Reyes Zavala, "El juego," *El Correo*, 25 Jan. 1907, 2, reel 6.

40. "Faltan brazos y sobran vagos," *El Correo*, 10 Jan. 1906, 2, reel 5. On ideas about prisons and prison reform in Mexico, see Robert Buffington, "Revolutionary Reform: The Mexican Revolution and the Discourse on Prison Reform," *Mexican Studies/Estudios Mexicanos* 9, no. 1 (Winter 1993): esp. 74–87.

41. "La vagancia," *El Correo*, 8 Feb. 1907, reel 6.

42. Moisés González Navarro, *La vida social*, in Daniel Cosío Villegas, *Historia moderna de México: El Porfiriato*, vol. 4 (México: Editorial Hermes, 1957), 422. Calls for vagrancy regulation in Parral were extensive; as examples, see "Dos verguenzas," *El Hijo del Parral*, 9 July 1899, 1, AM, caja 1901C; "Menesteros ó flojos," *La Nueva Era*, 5 Jan. 1902, 1, AM, caja 1902D; and "Perder el tiempo," *El Hijo del Parral*, 23 July 1905, 1, AM, caja 1905F.

43. "Notas oficiales," *El Correo*, 8 Nov. 1904, 1, reel 3.

44. Luis Terrazas, Gobernador, al jefe político, D. Rodolfo Valles, Parral, 25 June 1904, AM, caja 1900A.

45. "To Encourage Laboring Men: Gov. Creel Planning to Help Them to Get Their Own Homes," *Chihuahua Enterprise*, 14 Nov. 1908, 1.

46. Francisco Díaz, "Los artesanos informales," *El Correo*, 1 May 1905, 2, reel 4.

47. "Castigo para los artesanos informales," *El Correo*, 1 March 1906, 2, reel 5.

48. "Los vagos," *El Hijo del Parral*, 25 Oct. 1903, 1, AM, caja 1903C.

49. "Franquezas populares," *El Correo*, 14 Aug. 1906, 1, reel 5.

50. "Las fiestas de navidad," *El Hijo del Parral*, 14 Oct. 1900, 1, AM, caja 1902D. See also "Los fiestas anuales," *La Nueva Era*, 29 Sept. 1901, 1, AM, caja 1903H.

51. For a discussion of Terrazas' relationship with Díaz and his terms as governor, see Wasserman, *Capitalists, Caciques, and Revolution*, 36–42.

52. "Hace treinta años y despues de treinta años," *El Correo*, 13 April 1904, 1, reel 3.

53. Silvestre Terrazas, "Iniciativa contra el alcoholismo y la prostitución, presentada al I. Ayuntamiento por el Regidor 6° C.S. Terrazas," *El Correo*, 2 May 1903, 2, reel 2.

54. Ramo de Gobernación, num. 858, 16 June 1903, in AM, caja 1903A.

55. "Reglamento de cantinas," *El Correo*, 9 July 1903, 2, reel 2. See also: "Un decreto del Congreso del Estado," *El Correo*, 3 July 1903, 1, reel 2; "¡Ahora ó nunca!," *El Correo*, 21 June 1903, 1, reel 2; "Decreto sobre las cantinas," *El Correo*, 8 July 1903, 1, reel 2; and "Las cantinas," *El Correo*, 15 July 1903, 1, reel 2.

56. "Las primeras medidas," *El Correo*, 4 June 1903, 1, reel 2; "Un decreto del Congreso del Estado," *El Correo*, 3 July 1903, 1, reel 2; "Reglamento de juego," *El Correo*, 9 July 1904, 2, reel 3; and "Reglamento de juego," *El Correo*, 11 July 1904, 2, reel 3.

57. "En el Ayuntamiento," *El Correo*, 26 Sept. 1903, 1, reel 2; "El Reglamento de Tolerancia," *El Correo*, 27 Sept. 1903, 1, reel 2; "El Reglamento de Tolerancia, " *El Correo*, 3 Oct. 1903, 1, reel 2.

58. On Creel's rule in Chihuahua, see Mark Wasserman, *Capitalists, Caciques, and Revolution*, 131–38.

59. "Notas oficiales," *El Correo*, 19 Jan. 1905, 1, reel 4 and "Informe leido el 1° de junio de 1905 por el Gobernador Interino Constitucional del Estado C. Enrique C. Creel," *El Correo*, 2 June 1905, 2, reel 4.

60. "Aprehensiones," *El Correo*, 19 June 1905, 1, reel 4.

61. "Magnífica disposición," *El Correo*, 14 July 1904, 1, reel 3. For examples of complaints against cantinas and billiard halls, see "Las cantinas," *El Correo*, 18 July 1903, 1, reel 2; "Alarma entre los comerciantes," *El Correo*, 24 Jan. 1905, 1, reel 4; "El cierre del comercio en pequeño y los expendios de licores," *El Correo*, 26 Jan. 1905, 2, reel 4; "Billares y cantinas," *El Correo*, 1 Aug. 1905, 2, reel 4; "El cierre de las cantinas: Reformas al reglamento," *El Hijo del Parral*, 20 Nov. 1904, 2, AM, caja 1904A.

62. González Navarro, *La vida social*, 79.

63. "Contra la embriaguez," *El Correo*, 11 Aug. 1906, 1, reel 5.

64. "Contra el alcoholismo (discurso pronunciado por su autor en la Velada que organizó la Liga Antialcohólica en el Teatro de los Héroes)," *El Correo*, 14 Dec. 1906, 2, reel 5.

65. Agustín Páez, jefe municipal, Santa Bárbara to jefe político, Distrito de Hidalgo, 14 March 1908 in AM, caja 1908C.

66. Presidente municipal, Valle de Zaragoza to jefe político, Distrito de Hidalgo, 12 April 1904, AM, caja 1904A and presidente municipal, Valle de Zaragoza to jefe político, 20 Oct. 1904, AM, caja 1904J.

67. Miguel Domínguez to Ayuntamiento, Parral, 4 Aug. 1903, AM, caja 1903E.

68. Luis Terrazas, Governor to Rodolfo Valles, jefe político, Distito de Hidalgo, 25 June 1904 in AM, caja Decade 1900A.

69. Presidente municipal, Santa Bárbara to jefe político, 8 June 1903 in AM, caja 1903I.

70. Borrador de Acuerdos del Ayuntamiento–1900: Sesión ordinaria del día 21 de abril de 1900 in AM, caja 1900 Legislación.

71. Alain Corbin, *Women for Hire: Prostitution and Sexuality in France after 1850*, trans. by Alan Sheridan (Cambridge: Harvard University Press, 1990), 9–10.

72. Presidente municipal, Santa Bárbara to jefe político, Distrito de Hidalgo, 19 June 1903, in AM, caja 1903I.

73. Octaviano Ruíz to C. C Presidente y Vocales de la Junta Calificadora Municipal, 26 March 1900 in AM, caja 1900G; Padrón de las meretrices inscritas en el ramo de Tolerancia 1902, AM, caja 1902F.

74. Reglamento de Cantinas aprobado por el Y. Ayuntamiento de Hidalgo del Parral in Ramo de Gobernación, num. 858, 16 June 1903, in AM, caja 1903A.

75. Presidente municipal, Huejotitan to jefe político, Distrito de Hidalgo, 23 June 1903, AM, caja 1903J; on Santa Bárbara see presidente municipal, Santa Bárbara to jefe político, 8 June 1903, AM, caja 1903I.

76. Presidente municipal, Santa Bárbara to jefe político, 2 Aug. 1903, AM, caja 1903I.

77. Presidente municipal, San Isidro de las Cuevas to jefe político, 6 Aug. 1903, AM, caja 1903F and presidente municipal, Valle de Zaragoza to jefe político, 21 June 1903, AM, caja 1903I.

78. Miguel Armendáriz, presidente municipal, Balleza to jefe político, 14 Oct. 1903, AM, caja 1903G.

79. President municipal, Santa Bárbara to jefe político, 16 Oct. 1903, caja 1903I. For evidence of this new concern with alcohol see Presidente municipal, Santa Bárbara to jefe político, 8 June 1903, AM, caja 1903I; "Escandalitos en Santa Bárbara," *La Nueva Era*, 28 July 1904, 3, AM, caja 1904A and Presidente municipal, Valle de Zaragoza to jefe político, 20 Oct. 1904, AM, caja 1904J.

80. "Ventas clandestinamente," *El Correo*, 21 Jan. 1908, 1, reel 7 and Expediente: Varios corresondientes al mes de diciembre 1907, AM, caja 1907H.

81. Informe rendido por el Sr. Rodolfo Valles, jefe político del Distrito Hidalgo, ante el I. Ayuntamiento de Hidalgo del Parral, el día 1° de enero de 1907, in AM, caja 1907J.

82. Christopher Hill, *Society and Puritanism in Pre-Revolutionary England* (London: Secker and Warburg, 1964), 257–58.

83. For an example of state measures designed to "moralize" public officials in Hidalgo District see J. Cortazar to jefe político, Distrito de Hidalgo, 3 Aug. 1903, in Expediente: Parral, agosto 1903, AM, caja 1903L. Mark Wasserman concludes in *Capitalists, Caciques, and Revolution* that despite "progressive" reforms and benevolent projects, Creel presided over "a morass of corruption and governmental abuse" (133).

84. The uproar surrounding the robbery of the Banco Minero de Chihuahua, a Terrazas family enterprise, in March 1908 and the attention it received in *El Correo* makes more sense if interpreted in light of this preoccupation with moral reform. See Wasserman, *Capitalists, Caciques, and Revolution*, 53–58.

85. Knight, *The Mexican Revolution*, vol. 1, 30.

Chapter Eight

White-Collar Lima, 1910–1929

Commercial Employees and the Rise of the Peruvian Middle Class

David S. Parker

This study argues that salaried white-collar workers in Peru, in their collective struggle for better salaries, benefits, and working conditions, crafted a discourse that stressed an innate, almost God-given difference between middle-class empleados *and blue-collar* obreros. *Protective social insurance legislation passed in 1919 confirmed and gave legal force to this* obrero-empleado *distinction, and in so doing helped define what it meant to be "middle class" in Peru. The result was an organized middle class that was in some ways quite militant, yet that militancy was tied to a vision of white-collar distinctiveness that often undermined solidarity with manual workers.*

The year 1919 saw increasing social unrest throughout much of the world, and Peru was no exception. A general strike in January led President José Pardo to decree the eight-hour workday, and demonstrations for lower food prices ignited a wave of looting and mob violence in May.[1] Politics were equally unstable: on July 4, President-Elect Augusto B. Leguía carried out a coup rather than wait for Congress to confirm his victory. Amid the agitation, few paid much attention to a strike called one Saturday morning in late September. Led by clerks in the import-export firms, banks, and retail stores of Lima and Callao, the action was nonviolent, orderly, even polite. No mounted police were called in; in fact, the National Assembly voted to support the strikers' demands. The pickets, numbering some 1,500, went home as soon as business leaders agreed to arbitration.[2]

Only in retrospect did the September strike emerge as a landmark in Peruvian social history. It was the first major public demonstration to invoke the name of "the middle class," a concept virtually absent from the discourse of the previous century. White-collar workers had begun to assert a collective identity. They described themselves as natural leaders of the middle class, separate from the workers below and the oligarchs above. Their organized and vocal presence helped change the shape of Peruvian politics in the 1920s, and many of their demands were adopted in precedent-setting labor legislation.

The middle class has long received attention from students of modern Latin American history, and deservedly so. Hailed by some as a progressive, democratic force for change, criticized by others as a dependent, authoritarian ally of the status quo, few social sectors have aroused so much debate. It is all the more surprising, therefore, that an event like Peru's 1919 employee strike should remain but a minor historical footnote. While innovative social and cultural histories of elites, peasants, and urban workers continue to challenge accepted wisdom, research on the middle class lags behind. In an effort to fill the gap, this essay uses the records of Lima's white-collar workers to trace the emergence of a distinctly middle-class culture and consciousness in a major Latin American capital.[3]

THE WHITE-COLLAR EMPLOYEE IN LIMA SOCIETY

In the early twentieth century, Peru was not a manufacturing country. Agricultural and mineral exports provided a handsome income, while attempts to industrialize were thwarted by a combination of comparative advantage, transport costs that fell with the opening of the Panama Canal, government policy, and the elite's taste for imported goods.[4] Import-export commerce was one of Lima's principal economic activities, responsible for many of the largest fortunes and employing some 15 percent of the city's adult male population. Fewer than half that number worked in factories.[5]

By any measure, commercial employees comprised a significant part of the Peruvian workforce. Like other white-collar workers, they were known as *empleados*, a title that distinguished them from the blue-collar *obreros*. A broad range of people fell under the category of empleado. The wealthiest were accountants and executives in the banks and the largest commercial houses, many of them foreigners. They could live handsomely, and often came from respected families, well connected in society. The poorest tended to be clerks in small retail stores, many of whom worked fifteen or even eighteen hours a day, seven days a week, for the most meager of salaries.[6]

Across this spectrum, empleados shared a number of qualities. To begin, gaining white-collar employment was no easy matter. Requisite job skills included proper spelling and attractive penmanship, mathematical ability, and often some knowledge of bookkeeping, making a secondary education nearly indispensable. Even so, none of those talents sufficed without the all-important personal recommendation.[7] Many store owners so feared robbery and embezzlement that they carried insurance against losses from unscrupulous employees. Unless a friend or previous employer could vouch for an applicant's moral character, he was unlikely to be hired. As a result, recruitment typically followed family ties, political patronage, commercial contacts, school loyalties, provincial origins, or nationality. Even with good recommendations, many aspiring empleados had to begin as *meritorios*, working for up to three months on a trial basis, receiving a nominal wage or no pay at all.[8]

Paternalism colored every aspect of an employee's regime, beginning with basic vocabulary. The most common synonym for empleado was *dependiente* (dependent), while the employer was his *principal*. Empleados were also known as *servidores* (servants), and their seniority was called *tiempo de servicios* (time of service). Though many empleados did move from job to job, the relationship between a principal and his *dependiente* was assumed to be stable and lasting. Unlike professionals such as lawyers, engineers, or architects, most empleados worked without formal contracts specifying their salary or duties.[9] They were to carry out whatever tasks their employer might request, work related or not, and to put in overtime without remuneration. Absolute loyalty was expected at all times.

Those who rebelled against demands they deemed unreasonable filled the records of Lima's labor tribunals. Sales assistant Daniel Flores, feeling ill one day, told his superior that he was unable to stack and move cases in the warehouse. He was promptly fired. Typist Teodora Vega met the same fate when she left the office at 8PM against her boss's orders, though by law women were not supposed to work after that hour. Juan Marticorena was struck in the face by the owner of the pawnshop La Aurora, after complaining about the kind of work he was being asked to perform. In return, he threatened the man with a revolver kept on the premises.[10] For each of these cases, many more chose to obey their supervisors without debate.

Nevertheless, paternalism also worked in the employee's favor, because employers considered it a moral duty to provide for the well-being of their faithful servants. Some awarded pensions; others paid medical or funeral expenses. Many empleados depended on their bosses for interest-free salary advances to see them through times of need. Mutual loyalties often went very deep indeed, with *dependiente* and principal bound socially as well as economically through the institution of *compadrazgo* (ritual kinship).[11] Typical was the case of Antonio Fontana, who had worked for thirty-eight years in one man's store.

> Fontana was, for [his employer] Mr. Juan Nosiglia, not an empleado earning twelve pounds a month, but a friend, more than a friend, rather something like

a member of the family, who sometimes dined at their table. He had the complete confidence of his boss, which he never abused. That confidence, certainly very justified in the case of this empleado of notable honesty, reached the point that he had been authorized by Mr. Nosiglia to take from the warehouse whatever he might need, to be discounted later from his paycheck. [12]

Paternalism was accompanied by the firm belief that commercial employment meant a career with a future. The story of Augusto and Fernando Wiese was well known: from simple empleados in the Emilio F. Wagner & Co. import house, they had risen to become the firm's owners in 1915. [13] While their ascent was unusual, it was hardly unique. Banks and commercial houses relied upon internal training and promotion; biographies of the highest executives usually included a start at the bottom of the ladder. In smaller stores, a successful empleado might be given a share of the profits or named as a partner. Though only the lucky few reached top management positions, mobility up the ranks was the rule and the expectation. [14]

THE CULTURE OF RESPECTABILITY

The attraction of white-collar employment derived not so much from the prospect of mobility as from the empleado's relatively privileged place in Lima's social structure. To understand this point, it is necessary to look at the rules of class stratification as Peruvians themselves did. Sociologist Lowry Nelson described a common Latin American pattern when he wrote about Cuba in the 1940s:

> An arbitrary classification on the basis of income and occupation might . . . reveal a range of classes with a pattern not unlike that of the United States. However, on the more subtle socio-psychological basis . . . Cuban society can more easily be classified into two groups only, upper and lower—or perhaps it would not be too inaccurate to say those who hire servants and those who do not; or, if one wishes, those who work with their hands and those who work with their heads, or do not work at all. The latter are the heirs of the old aristocracy, the former, the heirs of the serfs and slaves. . . . This simple dichotomy of "upper" and "lower" is based primarily on tradition . . . rather than on differences in income and wealth, which are only secondary criteria. It is very likely that on the basis of occupation, there would be included in the upper group not only the wealthy and well-to-do, but also the professional workers of all kinds and the "white-collar" workers, even though among the latter there may be many with lower incomes than would be found among the skilled manual workers. [15]

This two-class order had the deepest of roots in Latin America's history. Nations forged in conquest, where Indians were organized and Africans imported to labor for a Spanish minority, Latin America had for centuries been divided between rulers and ruled, masters and slaves. Colonial law and custom provided for a theoretical division of society into estates (*estamentos*), castelike social groupings based on race and profession, each with different rights, duties, and privileges before the crown. Though the liberal republics of the nineteenth century legally abolished all but minor traces of the *sociedad de estamentos*, traditions forged over three centuries of Spanish rule did not die easily. [16]

In Peru, as elsewhere, those above the great social divide were known as *gente decente*, while those below were alternately *gente del pueblo*, *la plebe*, *las masas*, *los pobres*, *la clase trabajadora*, or after World War I, *el proletariado*. [17] Steve Stein has argued that, well into the twentieth century, Peruvian schoolchildren were taught that this social hierarchy was both inevitable and morally just. As one standard elementary textbook explained, "Urbanity greatly respects those categories established by nature, by society, and by God himself, and therefore it obligates us to give preferential treatment to some persons over others, according to their age, their social position, their rank, their authority, and their character." [18]

Nonmanual labor was a defining quality of the *gente decente*, along with such factors as race, family name, and education. Income was far less important. While the wealthy Chinese shopkeeper would not be considered a part of respectable society, a widow living in absolute poverty might still be *decente*, if she had a certain last name and kept up appearances.

The opposition between the *gente decente* and the *gente del pueblo* tended to be seen in rigidly dualistic terms, with no middle ground. Members of respectable society felt that they shared little in common with the great unwashed masses. Racial and cultural differences reinforced the sense of distance, as if the decent people and the multitude were distinct species of human being. Yet this caste-like dualism was more imaginary than real, the line of demarcation not always clear cut. If an artisan came to own his own shop, employed others, sent his children to private school, and invested in urban real estate, he could become a respectable proprietor—assuming that he belonged to the church and was not too dark-skinned. [19] Of course, decency alone did not win entry into the closed circles of the oligarchy, and no artisan was likely to see his son or daughter marry into one of the "better" families. Still, being above the great social divide meant that he could take a box in the theater, sit in one of Lima's smart cafes, spend a summer weekend at the beach resorts of La Punta or Barranco, even hold political office, without arousing scandal or criticism. In status-conscious Lima, where men dared not enter the central plaza unless they wore a jacket and tie, these were serious issues.

Predominantly white and educated, empleados were widely accepted as *gente decente*. [20] Two examples demonstrate this point. While industrialists held parties for their workers on the factory grounds or in a nearby hacienda, commercial owners honored their empleados at banquets in Lima's private clubs or fashionable restaurants, places likely to refuse entry to most manual laborers.[21] In the 1920s, a public housing plan called for two types of construction, one for obreros and one for empleados. The manual workers' dwellings allowed twenty-five square feet of space per person, while those for the employees gave forty square feet.[22] The proposal did not have to explain why the empleado required more space than the obrero; it was taken for granted that their needs were intrinsically different. Both cases show how the distinction between empleado and obrero went far beyond any mere census classification.

Empleados jealously defended their identification as gente decente, adhering as faithfully as possible to the norms of respectable society. Men cultivated the bearing of gentlemen, from their concern for personal honor and reputation—including familiarity with dueling protocol—to their practice of such aristocratic sports as cricket, tennis, and billiards.[23] Many empleados had their suits made from imported fabrics, even though Peru was a wool and cotton exporter with a domestic textile industry.[24] White-collar families sought to avoid those types of housing considered unbefitting decent people, and above all, the wife was not to work, children went to private school, and housework was done by a maid.[25]

Such was the case despite evidence that a large number of empleados were quite poor, surviving from paycheck to paycheck with little or no savings to cover an emergency. Even well-paid empleados frequently died in poverty, when sickness or forced retirement took away their livelihood.[26] Some owners came to the aid of their former *dependientes*; unfortunately, as white-collar advocate Daniel C. Urrea argued in 1915, these were the minority: "the commercial employee . . . always has before him the spectre of misery in his old age."[27] Indeed, social workers of the time reported on the problem of "the middle class poor," evidence that the term *middle class*, when it was used, referred not to an economic category but to a kind of social caste.[28] The middle class was that group of people not of the oligarchy but still *decente*, no matter what their income.

From this situation, in which social position did not necessarily reflect economic means, a particular culture arose. From the shooting club to the billiard salon, middle class culture was a reflection—some said an imitation—of an idealized elite lifestyle. But as contemporary observers were quick to point out, much of the Peruvian middle class lacked the income to support the type of housing, dress, and consumption expected of the *gente decente*. They were constantly accused of living beyond their means, keeping up appearances at the cost of tremendous sacrifice. Wrote Peruvian historian Jorge Basadre:

The tragedy of an important sector of the middle classes during the nineteenth and the beginning of the twentieth century derived from their heroic effort to approach the ranks of the aristocracy and differentiate themselves from the mass of workers or artisans. They were condemned to a lifestyle and to social rituals in their dress and appearance that were constantly beyond their objective possibilities. . . . Theirs was a life of intimate tragedies, carefully covered up.[29]

The fiction of the period is filled with stories of families who decorated their sitting rooms in great elegance but were unable to furnish the rest of the house; women who copied the latest European styles in cheaper fabric; men who pawned all their belongings to get a box seat at the theater because they could not bear to be seen anywhere else.[30] Nor were such observations limited to novels. Two municipal inspectors wrote about those who chose to dwell in dangerously overpopulated mansions (*casas de vecindad*, abandoned by their original owners, subdivided, and rented) rather than move into physically superior, but socially stigmatized, working class housing (rustic dwellings built on lots called *callejones*): "For unfounded preoccupations, for feigned social respect, they . . . prefer to live in such filthy and unhealthy conditions, in order to cloak themselves in the illusion of residence in a decent house."[31]

These and similar practices became a hallmark of the middle class in early twentieth-century Lima; to characterize such behavior, pundits coined the now classic Peruvianism, *huachafo*.[32]

WHITE-COLLAR ORGANIZATION

Given their identification with respectable society and their faith in the values of the elite, few empleados considered posing a direct challenge to the established economic order. They did organize, however, founding the Sociedad Empleados de Comercio in December 1903. Like other mutual-aid societies of the time, the SEC's principal objective was to cover members' medical and funeral expenses. Nevertheless, the organization had a political purpose from its inception, lobbying for enforcement of the municipal Sunday closing law.[33] In its early years, most empleados saw the SEC as little more than a life and health insurance policy, with dues instead of premiums. Fewer than half of its members voted in elections, and a much smaller number attended meetings. Leaders tended to be high-level functionaries, some of whom used their position as a stepping-stone to public office.[34] Over time, however, the organization slowly gained acceptance as an advocate for white-collar workers of all kinds, from bank clerks to bureaucrats. Its first significant campaign was in 1914, when the government unveiled a plan to tax salaries. By threatening a general employee strike, SEC leaders succeeded in defeating the proposal.[35]

Throughout its early history, the SEC emphasized the goals it shared with employers. Important political and business figures were made honorary members, while the major commercial enterprises helped finance the organization's first meeting hall. The society boasted that it provided company owners a valuable service by organizing classes to improve employee skills and by acting as a reference to guarantee the moral character of its members. As late as 1916, the SEC declared as its purpose "to cement upon solid bases harmony between bosses and employees, endeavoring that both might find the guarantee of their rights and commitments."[36]

This picture changed after World War I. Led by the SEC, empleados emerged as spokesmen for the middle class, highly critical of the economic elite. What brought about such a major transformation? For one thing, a significant commercial crisis starting in August 1914 as the war disrupted international trade and employees suffered pay cuts and unemployment.[37] The postwar era saw an unprecedented economic boom, but a boom that was accompanied by high inflation. While working class day-wages rose—fueled by the demand for construction labor—the more rigid empleado salaries remained constant. In some cases not even the wartime cuts were restored.[38]

Empleados were directly influenced by the organization and radicalization of the working class, as the anarchist message began to find resonance in a society shaken by economic crisis. Even more important, however, was a growing wave of elite reformism. Several major figures in government and business believed that unrest could be prevented by copying European models of labor legislation, fomenting cooperatives, and improving urban sanitation and hygiene. A new generation of politicians placed the "social question" at the top of their agendas; among them were men like Luis Miró Quesada and José Carlos Bernales, both active patrons of the SEC. Even "socialism," albeit poorly understood, took on a new respectability in elite circles, as demonstrated by the triumphant visit of Argentine socialist Alfredo Palacios.[39]

The unquestionable catalyst was the general strike for the eight-hour day, in January 1919. Against expectations, the government acceded to the workers' demands with little resistance, making Peru one of the early countries in South America to adopt the measure. Empleados did not play a central role in the strike, which was led by textile workers and stevedores. Retail shops and import houses closed their doors only because store owners feared general violence.[40] Nevertheless, as soon as President Pardo decreed the shorter workday, white-collar employees began to mobilize on an unprecedented scale. The reason was simple: as formally written, the eight-hour decree applied only to factory workers, igniting controversy over who was covered by the measure and who was not.

When the commercial houses made it clear that they were going to continue business as usual, empleados began to hold conferences and demonstrations to protest their unequal treatment.[41] In the climate of general discontent, a group of young employees came to exercise increasing influence within the SEC, leading the call to broaden the decree.[42] Citing the rising cost of living, they lobbied the government and employers for higher salaries and shorter hours. After several months passed without a response, employees in the port of Callao finally decided to walk off the job. The strike spread to Lima the following day.[43]

The empleados' rhetoric underwent an equally revolutionary transformation in 1919, as white-collar workers for the first time began to speak of a society divided by class. In its 1913 statutes the SEC did not once mention the word *class*, its stated purpose was to "raise the moral condition of its members, doing whatever possible to achieve the guarantees to which they have a right, by merit of the dignity with which they sustain their commitments as empleados."[44]

Yet by January 1919, a mere six years later, SEC communiqués had begun to describe the organization as the representative of a class in conflict, whose interests could only be defended through concerted action: "The Sociedad Empleados de Comercio of Lima and the Asociación General de Empleados of Callao believe it their duty to [give] their unanimous support in service of the vital interests of the social class that they represent: interests deeply affected by the growing rise in the cost of living, so noticeably marked since the beginning of the great war that just ended."[45]

At first glance, the changing language seemed to provide further evidence that commercial employees were taking their place in the emerging labor movement, abandoning paternalism, discarding traditional prejudices, and recognizing their common interest with all workers. On closer inspection, however, white-collar militancy belied a very different set of underlying attitudes. Though empleado demands had indeed taken on a new, class-conscious tone, it was a middle-class consciousness, largely oblivious to the cause of manual workers. In their speeches, white-collar activists used the terms *empleado* and *middle class* interchangeably, arguing that empleados made up the vast majority of the middle class: "The hour of revindication has arrived for the commercial employees, for the middle class in general."[46]

This rhetoric was also increasingly disseminated in the press: "Without a doubt, this movement of the middle class is justified. . . . If any social class merits special consideration, it is that within which are comprised the commercial employees, and also, those who hold the inferior posts in the [public] bureaucracy."[47]

Opinion-makers agreed that the empleados' campaign embodied the needs and desires of the middle class as a whole, even if the definition and boundaries of that class were left ambiguous. At any rate, they argued, they were not the needs of blue-collar workers, who had already received preferential treatment with the eight-hour day.

THE CLASS THAT MOST SUFFERS

Paradoxically, the discourse used to advance the claims of the middle class made sense only in context of the traditional, culturally defined categories of the *gente decente* versus the mass. As the nascent Association of Bank Employees stated on the eve of the 1919 strike:

> The so-called middle class, formed by employees of the public sector, banks, and commercial offices, is a group of men born into distinguished social classes, belonging at times to aristocratic families, possessing education and culture. But they are also men punished by fate, obliged to educate their children and support their families within the bounds of decency, and within conditions imposed by their social circle. This social class is the true victim of the grave economic situation; obligated to live in decent houses, to dress with relative elegance and to eat with some comfort, they are most affected by the rise in the cost of rents, clothing and food. Their income does not keep up with the constant rise in the cost of those elements required to maintain themselves within a social situation that, for their very modesty, they cannot possibly abandon.[48]

The assertion, in other words, was that inflation made it impossible for empleados to support the lifestyle demanded by their position as members of respectable society. Editorials echoed this claim, such as the following, which detailed the primordial difference between the empleado and the obrero:

> The [empleados] suffer the same slavery as the day-laborer in terms of the hours of work, and in many cases earn less, despite the fact that society burdens them with steep demands. The common worker, it is true, exhausts his forces on the job; but he is satisfied with his meal from the cheap food stand, his drink with friends in the corner bar and his room in the crowded tenement. In the home of the obrero the wife sells her cooking and the child hawks newspapers on the street. Completely different is the case of the empleado, who is always obliged to maintain, even if only in appearance and at the cost of every kind of personal sacrifice, the social position he inherited and which the life of social relations, as well as his own hope of getting ahead, make indispensable.[49]

The climate of inflation, labor agitation, and emerging empleado organization thus gave birth to one of the classic myths of the Peruvian middle class: that they suffered *more* from inflation than did manual workers, because their inherent social status left them no choice but to maintain a level of consumption that they could no longer afford. According to José Carlos Mariátegui, this assertion became commonplace after 1919, and it has remained a Peruvian cliché ever since.[50]

The brilliance of the myth was its ability to reconcile the irreconcilable. On the one hand, the idea of the suffering middle class bolstered empleado demands for better salaries, shorter hours, a Sunday holiday, and lower consumer prices—the typical labor agenda, which they shared with manual workers. On the other hand, it reinforced the insistence that empleados and obreros were different by nature, with inevitably distinct material needs. Nowhere in this framework was there room for the idea that a manual worker might need or even desire to live a "decent" lifestyle, nor for the remote possibility that an obrero might become an empleado or vice versa.

Moreover, the image of a middle class oppressed by inflation, trapped under the weight of obligatory expenses, could be used for a variety of political ends. Members of the economic elite fervently supported middle-class demands in the early months of 1919, noting that the poor empleados suffered in silence, participating in relatively little labor agitation, strikes, or violence. As conservative *La Crónica* editorialized: "Yes, the working class suffers from the incredible rise in the cost of living, but suffering just as much, or surely even more, is the so-called middle class, the 'bourgeoisie' so unjustly attacked by the agitators of today."[51]

Much ink was spent sympathizing with the poor, downtrodden empleado; the not-so-hidden agenda was to praise his stoic resignation, thereby condemning the obrero's assertiveness. This provided a way to oppose the manual workers' demands without abandoning a humanitarian public posture and self-image.

But the elite's eagerness to repeat employee claims that the middle class suffered the most, and suffered in silence, came to backfire against them. The young employees responsible for the September 1919 strike pointed out what should have been obvious:

In the article carried by today's *La Crónica*, it is said that "the middle class suffers more than the working class from the incredible rise in prices," and . . . it is suggested that the obreros achieve in another way (that is to say, by peaceful means) the ends that they pursue. . . . The worker has never achieved improvements of wages and other such benefits without recourse to the strike, and without exercising certain measures of pressure against the capitalists. . . .
Well, then, if we of the middle class, constituted in the majority by empleados, find ourselves in worse conditions than blue-collar workers, in spite of our being the brain of all organization, it is precisely for the lack of union and virility among us, that we do not demand by force what we are not given by right. The day that the employees would rise up and strike, they would be heard and attended in their just demands.[52]

When carried to its logical conclusion, the idea that the empleado was more oppressed than the obrero became nothing short of revolutionary. Instead of seeing the tendency to live beyond their means as a collective mid-

dle-class character flaw, the employees of 1919 argued that a "decent" lifestyle was a "demand of their environment," indeed, a requirement of white-
collar employment. Turning the old criticism on its head, the empleados
made a truly radical assertion: that as born members of the middle class, they
had the intrinsic right to a respectable living standard, however that might be
defined. This new middle-class consciousness was profoundly anti-egalitar-
ian, based upon belief in a natural social hierarchy; yet it provided the motive
and justification for the September strike.

THE STRUGGLE FOR PROTECTIVE LEGISLATION

The arbitration board charged with solving the 1919 conflict ruled that employees should receive an across-the-board pay raise and a limit on their
working hours. Employees did not win the eight-hour day, but stores were
obliged to close at 7PM, a provision that the SEC itself began to enforce. [53]
The conquests of 1919, however limited, inspired empleados to continue
organizing in pursuit of pensions and other protective legislation. These campaigns demonstrated the strengths, but also the limitations, of the new middle-class movement.

In early 1921, disgruntled employees in the semi-public, semi-private tax
collection agency tried to form a union. When the company refused to recognize the organization and fired its leaders, the SEC called a general white-
collar strike in defense of the principle of unionization. Few answered the
call, however, and the action was a resounding failure. Empleados had mobilized in 1919 to make demands on the government, but they were not ready
for a direct confrontation with employers over the abstract right to unionize.
In addition to their deep sense of respectability, bonds of loyalty still tied
them to their *principales*. The radical rhetoric of 1921 went against the grain
of their identity as a suffering but distinguished class. [54]

Similarly, employees failed in 1922 and 1923 to win passage of legislation designed to establish a mandatory pension system and to formalize the
rights of employees vis-à-vis their bosses. The Chamber of Commerce opposed the bill, which died a slow death in congressional debate. [55] In this
case, the empleados exerted little real pressure, merely filling the Senate
gallery and cheering on the protagonists as if the debate had been some kind
of sporting event. Wrote one columnist:

> In all the countries of the world, the middle class fights directly, head in the
> air, face-to-face with the enemy. Here it is a timid, cowed, oppressed class,
> with a poorly-understood idea of social action. Hated by plutocrats, ridiculed
> by millionaires, looked on with disdain by aristocrats, held as an enemy by
> obreros, it finds itself alone and isolated, enclosed in the house of cards that

are its prejudices and myths. They say nothing, they ask for nothing, they want nothing. They never raise their voice for fear of imposing. [56]

This criticism was perhaps unfair, because the failure of the 1921 strike had demonstrated the narrow line that empleados were forced to walk. Too little action slowed the pace of reform, but too much pressure undermined the foundation of empleado legitimacy: the ideology of the most oppressed class, suffering in silence. A more confrontational stance would have offended empleado sensibilities as members of the respectable half of society, and probably would have alienated elite opinion, eroding the support that the empleados' cause continued to enjoy. In the end, the SEC leadership chose to lobby for a more moderate law, leaving intact those elements of paternalism and personal loyalty that so characterized white-collar employment. This second bill, which had the explicit support of President Leguía, succeeded in winning congressional approval and was passed as Law 4916 in February of 1924. [57] Commonly known as the Ley del Empleado, Law 4916 provided the basis for a substantial part of Peru's labor jurisprudence, much of it still in force today. The law provided empleados with the following benefits:

1. Three months prior notice before firing, or in case of *despido intempestivo* (unannounced firing), payment of the corresponding salary.
2. Compensation for years of service, paid in a lump sum when the employee left the employer, based on a sliding scale roughly equivalent to two weeks' salary for each year of employment.
3. A life insurance policy provided entirely by the employer for all empleados with four years of service. If an employee died within the first four years, the *patrón* was to pay for a funeral "in accordance with the social status [*según la categoría y rango social*] of the deceased."
4. In the case of work-related illness or injury, employers were to pay 80 percent salary for the first two months, 60 percent the third month, 40 percent the fourth, and thereafter 20 percent, which the employee would receive for the rest of his life in the event of permanent disability. [58]

The Ley del Empleado presupposed and sought to preserve the stable, long-term relationship between employer and employee. Those who frequently changed jobs received few benefits, but people with many years of service in a single establishment could expect a large compensation, in lieu of a pension. The three months' notice arose from the idea that an empleado, if fired, found it especially difficult to obtain a new post. While manual workers were accustomed to job instability, white-collar employees shared an almost irreplaceable bond with their employers, or so it was argued. This vision of the "faithful servant" was similarly behind the lump-sum indemnification. Though employees saw the payment as a right earned over many years of labor, business leaders thought of it as a charitable duty, to assure that their *servidores* did not retire to, or die in, abject poverty.[59] Throughout debate on the bill, the special relation between employer and employee was repeatedly stressed. When one senator complained that the project gave the empleado benefits superior to that of the obrero, another responded, "The condition of the obrero is completely distinct from that of the empleado. The condition of the former in respect to the employer is circumstantial, not permanent like that of the empleado."[60]

Though the Ley del Empleado was rooted in paternalism, its effects were still transcendental. First of all, Law 4916 only applied to the nonmanual, ostensibly middle-class employee. Labor law froze the traditional categories of empleado and obrero into formal definitions, and bestowed upon one benefits that the other supposedly did not deserve or did not need. Thus, as law supplanted custom in deciding who was an empleado and who was not, law also supplanted custom in deciding who was *decente* and who was not. In effect, social classes became legal constructs for the first time in Peru's post-colonial history.

Secondly, Law 4916 provided that all empleados would receive the kinds of benefits that employers usually gave only to their most loyal, most senior employees. Under the new law, those benefits ceased to be rewards or charities: they were now rights that belonged to employees of all types, at all levels of hierarchy, in large firms and small. The effect was to grant empleados a degree of job security never before imagined. Even though the typical employee might have enjoyed a long-term relationship with his employer, it was another thing altogether when the owner could not fire anyone unless he was willing to pay three month's severance plus the compensation for years of service. Employers found it increasingly difficult to use the threat of firing as a way to discipline their workforce.

This aspect of the law sparked heated opposition from the business community. In a campaign launched against the measure, the Chamber of Commerce made it clear that employers had no problem providing benefits for their "good" employees. Unfortunately, the chamber argued, certain "inept, undisciplined and unscrupulous" employees took unfair advantage of the law, either putting no effort whatsoever into the job or going from office to office, intentionally trying to get fired in order to receive the three month's salary.[61] Owners began to interpret the law as restrictively as possible, and frequently tried to circumvent its provisions.

LEGISLATING SOCIAL CLASSES: EMPLEADOS AND OBREROS

Employer resistance took a number of forms, including a widespread effort to reclassify empleados as obreros. Not surprisingly, this sparked a series of legal conflicts over who enjoyed empleado status. The legislation had been approved with employees of the large import houses and banks in mind; it did not take into account the technicians, warehouse guards, hacienda administrators, foremen, mining work-gang leaders, and others whose work and social category fell within the gray area between empleado and obrero, or between empleado and domestic servant. Arbitration tribunals had to establish, case by case, who was an empleado and who was an obrero. It became clear for the first time that customary distinctions were inadequate, because they were not based on formal, objective rules that held up legally. Moreover, the rise of new occupations, especially technical jobs in mining and construction, played havoc with a system of stratification that traced its origins to an earlier, less diversified economy.[62]

The judges based their decisions on various criteria, the most important being the degree to which the duties performed were primarily intellectual versus manual. All claimants who could possibly support their status as an empleado tried to do so, often embellishing their job descriptions. A doorman emphasized the occasions on which he took money to the bank or made purchases for his boss, a mechanic called himself a "mechanical employee," the most senior of three telephone repair workers gave herself the title "chief of repairs section," and a live-in apartment handyman provided documentation showing that he was responsible for collecting rents and screening new tenants.[63] Employers played the same game, declaring in one case that a highway construction engineer performed services "of a technical nature," and in another that a draftsman only worked as a day laborer.[64] Some employers tried to deny their workers empleado status by shifting them from the monthly salary payroll (customary for empleados) to the day-wage payroll (customary for obreros).[65]

Job descriptions were often not enough to settle the obrero-empleado question, so the tribunals tended, albeit against the letter of the law, to take the characteristics of claimants into account. Education was a crucial factor: few illiterates won empleado status, and technicians with formal credentials had a better chance than the self-taught. Race could not but slip into the calculus: one night watchman, a Spaniard, won empleado status when indigenous Peruvians doing identical work did not.[66] Since European birth practically guaranteed consideration as one of the *gente decente* in Peru, this is perhaps not surprising.

Some defenses were brilliant. All workers in the Cerro de Pasco Copper Corporation, for example, carried identification cards in Spanish that identified each as "empleado no. N" of the company. The word *empleado* was clearly a literal translation from the English, used by that U.S.-owned and -operated mining concern with its generic meaning, covering both manual and nonmanual workers. Even so, one lawyer successfully used the ID card as material evidence to prove that a miner, by the company's own admission, was indeed an empleado and not an obrero.[67]

The most common court declarations combined aspects of the job description with characteristics of the worker, in search of a kind of argumentative overkill, as in the following:

> José León was neither an obrero nor a foreman but rather a "checker," whose occupation consists of ordering the transfer of cargoes from the warehouse to the convoy in order to send them on to their destination, recording each package on an ad hoc list. He was the one man responsible in case of the loss or misdirection of cargo; he earned a monthly salary of 85 *soles*, paid fortnightly, as were the other empleados. . . . Unlike foremen, a "checker" works at night and even on holidays without receiving overtime, and in past strikes the "checkers" have never intervened on the side of the workers nor have they taken the obreros' side in their negotiations with the Company.[68]

José León's attorney mounted a defense based on the job's intellectual nature, the level of responsibility, the mode of payment, and, significantly, workplace politics. Though it was uncommon for claimants to refer to their political or strike behavior in order to argue empleado status, his case underscored how the law rewarded those employees who insisted that they were distinct from obreros.

Empleados responded in contradictory ways to their new legal rights. On the one hand, disputes over interpretation of the law drove a wedge between the business community and the white-collar organizations, pushing empleados toward a more radical line and undermining the harmony that they had once claimed to seek with employers. Tensions were felt not only during peak moments of confrontation, as when the Chamber of Commerce tried to repeal or circumvent major portions of the legislation, but also in daily interaction on the job. Employers complained about the erosion of discipline, while empleados countered that their bosses would falsely accuse them of theft or some other offense in order to avoid paying indemnifications. Differences that might have been solved amicably, it was charged, now went to court.[69] Some arbitration cases generated heated rhetoric, as in that of a department store employee who complained about the "abuse of the capitalist against the little empleado."[70]

On the other hand, the actual content of the legislation had an opposite effect. With compensation claims based on the time of service to a single employer, the law perpetuated the ideal of mutual loyalty and defended a way of life that could not easily be reconciled with strikes or trade unionism. Indeed, many of the law's most fervent supporters considered it little more than a guarantee that employers would treat their empleados with the kindness that tradition dictated and that "good" employers willingly gave. The conflicts that arose were rationalized as the machinations of a few "bad" employers, even when the Chamber of Commerce led the siege.

An excellent example is the case of Antonio Fontana, the man who had worked for thirty-eight years in Juan Nosiglia's family business, and who had been allowed to take whatever he needed from the warehouse. Sometime after his employer's death, Fontana notified the new boss, Juan Nosiglia Jr., that he wished to retire and receive his indemnification for thirty-eight years of service. The young Nosiglia fired him, refusing to pay compensation because Fontana had allegedly stolen a pair of shoes. Fontana claimed he had taken them on account, as always. Significantly, the article in Fontana's defense spoke not of the employee's legal rights but of the hard-heartedness of Juan Nosiglia Jr., who had shamelessly reneged on a moral obligation to his father's trusted servant: "[T]he situation of Fontana should be defended not only by the law, but also by the recognition of his bosses. But—and this is the tragedy—the poor, elderly man has been deprived of . . . this recognition, and so his only hope is that justice be done by those who enforce the law."[71]

More important, the Ley del Empleado gave permanence to a division of society based on the distinction between manual and nonmanual labor. This could not help but erode any grounds for a broad labor alliance, especially if an empleado like José León could use a demonstrated lack of solidarity with obreros as evidence to prove his status and claim his benefits. In fact, some empleados cited the new legislation expressly to discredit and demean those "below them" in the hierarchy, as in this letter from a time-keeper to the company director:

> I can only protest, Mr. Superintendent, that in order to fire me from my position you have invoked the affirmations of a drunken watchman, whose word could never prevail, given his sad condition of domestic (in accordance with paragraph "A" of Article 2 of the reglamentation of Law 4916), over the affirmations of a man of honor and a conscientious employee, who in his thirteen years of service to the company, has never given his superiors any reason for complaint.[72]

The law justified traditional prejudice, reiterating the idea that obreros and empleados were two different kinds of people, and that only empleados were *gente decente*, members of the middle class. In the end, supposedly "progressive" labor legislation crystallized and preserved a caste-like conception of society, with roots deep in Latin America's colonial heritage.[73]

EMPLEADOS AND THE NATURE OF THE MIDDLE CLASS

The historical role of the middle class in Peru, as in the rest of Latin America, has typically been described in one of two ways. The progressive theory saw the middle class as a force for change, fully conscious of its interests, willing to ally itself with the working class in order to combat oligarchic domination. The dependent theory has seen the middle class as a loyal appendage of the upper class, on whom it relied for jobs and favors. The dependent middle class emulated the elite and shared its view of the world, including disdain for (and fear of) the masses. Most alternative theories combined the two visions, painting a middle class that wavered between progressive and dependent as it adapted to circumstances. In every case, however, progressive and dependent attitudes were thought of as diametrical opposites, an assumption that is logical, but wrong.

The experience of the Peruvian empleado illustrates the complexity of a middle class that was simultaneously progressive *and* dependent. On the one hand, because their society generally considered them part of the *gente decente*, empleados lived in a cultural milieu suffused with elite values and ideals. In such matters as housing, dress, food, and leisure, the upper class was their reference point: they had no other. Paternalism and the ideal of loyal service bound employees to their bosses, while the tradition of internal promotion (and hence, the chance of upward mobility) legitimized their aspirations and their identification with those above them. On the other hand, the economic demands of membership in respectable society were often well beyond an employee's modest means. Those culturally defined "necessities" were a heavy financial burden, especially in times of inflation. Because employees could not rely upon their bosses' generosity alone to provide for a lifestyle befitting their perceived social station, they were left with little choice but to join together and take action on behalf of concrete material demands.

Lima's employees gradually, perhaps reluctantly, adopted working-class methods of organization and struggle, including the union and the strike. In some cases they joined forces with blue-collar workers. At no time, however, did their action signify a true identification with the proletariat. Employees consistently claimed that they, the middle class, were the ones who suffered most from the rising cost of living. They were naturally distinct from the working class, so the argument went, and their basic necessities were, by definition, greater. The ideology of the most-oppressed middle class took firm root in Peruvian political culture, enabling empleados to continue seeing themselves as part of society's respectable half, even while they joined blue-collar workers in the streets. This vision strongly influenced Peru's early labor law, cementing the obrero-empleado division as a permanent facet of that nation's social organization. In sum, the empleados successfully defended their interests while they preserved a basic identification with the elite. From their point of view, this was anything but dependence: it was a hard-fought and well-deserved victory.

NOTES

This chapter was previously published in the *Hispanic American Historical Review* 72, no. 1 (February 1992): 47–72.

1. Peter Blanchard, *The Origins of the Peruvian Labor Movement, 1883–1919* (Pittsburgh: University of Pittsburgh Press, 1982), 148–59; Denis Sulmont, *El movimiento obrero en el Perú, 1900–1956* (Lima: Pontifica Universidad Católica del Peru, Fondo Editorial, 1975), 80–94; Peter F. Klarén, "The Origins of Modern Perú, 1880–1930," in *The Cambridge History of Latin America*, ed. Leslie Bethell, vol. 5, *c. 1870 to 1930* (Cambridge: Cambridge University Press, 1986), 624–31; Jesús Chavarría, *José Carlos Mariátegui and the Rise of Modern Peru, 1890–1930* (Albuquerque: University of New Mexico Press, 1979), 21–24; Piedad Pareja Pflucker, *Anarquismo y sindicalismo en el Perú (1904–1929)* (Lima: Ediciones Rikchay Perú, 1978), 41–61; Manuel Burga and Alberto Flores Galindo, *Apogeo y crisis de la república aristocrática* (Lima: Ediciones Rikchay Perú, 1980), 150–54.

2. These events are described in Jorge Basadre, *Historia de la República del Perú*, 7th ed., (Lima, 1983), vol. 9, 421–22; and Ricardo Temoche Benites, *Cofradías, gremios, mutuales y sindicatos en el Perú* (Lima, 1987), 214–15. There were actually two strikes in Lima, each a day long. The first was on 20 September 1919, the second on 18 December after arbitration talks broke down. The Callao strike lasted over a week. No estimate was made of the number of employees who stayed off the job, but the figure of 700 demonstrators in Lima and 800 in Callao comes from *El Tiempo* (Lima), 20 Sept. 1919, 2, 7.

3. I am indebted to the Asociación de Empleados del Perú, formerly the Sociedad Empleados de Comercio, for access to their extensive private archive.

4. Rosemary Thorp and Geoffrey Bertram, *Peru 1890–1977: Growth and Policy in an Open Economy* (New York, 1978), 167–212; Ernesto Yepes del Castillo, *Perú 1820–1920: un siglo de desarollo capitalista* (Lima, 1972), 146. On the importance of commerce, see Alexander Garland, *Peru in 1906, with a Brief Historical and Geographical Sketch* (Lima, 1907), 211, 230–31; Francisco García Calderón, *Le Pérou contemporain* (Paris, 1907), 147–52. On the rage for European products and styles, see Chavarría, *José Carlos Mariátegui*, 15–21; Aurelio Miró Quesada Sosa, *Lima: Ciudad de los reyes* (Buenos Aires, 1946), 89–91; Fernando Romero, *Evolución industrial y educación técnica* (Lima, 1951), 30–35. The elite so desired imported goods that one government official advised Peruvian factories to place counterfeit foreign labels on their products in order to boost domestic sales. See Carl Frederick Herbold, Jr., "Developments in the Peruvian Administrative System, 1919–1930: Modern and Traditional Qualities of Government Under Authoritarian Regimes," (PhD diss., Yale University, 1973), 117.

5. The 15 percent figure is based on census data. Peru, Ministerio de Fomento, Dirección de Salud Pública, *Censo de la Provincia de Lima (26 de junio de 1908)* (Lima: Imprenta de "la Opinión Nacional," 1915), 914–25; Peru, Ministerio de Hacienda, Dirección de Estadística, *Resumen del Censo de las Provincias de Lima y Callao levantado el 17 de diciembre de 1920* (Lima: Imprenta Americana, 1927), 174–82; Carlos P. Jiménez Correa, *Censo de las Provincias de Lima y Callao levantado el 13 de noviembre de 1931* (Lima: Imprenta Torres Aguirre, 1932), 196. The census categories are explained in David S. Parker, "The Rise of the Peruvian Middle Class: A Social and Political History of White-Collar Employees in Lima, 1900–1950" (PhD diss., Stanford University, 1990), chap. 1.

6. On the importance of the *empleado-obrero* distinction, see Stanley M. Davis, "Empleados and Obreros," in *Workers and Managers in Latin America*, ed. Stanley M. Davis and Louis Wolf Goodman (Lexington, MA: D.C. Heath, 1972), 31–34. For Peru: David Chaplin, *The Peruvian Industrial Labor Force* (Princeton: Princeton University Press, 1967), 83–87; James

Payne, *Labor and Politics in Peru: The System of Political Bargaining* (New Haven: Yale University Press, 1965), 163–65; David G. Becker, *The New Bourgeoisie and the Limits of Dependency: Mining, Class and Power in "Revolutionary" Peru* (Princeton: Princeton University Press, 1983), 282–83, 298–99. For Chile: Alan Angell, *Politics and the Labour Movement in Chile* (London: Oxford University Press, 1972), 66–69. Biographies of successful, high-level employees appear in Artemio Pacheco B., *Cabezas dirigentes del alto comercio del Perú* (Lima: Cámara de Comercio, 1923); José Reaño García, *Historia del leguiismo: sus hombres y sus obras* (Lima, 1928); *Diccionario biográfico del Perú*, 1st ed. (Lima: Escuelas Americanas, [1943 or 1944]); Oscar F. Arrús, "El movimiento financiero del Perú," in *El Perú en el primer centenario de su independencia* (Buenos Aires: Sociedad de Publicidad Sudamericana, 1922); *La Mesocracia*; *El Empleado*; *Ilustración Obrera*; *Mundial*. *Ilustración Obrera* 60 (Apr. 1917), 5–6. Many of the details of white-collar contracts and work regimes were found in the records of labor disputes involving empleados. For example: Daniel Flores vs. Luis Gotuzzo y Cía, 1925, no. 579; Carlos Carrasco vs. Jacobo Cassis, 1924, no. 349; Archivo General de la Nación, Lima (hereafter cited as AGN), Sección Poderes Públicos, Ministerio del Trabajo, Expedientes Laborales Varios (hereafter cited as ELV).

　　7. The public employee's dependence upon the political connection was a notorious cliché: the literature here is virtually endless. See Víctor Andrés Belaúnde, "La crisis presente" (1914) in *Meditaciones peruanas*, 2nd ed. (Lima: P.L. Villanueva, 1963), 97; Abelardo Gamarra ("El Tunante"), "Pepito de las cunas," in *Lima: unos cuantos barrios y unos cuantos tipos (al comenzar el siglo XX)* (Lima, 1907), 34–40; idem, "Los Felicianos," "Una de tantas familias," "No hay en qué trabajar," and "Juan Pichón," in *Cien años de vida perdularia* (Lima: Casa de la Cultura del Perú, 1963); Joaquín Capelo, *Sociología de Lima*, 4 vols. (Lima: Imprenta Masías, 1895), vol. 2, 120; and Oscar Caballero Fischer, "S. M. La tarjeta de recomendación," *El Empleado* 113 (Jan.–Feb. 1948), 23. The critique is discussed in Herbold, "Peruvian Administrative System," 65, 77, 84–85. Getting a white-collar job in the private sector followed many of the same rules of paternalism and personal contacts.

　　8. *El Tiempo* (Lima), 30 Mar. 1922, 3; 31 Mar. 1922, 3; José M. Harrisson, "Refutando un cargo contra la clase media," *El Empleado* 15 (May 1937), 8. The *"fianza de empleados"* was offered by several insurance companies: see the ad placed by the Compañía de Seguros "Rímac" in *Ciudad y Campo y Caminos* (Nov. 1927). For sample letters of recommendation: J. L. Zuzunaga vs. Patricio Zembrano, 1927, no. 1699, AGN, ELV. On the role of nationality in job recruitment: *La Defensa* (Lima), 16 Oct. 1927, 1. On solidarities among immigrants from the same region of Peru: Eudocio Ravines, *La gran estafa* (Santiago: Editorial del Pacífico, 1954), 84. A model letter from a person seeking work as a *meritorio* in a bank appears in *La Defensa*, 16 Apr. 1927, 2.

　　9. J. L. Zuzunaga vs. Patricio Zembrano, 1927, no. 1699; Juan Sarria vs. E. & W. Hart, 1926, no. 1407; AGN, ELV. The argument also appeared in debate over empleado legislation. Peru, Cámara de Diputados, *Diario de los Debates, Congreso Ordinario 1922*, 949–53.

　　10. In order: Daniel Flores vs. Gotuzzo y Cía, 1925, no. 579; Teodora Vega vs. Sociedad Anónima de Productos Nacionales "La Corona," 1929, no. 1588; Juan Marticorena vs. Juan A. Cavarelli, 1926, no. 993; AGN, ELV.

　　11. On company pensions, see for example *La Mesocracia* no. 1 (20 Oct. 1923), 21; no. 3 (5 Jan. 1924), 17. On funerals, see Sociedad Empleados de Comercio (hereafter cited as SEC), Actas Generales, vol. 2 (1915–1920), 25 Oct. 1915, 29; 18 Nov. 1915, 39. Evidence of *compadrazgo* (ritual kinship) between employers and empleados can be found, among other places, in Juan Marticorena vs. Juan A. Cavarelli, 1926, no. 993, AGN, ELV.

　　12. Clipping from *La Sanción* (n.d.) submitted as evidence in: Antonio Fontana vs. Juan Nosiglia, 1927, no. 554, AGN, ELV.

　　13. "De empleado a patrono," *La Mesocracia* no. 2 (1 Dec. 1923), 21.

　　14. Joaquín Capelo noted in 1895 that unlike public employees, skilled commercial employees often rose to become important functionaries. Capelo, *Sociología de Lima* II, 119. That young empleados could realistically aspire to executive positions is noted in a speech by the president of the Sociedad Empleados de Comercio in *La Mesocracia* no. 5 (Mar. 1924), 9–10. See also the biographies cited in Pacheco, *Cabezas dirigentes*, as well as those of Nicanor Salazar Castillo in *El Empleado* no. 4 (June 1936), 13; and J. Abadia in *Mundial* (1 Dec. 1922).

For the case of one commercial house owner distributing Lp. 2,500 out of company profits as an employee bonus: SEC to Vda. de Piedra e Hijos, Lima, 9 Aug. 1918, SEC Correspondencia Varios (1915–1920), 209. In another example, the widow of the former owner of the *Bazar Cisne* turned the shop over to two empleados of long standing. *El Empleado* nos. 72–73 (Mar.–Apr. 1942), 3.

15. Lowry Nelson, *Rural Cuba* (Minneapolis: University of Minnesota Press, 1950), 159.

16. On the importance of caste in Peruvian social structure: Fernando Fuenzalida Vollma, "Poder, etnía y estratificación social en el Perú rural," in José Matos Mar et al., *Perú: hoy*, 3rd. ed. (Mexico, 1975), 75–85; José Mejía Valera, "La estratificación social en el Perú," *Cuadernos Americanos* 23, no. 2 (1964): 107–17; Carlos Delgado, *Problemas sociales en el Perú contemporáneo* (Lima: Campodónico Ediciones, 1971), 48; José Sabogal Wiese, "Las clases medias en el Perú," *Economía y Agricultura* (Lima) 2, no. 8 (Oct. 1966): 343–44; Roberto MacLean y Estenos, *Genesis y telesis social en el Perú* (Lima: Libreria y Imprenta Gil, 1942), 117–21; José Luis Bustamante y Rivero, "Las clases sociales en el Perú," *Revista* (Arequipa) 49 (1961), 31–32, 36–39.

17. An excellent treatment of the division of society between *gente decente* and *gente del pueblo*, based on Buenos Aires of the late nineteenth century, is James R. Scobie, *Buenos Aires: Plaza to Suburb, 1870–1910* (New York: Oxford University Press, 1974), chap. 6. Similar arguments are presented for Mexico in William H. Beezley, *Judas at the Jockey Club and Other Episodes of Porfirian Mexico* (Lincoln: University of Nebraska Press, 1987), 5–6; and for Peru in Magali Sarfatti Larson and Arlene Eisen Bergman, *Social Stratification in Peru* (Berkeley: Institute of International Studies, University of California, 1969), 113.

18. Manuel Antonio Carreño, *Manual de urbanidad y buenas maneras* (Lima, 1966), 39, cited in Steve Stein, "Popular Culture and Politics in Early Twentieth-Century Lima," *New World* 1:2 (1986): 75.

19. On the ability of artisans to gain their independence and enter respectable society, see Santiago Basurco and Leonidas Avendaño, "Informe emitido por la comisión encargada de estudiar las condiciones sanitarias de las casas de vecindad en Lima, primera parte," Peru, Ministerio de Fomento, Dirección de Salubridad, *Boletín* 3, no. 4 (30 Apr. 1907): 32. Also Steve Stein, *Lima obrera 1900–1930*, 3 vols. (Lima: Ediciones El Virrey, 1986), vol. 1, 35.

20. Empleados were categorized by race in the 1908 census: White, 3354; Mestizo, 1599; Indian, 594; Black, 41; Asian, 982 (Peru, *Censo de 1908*, 914–25). In Lima as a whole, non-whites outnumbered whites by almost two to one, making commercial employees substantially whiter than the average.

21. Reports of these banquets (known as *agasajos*) appeared regularly in *La Mesocracia*, *El Empleado*, and *La Defensa*.

22. Alberto Alexander Rosenthal, *Estudio sobre la crisis de la habitación en Lima* (Lima: Imprenta Torres Aguirre, 1922), 18.

23. Duels are discussed in SEC, Actas Directivas, vol. 2 (1919–1924), 22 Dec. 1921, 165; 16 Mar. 1922, 185; 4 Apr. 1922, 192–93; *El Tiempo* (Lima), 25 Mar. 1922, 5. When the SEC was donated a vacant lot, members voted to erect a tennis court. *La Mesocracia* no. 2 (1 Dec. 1923), 15. Tennis was certainly a sport of the elite in Peru, as noted in Cipriano A. Laos, *Lima: ciudad de los virreyes (el libro peruano) 1928–1929* (Lima: Editorial Perú, 1927), 199, 212, 379. On the popularity of billiards and its presence in the aristocratic "National" and "Phoenix" clubs, see Laos, *Lima*, 371. The billiard table in the SEC meeting-hall was by some accounts the organization's greatest asset (SEC, Actas Directivas, vol. 2, 26 Feb. 1920, 45, 47).

24. See the advertisements in various issues of the empleados' regular publication, *La Mesocracia* (1924).

25. Joaquín Capelo, cited in Richard Morse, *Lima en 1900: estudio crítico y antología* (Lima: Instituto de Estudios Peruanos, 1973), 81. A typical empleado's budget, reproduced in *¡Ya!* 16 (July 1949), 18–19, provides evidence that such customs survived well into the 1940s.

26. Not atypical were the cases of two charter members of the Sociedad Empleados de Comercio, who at an advanced age were taken ill and left so poor that they could no longer pay their dues. See SEC, Actas Directivas, vol. 1 (1903–1918), 3 Sept. 1916, 253–54; vol. 3 (1924–1932), 26 Feb. 1924, 5; Sociedad Empleados de Comercio, *Memoria Anual 1916*, 5–6.

27. Sociedad Empleados de Comercio de Lima, *Discurso pronunciado por el socio honorario de la institución, D. Daniel C. Urrea, en la conferencia ofrecida en honor de los empleados de comercio de la república el 8 de mayo de 1915* (Lima: Liberia e Imprenta Gil, 1915), 15–16.

28. Basurco and Avendaño, "Informe, primera parte," 6.

29. Jorge Basadre, "La Aristocracia y las clases medias civiles en el Perú republicano," *Mercurio Peruano* 44 (1963): 466–67.

30. Capelo, *Sociología de Lima*, vol. 2, 184–92; vol. 3, 261, 278–79; Manuel Moncloa y Covarrubias, *Las Cojinovas: costumbres limeños . . . cursis* (Lima: Badiola y Berrio, 1905), esp. 24–25; Abelardo Gamarra ("El Tunante"), "El museo de las desdichas, o las casas de préstamo," in *Rasgos de pluma* (Lima: Torres, 1889), 108–10; Manuel Beingolea, "Mi corbata," in *Bajo las lilas, cuéntos pretéritos, selección* (Lima: Editorial Jurídica, 1967), 93–102; Basadre, "Aristocracia y clases medias," 467.

31. Basurco and Avendaño, "Informe, primera parte," 6–7; idem, "Informe emitido por la comisión . . . segunda parte," Perú, Ministerio de Fomento, Dirección de Salubridad, *Boletín* 3, no. 5 (31 May 1907), 65–66.

32. *Huachafo* and *huachafería* described the poor taste of the social climber, the unsuccessful attempt to don the trappings of elegance or culture. Unlike the Spanish *cursi*, *huachafo* more typically referred to an economically struggling middle class than to a wealthy but uneducated *nouveau riche*. For more on the origins and meanings of the word, consult the following: Willy F. Pinto Gamboa, *Lo huachafo: trama y perfil (Jorge Miota, vida y obra)* (Lima: Editorial Cibeles, 1981); Sebastián Salazar Bondy, *Lima la horrible* (Lima: Ediciones Peisa, 1974), 117–18; Federico Schwab, "Lo huachafo como phenómeno social," *Peruanidad* 2, no. 5 (Mar. 1942), 401–3.

33. The concern with *descanso dominical*, or the Sunday holiday, was present from the organization's inception. SEC, Actas Directivas, vol. 1, 17 Dec. 1903, 2; Sociedad Empleados de Comercio, *Reglamento* (Lima, 1913), art. 3; *Memoria Anual 1913*, 3–4; *Memoria Anual 1914*, 5–6; *Memoria Anual 1915*, 9–10; *Memoria Anual 1916*, 10.

34. Sociedad Empleados de Comercio, *Memoria Anual 1913*, 2.

35. *La Prensa* (Lima), 22 Jan. 1915, 2. Sociedad Empleados de Comercio, *Memoria Anual 1915*, 5–6. Basadre, *Historia de la República* IX, 84.

36. On honorary members, for example: SEC to Germán Loredo, 26 Dec. 1904, SEC Correspondencia Institucional (1904–1916), 70–71. Passing the hat among employers was discussed in the very first session of the directorate. SEC, Actas Directivas, vol. 1, 17 Dec. 1903, 1. Also Sociedad Empleados de Comercio, *Discurso pronunciado por . . . Urrea*, 18; *Memoria Anual 1913*, 7; *Memoria Anual 1914*, 6. Sociedad Empleados de Comercio, flyer dated 15 Oct. 1916; Biblioteca Nacional, Sala de Investigaciones, Colección de volantes y hojas sueltas (hereafter cited as CVHS).

37. The World War I economic crisis is analyzed in Bill Albert, *South America and the First World War: The Impact of the War on Brazil, Argentina, Peru and Chile* (Cambridge: Cambridge University Press, 1988). For primary materials, see *Exposición del gerente de la Compañía Recaudadora de Impuestos, Sr. D. José Carlos Bernales* (Lima: Imprenta "Artistica," 1917), 10; and *Almanaque de "El Comercio," 1915*, 86–93. On empleado efforts to limit the impact of unemployment and pay cuts: SEC, Actas Directivas, vol. 1, 28 Sept. 1914, 208; Sociedad Empleados de Comercio, *Memoria Anual 1915*, 4–6.

38. Oscar Arrús, "El costo de la vida en Lima," in *El costo de la vida en Lima y causas de su carestía* (Lima: n.p., 1927), also reprinted in Wilma Derpich, José Luis Huiza, and Cecilia Israel, *Lima años 30: salarios y costo de vida de la clase trabajadora* (Lima: Fundacíon Friedrich Ebert, 1985), 111–36. See especially 134–35.

39. Guillermo Rochabrún, "Las ideas socialistas en el Perú," *Los Caminos del Laberinto* 4 (Dec. 1986): 3–7; Herbold, "Peruvian Administrative System," 69–87; Luis Miró Quesada, *Albores de la reforma social en el Perú* (Lima, 1966), esp. 138; José Carlos Mariátegui, "Bolshevikis, aquí" and "Los delegados del pueblo," in Alberto Flores Galindo, ed., *El pensamiento comunista 1917–1945* (San Isidro: Mosca Azul Editores, 1982), 50–56. On the Palacios visit: Juan Gargurevich, *La Razón del joven Mariátegui: crónica del primer diario de izquierda en el Perú* (Lima: Editorial Horizonte, 1978), 103; SEC, Actas Generales II, 19 Dec. 1918; *El Tiempo*, 30 Apr. 1919, 2; 13 May 1919.

40. When the eight-hour movement erupted, the SEC was busy discussing the unrelated issue of alleged Chilean aggression against Peruvian employees in the disputed territories of Tacna, Arica and Tarapacá (SEC, *Actas Generales*, vol. 2, 19 Dec. 1918). The store owners' fear of violence is noted in *Variedades* (Lima) 14, no. 568 (18 Jan. 1919): 39–46.

41. Asociación General de Empleados (Callao: Imprenta "El Progresso"), *Memoria Anual, Año II* (Lima, 1919), 18–24, esp. 22; *La Prensa*, 16 Jan. 1919, 4; 17 Jan. 1919, 3; 19 Jan. 1919, 3; 24 Jan. 1919, 3; 25 Jan. 1919, 2.

42. The young radicals' most active spokesman was Eudocio Ravines, an accountant in a hardware store, who a decade later would found the Peruvian Communist Party. Their struggle for control of the SEC is followed in *La Razón* (Lima) between 18 June and 22 July 1919. See also Ravines, *La gran estafa*, 87–88; Ricardo Martínez de la Torre, "El movimiento obrero en 1919," part 3, *Amauta* 19 (Nov.–Dec. 1928), 64–65.

43. SEC, *Actas Generales*, vol. 2, 18 Sept. 1919, 273–75; 19 Sept. 1919, 276–81; SEC Archive, Libro de Actas de la Asociación General de Empleados (Callao); *El Tiempo* (Lima), 13 Sept. through 1 Oct. 1919; 4 Dec. 1919, 5; 18 Dec. 1919, 4; 19 Dec. 1919, 2–3.

44. Sociedad Empleados de Comercio, *Reglamento* (Lima: Imprenta F. García Grilló, 1913), art. 3.

45. *La Prensa*, 24 Jan. 1919, 3.

46. *La Prensa*, 25 Jan. 1919, 2.

47. *La Crónica* (Lima), 17 Jan. 1919, 3.

48. *El Tiempo*, 27 Sept. 1919, 3. Minor liberties have been taken in translation for the sake of clarity. Note the constant use of the word "obligated." The Spanish *obligado* could easily have been translated as "compelled" or "forced." The idea that a person could be forced to enjoy a particular level and type of consumption may be difficult to swallow, but this was central to the employees' argument.

49. *La Prensa*, 17 Jan. 1919, 3.

50. José Carlos Mariátegui (1894–1930) wrote about the empleados in *Mundial*, 21 Oct. 1927. The column has since been reprinted as "La organización de los empleados" in *Ideología y política* (Lima: Libería Editorial "Amauta," 1969), 189–92. See also Burga and Flores Galindo, *Apogeo y crisis*, 182.

51. *La Crónica*, 30 May 1919, 2.

52. Quote taken from a letter that empleados reportedly sent to the Lima papers in 1919, cited by Martínez de la Torre, "El movimiento obrero," 64–65. A letter with somewhat similar content, probably written by Ravines, was signed pseudonym "Boris" and published in *La Crónica*, 21 Jan. 1919, 11.

53. The arbitration agreement was published in *El Tiempo*, 28 Dec. 1919. SEC participation in its enforcement is recorded in Sociedad Empleados de Comercio, *Memoria Bienal 1921–22*, 11–12.

54. Accounts of the 1921 strike are taken from the following sources: SEC, *Actas Generales*, vol. 3 (1920–1925), 18 Jan. 1921, 28–34; Actas Directivas, vol. 2, 5 Jan. 1921, 82–83; 12 Jan. 1921, 84–86; 24 Jan. 1921, 87–88, 2 Mar. 1921, 93; *La Prensa*, 18 Jan. 1921, 5; 20 Jan. 1921, 8; 4 Feb. 1921, 3; 15 Feb. 1921, 5–6; 16 Feb. 1921, 4; 17 Feb. 1921, 2; 21 Feb. 1921, 5; 23 Feb. 1921, 7; 24 Feb. 1921, 7. Conservative criticism of the SEC leadership's handling of the strike can be found in "Manifiesto a los Empleados de Comercio," February 1921, CVHS. The directorate, including Vice President Eudocio Ravines, was forced to resign. See SEC Actas Generales, vol. 3, 5 Mar. 1921, 38–40.

55. The text of the proposal is reproduced in Peru, Cámara de Diputados, *Diario de los Debates, Congreso Ordinario 1922*, 894–98. For debate: ibid., 45–46, 440, 907–15, 935–40, 948–54, 974–78, 987–91, 999–1007, 1014–20. Favorable editorials appeared in *El Tiempo*, 5 Feb. 1922, 2; 6 Feb. 1922, 1–2; 16 Feb. 1922, 2; 17 Mar. 1922, 3; 23 Oct. 1922, 4. On the role of the Chamber of Commerce, see Jorge Basadre and Rómulo Ferrero, *Historia de la Cámara de Comercio de Lima* (Lima: Santiago Velarde, 1963), 137–38. Its counter-proposal was published in *El Comercio* (Lima), 3 Oct. 1922. See also *El Tiempo*, 5 Feb. 1922, 2; 4 Oct. 1922, 1; 15 Oct. 1922, 10; *La Prensa*, 6 Oct. 1922. SEC criticism of the Chamber of Commerce can be found in *El Tiempo*, 22 Oct. 1922, 6.

56. *El Tiempo*, 23 Nov. 1922, 4.

57. José M. Ramírez Gastón, *Mi lucha por un ideal social: la ley 4916, básica de la legislación del empleado del Perú, primera en América, y la seguridad social* (Lima: Editorial "La Confianza," 1966); Abel Ulloa Cisneros, *Leguía: apuntes de cartera 1919–1924* (Lima: n.p., 1933). Law 4916 and subsequent amendments are compiled in several places. See Peru, Ministerio de Fomento, *Ley del empleado no. 4916 y sus ampliatorios no. 5066 and 5119, reglamento de las precedentes leyes* (Lima: Imprenta "El Tiempo," n.d. [1928 or 1929]); S. Martínez G., *Ley del empleado particular* 2nd ed. (Lima: Imprenta "El Carmen," n.d., published sometime after 1983). Also Napoleon Valdez Tudela, *Comentarios a la legislación social peruana* (Lima: Imprenta D. Miranda, 1958), 211–14.

58. Martínez, *Ley del empleado*, 7–10.

59. Congress passed the law without settling this most important question. Peru, Senado, *Diario de los Debates, Congreso Extraordinario 1923*, 599–605. The ambiguity spawned a number of subsequent conflicts, the most important being whether or not employees who resigned voluntarily received compensation. These issues are covered in Parker, "Peruvian Middle Class," chap. 3.

60. Peru, Senado, *Diario de los Debates, Congreso Extraordinario 1923*, 608.

61. Henry Grandjean vs. Gran Hotel Bolívar, 1927, no. 641, AGN, ELV. See also Basadre and Ferrero, *Cámara de Comercio*, 138.

62. The problem was quickly perceived by the officials involved in enforcing the new law, and this increased pressure for reglamentation. Inspección Fiscal de Bancos, "Informes" 1926, AGN, O.L. Series, no. O.L. 845–1527. Also Manuel M. Chávez Fernández, *Jurisprudencia de la ley del empleado: leyes, decretos y fallos arbitrales concernientes a la ley 4916* (Lima: Imprenta Americana, 1925).

63. In order: Victoriano Gallúes vs. Compañía Peruana de Vidrio, 1927, no. 624; Tomás Viacava vs. Empresas Electricas Asociadas, 1925, no. 1633; Otila Casagrandi vs. Compañía Peruana de Teléfonos, 1926, no. 343; Emilio Cisneros vs. Geo. L. Sellé, 1927, no. 308; AGN, ELV.

64. Miguel Acosta Cárdenas vs. Empresa Agrícola Chicama, 1926, no. 47; S.E. Deza vs. Cerro de Pasco Copper Corp., 1926, no. 500; AGN, ELV.

65. Walter Simm vs. The Foundation Co., 1928, no. 1398, AGN, ELV. Some empleados considered transfer to the day payroll grounds for quitting, not only for the loss of empleado benefits but just as importantly for its symbolic meaning (*La Defensa*, 16 Apr. 1927, 1).

66. On illiterates: Eulalio Podestá vs. la Casa Sanmartí, 1927, no. 1162; Cirilo Vásquez vs. Empresas Eléctricas Asociadas, 1927, no. 1614; Valerio Camargo vs. Cerro de Pasco Copper Corp., 1928, no. 384; AGN, ELV. On technicians: Hermanos Castañeda vs. Hacienda Pomalca, 1927, no. 1723; Saul Bonilla Collazos vs. Compañía Minera Santa Inés, 1928, no. 159; AGN, ELV. On the Spaniard: Victoriano Gallúes vs. Compañía Manufacturera de Vidrio del Perú, 1927, no. 624, AGN, ELV.

67. César Castillo vs. Cerro de Pasco Copper Corp., 1927, no. 282; Carlos Coni vs. Cerro de Pasco Copper Corp., 1927, no. 346; AGN, ELV.

68. José E. León vs. Empresa del Ferrocarril Central del Perú, 1924, no. 851, AGN, ELV.

69. *Proyecto del Presidente de la Cámara de Comercio del Callao, Sr. Manuel Diez Canseco, sobre la reforma de la legislación relativa a los goces de los empleados de comercio* (Callao: Tipografia "Lux," 1927), 7–8.

70. Eduardo Craff vs. A. F. Oechsle, 1925, no. 368, AGN, ELV.

71. Antonio Fontana vs. Juan Nosiglia, 1927, no. 554, AGN, ELV.

72. César Augusto Zevallos vs. Cerro de Pasco Copper Corp., 1929, no. 1691, AGN, ELV.

73. These legal definitions survived well into the 1960s, influencing Peruvian social policy to this day. See Parker, "Peruvian Middle Class," chap. 5, epilogue and conclusion.

Chapter Nine

Domesticating Modernity

*Markets, Home, and Morality in the Middle Class in
Rio de Janeiro and São Paulo, 1930s and 1940s*

Brian P. Owensby

*In this piece, historian Brian Owensby draws on archival and literary sources
from the 1930s and 1940s to explore how the "experience and meaning of
being middle class" in Rio de Janeiro and São Paulo changed with the rise of
modern market culture and heightened economic and social competition. As
"collar-and tie" employees and liberal professionals faced growing insecurity
in their lives, they adapted old ways and invented new ways of differentiating
themselves from those "below them." Owensby focuses especially on the rise
of an ideology of middle-class domesticity, and connects that vision to a politics torn between apathetic antipolitics and deep-rooted moralism. He is the
author of* Intimate Ironies: Modernity and the Making of Middle-Class Lives
in Brazil *(Stanford University Press, 1999).*

In a modest but comfortable home in São Paulo late one afternoon, the voices
of two brothers are dying down from a long and disruptive debate about
politics. Carlos, diligent bookkeeper at a downtown commercial firm and
elder of the two, simply cannot understand his brother's attraction to radical
politics. Alfredo, rebel with numerous causes and on the run from police, has
insisted all along that he, unlike his brother, lives for an ideal. With nothing
more to say to each other, they allow their long-suffering mother the last
word. Pausing for a moment in her endless chores, Dona Lola asks Alfredo,
plaintively, "Don't you think you can find happiness in a peaceful home
life?"

This scene never actually happened. Carlos, Alfredo, and Dona Lola are
characters in Leandro Dupré's 1943 best-selling novel titled *There Were Six
of Us,* described by one reviewer as the "perfect middle-class novel . . .

because of the author's faithfulness to middle-class types, to the thinking of the social group to which she belongs."[1] What is significant here is the symbolic coupling of home, politics, and middle class. For, in most cases, the many who read this book probably were not very different from the people depicted in the scene itself—white-collar employees and professionals and their families in São Paulo and Rio de Janeiro.

By the early 1940s, these people (and others) understood that modern Brazil was strikingly different from Brazil before 1930. Through the decades after 1900, the supple bonds of agrarian patriarchalism had loosened in the face of economic expansion, urbanization, and industrialization. In politics, dissident elites and their urban allies had launched a series of revolts in the 1920s that culminated in the nearly bloodless revolution of 1930 against the elites who had monopolized political structures since the 1890s. It was a revolution of disappointed expectations for many white-collar Cariocas and Paulistanos who watched its promise of a more participatory and peaceful politics tarnish in a corrosive atmosphere of right- and left-wing extremism and revanchism by elites aspiring to restore the old regime.

The new Brazil also differed from the old in that class had become a defining feature of Brazilian politics in preceding decades. Between 1917 and 1921, anarchists led a series of unprecedented general strikes. The Communist Party was founded in 1922. In the 1930s, militant labor unions demanded a voice, and by the early 1940s, President Getúlio Vargas seemed ready to court their favor, easing restrictions on labor activity in the *Estado Novo* (New State), the authoritarian regime that took power in 1937.

In this context, Dupré allowed Dona Lola to represent the peace and quiet of the home that seemed in such sharp contrast to the clangor of society beyond the walls. Much more than just a yearning for domestic tranquility, she, and her son Carlos, stood for a kind of counterideal to Alfrêdo's radicalism, and by extension, to politics more generally. Through her selfless actions, soft words, and spirit of resignation, she embodied the proposition that home life could be a refuge from the confusion of *a rua,* the public and vaguely dangerous space of the street, broadly understood, where markets, interests, and politics were the order of the day.[2] In a sense, the middle-class home as depicted in Dupré's novel was the flip side of the perceived disorder of the outside world, and as such, it serves as a powerful metaphor for understanding the ways in which the middle class in Brazil's larger cities related to the dramatic changes of their rapidly modernizing society. This fugue between inside and outside, order and disorder, I contend, resonated deeply in middle-class lives. In the face of dramatic change and as social danger was being recast in class terms, the middle class came to be its own symbol of social peace. This symbolism defined the central paradox of the middle-class condition during these years—living by an idealized, almost mythological role that could never be achieved.

I begin this article with a detailed consideration of the experiential and mental universe of labor and consumption markets for middle-class Brazilians. I am principally concerned with the ways a modern market mentality converged with traditional notions of social hierarchy to give certain people in Rio de Janeiro and São Paulo new means of distinguishing themselves from those below them, even as it created enormous insecurities and uncertainties that helped define the experience and meaning of being middle class. I will then examine the emergence of a vision of domesticity keyed to the advantages and dilemmas of middle-class life in a modernizing market society in which class was becoming a central axis of social experience and identity. I will conclude by connecting this vision of domesticity to the wider sphere of politics in a class society.

It is by now a cliché that the middle class is difficult to define. The problem lies in the insistence on an a priori definition, whereas any historically concrete middle class (and probably any social grouping) must be found in the details of a given historical period. In the context of the expansion of and crisis in the coffee export economy, incipient industrialization, and growth of the public sector, the sons and daughters of declining *fazendeiros* [large landowners] and of immigrants and native Brazilians who had worked their way up out of an indistinct mass of manual laborers and literate poor converged in an emergent middle class between roughly 1850 and 1930.[3] For the two decades after 1930 . . . the cities of Rio and São Paulo were the center of gravity of middle-class experience. That experience may be characterized in terms of the lifeways of families headed by white-collar *(colarinho e gravata),* salaried employees, and professionals who did not engage in manual labor, and who were overwhelmingly white or light skinned.[4] These were people who had some education beyond primary school and who possessed a level of culture—manners, speech, and behavior—that set them apart from workers. They generally enjoyed a higher standard of living than the families of most manual workers, but by no means were wealthy.

This static sketch is less than half the story. More important than the laundry list of occupations it implies—commercial and bank clerks, teachers, doctors, lawyers, engineers, government employees, journalists, accountants, bookkeepers, office professionals, salesmen, managers and supervisors—is that middle-class Brazilians were people who lived economic and social lives oriented to dynamic aspects of a competitive society under the constraints of their economic condition. As such, their social lives were defined by the anxiety and aspiration of labor market competition, by a preoccupation with social mobility (upward as well as downward), and by their access to a vibrant new consumer market for manufactured goods beyond the experience of most poorly paid workers. Middle-class lifeways, then, partook of and contributed to the emergence of a "competitive social order" after the mid-nineteenth century. At the same time, they remained deeply tied to the cultural legacies of patrimonialism, patronage, and hierarchy, in the context of capitalist development rooted in Brazil's role in the global economy.[5]

Finally, a middle class (or for that matter, any class) is much more than a statistical matter.[6] It is as much state of mind as objective condition, as much a matter of becoming as a specific social station. Yearnings and fantasies are as important as the material conditions of everyday life. As such, I conceive of the Brazilian middle class in this period as a field of opportunity and potentiality for patterned behavior and self-identification rooted in the discourses and experiences of markets, homes, and politics.[7]

SECRETS OF THE MARKET

A young man placed an advertisement in São Paulo's major daily newspaper on Wednesday, Friday, and Sunday, 20, 22, and 24 May 1936, proffering his services as an office assistant.[8] His two main selling points were that he had a diploma from the highly regarded Alvares Penteado Commercial School, and that he had considerable experience in the Triangle, São Paulo's booming commercial district. He could be reached at a post office box, but gave no name (probably because he was already working at a firm and did not want it known that he was job-hunting). While in later years employment ads were much more likely to originate with employers than job seekers,[9] this young man's attempt to offer himself in an open fashion bespoke the growing sense of competition that was coming to dominate white-collar labor markets in Rio de Janeiro and São Paulo.

This job seeker was only one among tens of thousands. Bank and commercial clerks, teachers, public functionaries, lawyers, and doctors all must have thrilled at and complained of the "extraordinary intensification of the struggle for life" during the 1930s and 1940s.[10] The idea of competition as a defining feature of social life percolated through urban culture more generally as advertisers aimed sales pitches at young, white-collar men, hawking everything from night schools ("Prepare yourselves for the struggle!"), to brain tonics ("In the turbulence of modern life victory goes to those with strong brains!"), to razors ("Winners shave daily with Gillette!"), to life insurance ("With each passing day the struggle for life is getting harder. Today, competition is a harsh reality").[11]

The perceived harshness of competition had ambiguous effects within the social order. Education came to be more prized than ever before, since it was so often the ticket for admission into a respectable white-collar job, as the young Alvares Penteado man had recognized. Yet, even as modern aspects of market culture were taking root, older growth did not wither. Personal connections, institutionalized in the *pedido* (letter of request) and *pistolão* (letter of recommendation), continued to inform the expectations, anxieties, and strategies of those who navigated the turbulent straits of a tight labor market.[12] Thus, candidates taking the examination for a government position also might seek out a patron to help them in a white-collar work world in which meritocracy and patronage were alternative strategies for getting a leg up.

A dense mass of men concentrated in Rio's and São Paulo's white-collar labor markets now competed for respectable, nonmanual work as a matter of course. A generalized sense of competition for these jobs existed in Brazil's larger cities throughout the nineteenth century. In an export-oriented slave economy, only a few could do more than imagine the possibilities of finding a job that would give them security. But with the late nineteenth-century expansion of the coffee export economy, the urbanization and industrialization of the early twentieth century, and the bureaucratization of government, opportunities in the white-collar sector grew. Consequently, ever greater numbers of men and women began to dream of securing a place for themselves in Brazil's finely calibrated social hierarchy.

In the face of growing competitiveness, the long-standing Brazilian preoccupation with status and social position became pervasive. White-collar publications constantly referred to the twin pillars of Brazilian social distinction—the differences between manual and nonmanual work, and between the *culto* and the *inculto* (loosely, the cultured and the uncultured). For example, bank clerks, public functionaries, lawyers, teachers, journalists, accountants, and doctors insisted that they were intellectual workers. Even the lowliest commercial clerks set themselves off from the "brutish, unthinking, silent mass," since they were a "civilized" part of Brazil's middle class.[13] Indeed, the easy glissade from a simple manual-nonmanual dichotomy into notions of cultural elevation and competence was a crucial aspect of the way in which middle-class men defined themselves in the social hierarchy. Thus, civil engineers set themselves off from skilled manual workers, who in many cases performed the same work, by their "general culture," which workers "unhappily lacked."[14] This boundary was carefully patrolled, and white-collar organizations sought to reinforce it during the 1930s and 1940s by building libraries and classroom complexes to "cultivate their intelligence," so that members might become *"homens cultos"* (cultivated men) by attending to the "cultural level of [their] spirit[s]."[15]

The ballooning notion that it was now possible to get ahead in life must be understood in this context. When publications of white-collar organizations urged members to embrace the idea of "always try[ing] to move up a little more," something far more basic was at stake than simply money.[16] For the dream of moving up implied the nightmare of dropping down in the social scale, a fact that prompted one author to dedicate his book on the problems of the middle class to those who lived between the "hope of rising"

and the "fear of falling," with heavier emphasis on the latter than the former. [17] The interplay between hope and fear was captured in an advertising
campaign of the 1930s and 1940s, in which an insurance company trucked in
the anxieties of insecure people. The basic motif changed from time to time,
but the message of these small melodramas was always the same: The father
who failed to buy life insurance for his son was to blame for the fact that now
the child shined shoes (or carried bags, or worked in a factory—labor identified with illiterate and darker skinned people) rather than went to school,
since the "educated and the capable always win!" [18]

Winning did not mean merely the holding of a particular job. Consumption was another axis along which people in an emerging middle class experienced expanding markets. Before 1920 in Brazil, virtually nothing existed
that might pass for a consumer market. *Donas de casa* (housewives) bought
most household goods from peddlers, local merchants, or vendors, so that
routine, personal relationships were as important to the experience of consumption as the arm's-length anonymity of mass markets. The well-to-do in
Brazil's largest cities were the thin edge of a transformation in the 1920s. [19]
By the 1930s, middle-class households also were being targeted by advertisers for everything from beauty products to electric appliances, and were
shopping in the Mappin Department Store, through whose doors only the
well-heeled had passed before 1930.

Of course, the idea that material possessions connoted status was hardly
new. After 1920, however, urbanization, rising incomes and sheer numbers
led to a dramatic intensification of the pursuit of status through consumption.
Emblematic of just how central consumption had become in middle-class
lives during the 1930s and 1940s, a 1945 domestic advice book called *My
House* admonished women that "knowing how to buy is an art, it is indispensable knowledge for every good *dona de casa*." [20]

What were middle-class housewives buying with the money their husbands (and sometimes they themselves) earned, and what did it mean? For
the growing mass of people who harbored the desire to rise above the common rabble of *inculto* manual workers, clothes and cultural projection took
on heightened importance. Advertisements, especially those aimed at middle-class men and women, focused on status concerns. Conflating needs and
desires, fashion columns and ads for clothes and sewing machines insisted
that women could be "modern and elegant" without extravagant expense. [21]
They seem to have enjoyed some success. Market surveys conducted in the
mid--1940s indicate that middle-class women spent significantly more on
clothes and beauty products as a proportion of income than did poor or
working-class women. The same study suggested an equally powerful yen
within the middle class to be *culto*. Middle-class families outspent both rich
and poor as a proportion of household income in acquiring cultural goods—

schooling, books, magazines, encyclopedias—despite severe budgetary limitations.[22]

However, it was the dramatically expanded availability of consumer durables—radios, record players, refrigerators, carpets, sewing machines, typewriters, telephones, even cars—that marked the dawn of a consumer culture in urban Brazil. Consumption of these goods seemed to carry a social significance far beyond their utilitarian value, combining the impulse to modernity with a new way to project status. Advertisements hint at what was going on. As early as 1932, for instance, General Electric announced that its marvelous appliances were for "modern homes, the homes of families where the idea of comfort is linked to thrift."[23]

Through the 1930s, the most sought after of such marvels was the radio. One magazine proclaimed in 1935 that all "modern homes" had to have one.[24] A 1937 Philco ad linked radios to an elevated social status, picturing a gathering of distinguished looking people in long dresses and tuxedos, sipping champagne, sitting around a wood cabinet with large speakers.[25] Public functionary José Moacir de Andrade Sobrinho agreed in 1940 that a radio (and then a refrigerator) was the "next big expense" after rent, clothes, and a maid.[26] And by 1944, one commentator argued that a "dignified" lifestyle implied the ownership of a radio, and other "indispensable products that progress is furnishing."[27]

Of course, status claims based on the ownership of particular products were inherently unstable. For example, by the mid-1940s, ownership of a basic radio set was no longer sufficient to mark status, since many workers could own one.[28] Even at this early stage, the logic of consumerism, the constant pressure to own the latest model, the fanciest style, the newest gadget to keep up with peers and ahead of those behind, was already apparent. As one man put it in 1947, "There is always more things to buy and consume, there is always a desire to better one's standard of living."[29]

It is possible to glimpse just how deeply a consumer mentality had penetrated the middle class by the 1940s. One market study revealed that 75 percent of middle-class women said they paused at the window displays of Casa Canada, an upscale apparel store in Rio and São Paulo, to window shop. There is nothing remarkable in this, except that only 25 percent of wealthy women and a bare 2 percent of poor women claimed to do so.[30] A comparison of the different experiences implied here is illuminating. Because rich women simply could stride into the store, knowing that they could afford to buy, window shopping as daydream was not part of their experience. Most poor women, on the other hand, probably did not even bother to waste time on something so clearly outside the realm of their economic possibility. But, something in the image of a middle-class housewife breaking stride at a display window, longing for something not altogether unimaginable but nevertheless beyond financial reach, bespeaks the constitutive dilemma of middle-class consumption.[31]

Retailers were alive to this dilemma, and openly exhorted people to spend beyond their means. Consumer credit companies began to spring up, and by 1940, one was telling its potential customers, "If you have money . . . buy! If what you have at the moment is not enough, buy anyway."[32] Many took advantage of such offers, as is clear from frequent allusions to middle-class indebtedness throughout the 1930s and 1940s. How else, after all, was a bookkeeper to afford a radio that cost two or three times his monthly salary?

Traditional concerns for status intensified the strain between limited budgets and new consumption opportunities, especially among the middle class, who, as one observer noted in the mid-1950s, "put the emphasis on hierarchy."[33] Thus, the ability to consume up to one's social level was far more than merely keeping up with the Joneses. Above all, it was a question of securing a place in a hierarchical order that defined social identity and conditioned access to education, connections, and jobs. This is what accounts for the plaints of white-collar employees and professionals insisting that they were entitled to a lifestyle commensurate with their "higher place in the social scale."[34]

Indeed, a great wailing and gnashing of teeth often could be heard over the fact that "hundreds and thousands of manual workers" were earning more than certain white-collar employees and professionals.[35] What matters here is less the accuracy of such statements than the indignant air of scandal at the image of well-scrubbed, reasonably educated lawyers, doctors, teachers, or bank employees making less than some janitors, doormen, stonemasons, soccer players, or factory workers.[36] This was the fear that lurked in the souls of people who were coming to believe that they had something to lose, and who hoped and expected that all who heard their jeremiads would sympathize with the victims of an unjust remunerative scheme that flew in the face of the accepted ordering of occupations.

Financial insecurity, then, far from attenuating the distinction between the middle class and working class, seemed to reinforce it. The tensions and ambiguities of this situation were a defining feature of middle-class life during this period, as market researchers recognized when they concluded in 1946 that the middle class, which "yearn[ed] for a better representation and struggled desperately to keep up appearances," was worse off than workers, who "did not have greater social obligations."[37]

SMALL WORLD OF THE HOME

The tight knot among market forces, straitened budgets, new opportunities, and traditional concerns for hierarchy and status was a dominant reality of middle-class homes during the 1930s and 1940s. These homes generally comprised a husband, a wife, children, and usually a single servant. Within them, middle-class *donas de casa* might work at the tangle, loosening here, cinching there, without ever being able to undo it altogether. During the 1930s and 1940s, this thankless task came to represent the central dilemma of middle-class life—how to secure domestic order and respectability in the face of limited resources.

At mid-century, women could no longer be seen as living a secular cloister. If through the nineteenth and into the twentieth century women of the respectable classes had been identified almost exclusively with a domestic space largely sealed off from the outside world,[38] by 1940, their situation had changed considerably. Since the 1920s, it had become more common for women from middle-class families to take office jobs. Going to work meant being out in *a rua,* with all its allures and opportunities. Moreover, during the 1930s and into the 1940s, movies, car rides, fashion, modern romance novels, magazines, advertisements, radios, shopping, Samba, and dancing were all available to young women in a way they had not been before, perhaps making traditional roles seem confining and narrow.

Yet the break with the past was not so sharp.[39] Most women who worked outside the home did so only until they married, or for limited stints to help their families through a tough financial period. While considerable numbers of women became teachers and social workers, most employed women worked at routine jobs, such as typing, that paid poorly. In addition, women who worked outside the home were not exempt from the burdens of maintaining a household. Thus, within the constraints set by Brazilian society at the time, for every young woman who dreamed of becoming a teacher, there were probably several more who preferred the role of wife, mother, and homemaker.

Nor did staying at home isolate *donas de casa* from the currents of the times. Consumer culture did not remain respectfully at the doorway. Advertisers avidly competed for women's attention through images projected in magazine, newspaper, and radio ads: women in cars, women as beaming housewives, women as the bosses of their servants, women confidently negotiating *a rua,* women as slinky, independent, and self-assured. Women were targeted as "buyer[s] par excellence,"[40] and market surveyors seemed to take women's attitudes toward consumption more seriously than those of men.

Not incidentally, consumption offered middle-class housewives a further means of separating themselves from working-class women and a vicarious means of sidling up to the rich. Ads for beauty products during the 1930s and 1940s told women to make themselves healthy, beautiful, and seductive through potions, makeup, and clothes in "this century of dynamism and progress."[41] Working-class women were much less likely to read the magazines in which these ads appeared. As a result, market researchers generally excluded poor or working-class women from market studies on perfume, deodorants, and other beauty and personal hygiene products. Consumption, then, was a way middle-class *donas de casa,* like their collar-and-tie husbands, could secure and project status compared to those beneath them in the social hierarchy.

But the *dona de casa's* role went beyond shopping. For while a wife could work outside the home if necessary, her ability to stay at home was itself a badge of status for her husband and herself. Moreover, *donas de casa* were deeply implicated in the task of securing a family's social position. Housekeeping manuals, magazines aimed at women, and novels set in middle-class homes all stressed thrift, suggesting the many ways an imaginative housewife could stretch the family budget to ensure a "solidly settled economic base."[42] According to these sources, a housewife should mend old clothes, learn to make new ones, shop comparatively, make creative use of leftovers, manage the maid, and insist on "extraordinary cleanliness." One author explicitly equated men's and women's work: "[T]here is no less value in the woman's role [than the man's]. . . . Managing the house, raising the spirit of the children, monitoring expenses, economizing, seeing to the moral and material well-being of the children and husband, all these make feminine activities at least as important as masculine ones."[43]

The question is, important for what? Housekeeping manuals and other sources bespeak a subtle change in women's roles in the home.[44] While the home was a site of status seeking in a market society, it was also supposed to be a refuge from the harshness of a competitive world outside the domestic sphere. *Donas de casa* stood at the boundary between the two. In this view, wives could respond to the importunities of labor and consumer markets by economizing and by creating a tranquil atmosphere to which their husbands could come home. Such an understanding of domesticity gives pause, for the implicit rationale was economic rather than patriarchal. Owing her husband tenderness and patience as well as obedience, a wife's obligation in a more conjugal family was being conceptualized in terms of the family's broader relationship to a market economy, not only in terms of an inherent duty to a husband.[45] Traditional roles had hardly collapsed—husbands continued to lean on patriarchy to assert their authority at home. Still, these manuals and magazines suggest that the relationship between men and women was changing in complex ways, accommodating rather than negating market forces, even as traditional gender relations were influencing the character of the market.

There is an obvious tension between home as place of repose and calm and as a place where the never-ending struggle to secure and maintain a position in the social hierarchy was played out. Thrift as the organizing principle of middle-class homes was therefore ambiguous, both as concept and in practice. It was one way *donas de casa* could help their families consume up to their social level. At the same time, it was pregnant with an implication of social inferiority. For the middle class, the very need to economize made their households seem more like homes of the poor than like those of the financially secure.

Housekeeping manuals and magazines responded by trying to make thrift a virtue. One writer on matters domestic, for instance, vehemently denied that thrift was proof of inferiority. Certainly, women who spent "hours and hours" beautifying themselves to the neglect of their children were not to be admired, although even "frugal women" could not afford to ignore their appearance, since their social position demanded more of them than of "working-class women or women of the people."[46] Yet good *donas de casa* should not make the mistake the rich so often did, emphasizing luxury over "equilibrium in finances." This was particularly so in regard to children, as the inexcusable ostentation of the monied often "rent the harmony" of their homes and produced "disordered" children.[47] Wealth, in other words, was no guarantee of and hardly necessary to happiness—it might even be inimical to it—for "modest lives" could be happy by adopting a "middle way" of thrift and simplicity.[48]

A distinctive sensibility regarding the nature and purpose of the home in personal life and wider society seems to have underlain this vision of domesticity. Ideally, order, discipline, harmony, equilibrium, comfort, tranquility, stability, and a sound morality were goals to be striven for in the domestic sphere. Their opposites—disorder, disharmony, disequilibrium, disorganization, and immorality—were to be avoided at all costs. Religion was indispensable, as much a source of practical morality as a matter of belief, articulating a social position for those who were neither rich nor poor. The idea was that people of moderate means could create home lives morally and spiritually, if not materially, superior to those of the rich. In doing so, they could secure themselves against those below who lacked the resources to create ordered, moral, and tranquil home lives.

At the same time, the idealized middle-class home of housekeeping manuals, magazines, and novels implied a (limited) sense of being in control of one's own destiny, in sharp contrast to the indomitable chaos of the turbulent world outside. As one author put it in 1945, the home was a safe harbor where the family could "choose its relationships, determine its own program for life, and ensure the proper upbringing of children by avoiding futile and pernicious contacts with society."[49] In short, for those with the means and inclination to discipline themselves to economy and the middle way, home could be a place where a feeling of independence and autonomy, however tenuous, could be lovingly cultivated.

Dissonance between the home as site of status seeking and home as refuge from the outside world obliquely indicates the challenges middle-class *donas de casa* faced in a market society. We cannot know how many or exactly how housewives read the manuals and magazines that purveyed these views. Ample evidence testifies that middle-class men and women persisted in trying to imitate the rich, often eschewed frugality, and commonly refused to content themselves with their modest positions—precisely the sorts of bad habits they were supposed to avoid. The point of examining these sources, therefore, cannot be to reveal an authentic description of middle-class home life.

Nevertheless, these manuals and magazines exposed the broad dilemmas of middle-class economic and social lives. Homes could be tempestuous places amidst the swirl of desires and fears rooted in the middle-class relationship to market forces. Manuals and magazines, and novels more indirectly, indicate that one way middle-class people could confront this fact was to try to organize their home lives according to an ideal that prized thrift, order, and morality. The middle class honored values cheap enough to be affordable, but difficult enough to maintain that the vast bulk of the working-class poor could not measure up.

POLITICAL ORDER THROUGH MORALITY

Were there resonances between the inner tensions and contradictions of idealized middle-class home life and the broader politics of class by the mid-twentieth century? An answer does not lie in the direction of identifying middle-class political leanings for one party or another, or spelling out a supposedly distinctive middle-class political program. Indeed, contemporaries believed that there was no distinctly middle-class political position at the level of national politics. It was commonly lamented in the 1940s that the middle class had been "left out" of the postwar political equation, their interests subordinated to those of "proletariat and bourgeoisie."[50] A spokesman for middle-class interests concluded in the mid-1950s that whereas "the working class is united and strengthens itself through its *sindicatos*" and "employers, with the resources they have, find ways of defending their interests . . . our middle class is completely abandoned to its own fate, forgotten by politicians, at the margin of public life, relegated, alas, to a secondary plane."[51] And though the responses surely had many different meanings, it is worth noting that 83 percent of middle-class São Paulo residents polled in 1948 said they were not interested in politics.[52]

From this apparent lack of political enthusiasm, we need not conclude that the middle class was politically irrelevant. Even though middle-class individuals were deeply ambivalent about associational life,[53] and without a party of their own or a highly visible spokesman for their interests, they set their signatures to the social and political order in manifold ways. They were clients to powerful politicians, patrons to poorer people, social workers, educators, bureaucrats, labor lawyers, journalists, and others who ministered to the working class through their work. Still, it is worth taking seriously the notion that large numbers of middle-class people felt themselves to be excluded from national political institutions by 1950, or at least betrayed no particular inclination to active political participation. Paschoal Lemme, a left-leaning schoolteacher, is emblematic. In explaining his lack of political involvement during the 1930s, perhaps the period of most intense middle-class political engagement at that time, he had this to say:

> I was not affiliated with any political organization, nor was I involved in any kind of party militancy. My work and tasks at the Secretariat of Education and Culture of the Federal District and at the Educational Inspector's office of the Mate of Rio de Janeiro, plus my family responsibilities, left me no time to devote to other activities. But it was not just a matter of time, as I never had any intention of associating with a political party. [54]

One easily imagines any number of *donas de casa* expressing a similar lack of interest in political activity, especially given the historical exclusion of Brazilian women from activity in the public spheres. [55]

While most were not as self-conscious as Lemme, people sharing this outlook likely saw collective action for broader class and political ends as a kind of sideshow to the real challenges of life in a rapidly modernizing social order. For them, individualized striving in the labor market and in the home was a better option than politics for attaining the good life—or at least the best life they could hope for. Commentators professing a concern for the middle class worried about the consequences of what was perceived as a widespread sentiment. João Lyra Filho, the author of *Problems of the Middle Classes*, argued in 1942 that the "competitive spirit" was breeding an intractable "individualist sentiment" that undermined collective action. And a lawyer's clarion call for defense of the middle class in the 1950s concluded that the "middle class, by its character, has a marked individualist tendency. It is more concerned with its own affairs, individually, than with defending itself through professional organizations or group associations." [56]

An approach to understanding politics in this situation is to focus on political sensibilities—the nexus of valuations, preferences, and ideals underlying political attitudes. These were the raw materials from which politicians and ideologues fashioned the messages delivered by political parties and the state. Such deeper political currents are relevant to understanding both the broad bands of people who remained outside institutional frameworks as well as those who ventured into the political arena. [57]

One of the housekeeping manuals already analyzed provides an immediate sense of the connection I wish to make between domesticity and politics. Serrano, in *Notions of Home Economics* (1954), repeated much of what she had said in her 1945 *My House* and echoed the tone of magazines such as *O*

Cruzeiro and *Vida Doméstica.* She argued that the housewife's social mission was to "try to improve human society" by "combating egoism" and "correcting the asperity of the masculine character."[58] The message was clear: *donas de casa* could have an important role in ensuring order, equilibrium, and morality in society at large through their activity in the home.

Lyra, in *Problems of the Middle Classes*, also linked the values of middle-class home life to broader social and political concerns. If only the middle class could develop a "habit of thrift," he declared, and live by "moral discipline," they would feel no need to "dispute what others have" and would contribute thereby to the "tranquility of a life of peace and comfort, that would permit harmony among men." Essentially, this was a matter of organizing the home properly, for "the family is the most stable force for consolidating the social order" and for ensuring a "serene world [of] collective calm."[59]

One of the richest sources for teasing out the meaning of Serrano's and Lyra's words is novels specifically about the middle class written during the 1930s and 1940s.[60] These books, some with titles such as *Petit Bourgeois* and *Middle Class,* contain an implicit conceptualization of the relationship between domesticity and politics. They allow a glimpse of the gossamer threads linking personal life to political sensibilities. This coupling of home and politics, just one among many competing visions of the good society, describes a political dimension intersecting the ideologies and concrete programs usually associated with the politics of class. It also illuminates ways those outside institutional politics could make sense of politics in the intimacy of personal and private lives.[61]

Written in a self-conscious style of social realism, these stories revolve around the clash between the domestic ideal and the harsh world of economic competition and political turbulence outside the home. A number of them recount the slow fall of young middle-class men who allow themselves to be seduced by the allures of radical left-wing politics. Some characters find themselves shattered and alone at the end of the book, having abandoned middle-class identities for the illusion of a pointless and ultimately unrealizable solidarity with workers. Others wake up in time to the error of their ways.[62]

Nor do these books excoriate only radical politics. Mainstream partisan politics is seen as a dark force antithetical to higher moral purpose and the greater good of society. At root, the problem lies in the egoism of economically powerful elites and the *politiqueiros* (corrupt politicians) who treat politics as an arena for little more than personal advancement, without regard for social peace or the good of the nation.[63]

The only hint of an answer to the quandary of politics in these books is to depict the middle class as the moral center of gravity that can hold society together in the face of the centripetal force of the age—the struggle between capital and labor.[64] From the perspective adopted in these stories, the immorality of the powerful leads them to ignore the legitimate demands of the working class, which responds with the minatory roar of the oppressed. The resulting class struggle upsets social equilibrium and harmony. It is for this reason, says a character in one of the books, that society must "attend to the formation of the middle class,"[65] as there is no other way to avoid open class warfare. Crucially, the lexicon of social peace employed in these novels is identical to the language used by housekeeping manuals to describe a proper home—order, equilibrium, harmony, morality. In short, only a moral politics mediated by a politically neutral middle class can keep the antagonists from each other's throats.

In these stories, the home has a distinct political status. Women play a leading role in securing social peace—not in spite of, but because of, their alienation from the hurly-burly of politics.[66] Mothers, wives, and girlfriends in tightly rendered domestic persona represent intimate counterpoints both to working-class radicalism and to the corruptions of elite politics. Young middle-class men who should know better invariably break with girlfriends or trouble their mothers' sleep in the process of becoming left-wing radicals.[67] Wives become paragons of virtue and moral rectitude in the same measure as husbands become moral monsters in politics, the board room, the drawing room, and the bedroom.[68] Symbolically, these women are conservators of order and morality, at home as well as in society at large.[69] Through them, men who properly value the life of home and family could participate in the mission of securing society's moral center. All others merely contributed to a dangerous social disharmony.

Political moralism shared the ambiguities of middle-class life more generally. The overall message of these books is that the middle class could serve as a force for stability and conciliation in a society riven by struggle and conflict among classes. Yet, the stories offered no means by which this morality could be brought directly to bear on political issues. Political action itself was morally suspect, so that the intrinsic force of morality alone was supposed to redeem the political sphere. The error of the other classes, the two combatants, was their failure to recognize the redemptive power of a morality operating above politics.

This view of politics is not so curious. A remarkable aspect of these books is the utter absence of a viable collective political experience for middle-class people. All politics amounted to unacceptable radicalism or entanglements with the corruptions of *politicagem* (political chicanery). Hedged in by powerful antagonists—employers and workers—battling for control of the material world and lacking a collective expression of their own, middle-class characters in these books see no realistic way of competing with capital and labor in the political sphere. Instead, they anchor their political outlook where they feel they have a modicum of control—the intimate life of family and home, where they can avoid "futile and pernicious contacts" with society.

Moreover, the very ideal of middle-class domesticity portrayed in the novels seems at odds with a meaningful sense of collective action. At the core of this vision was a concern for status, mediated through labor and consumption markets. Unlike collective politics, political moralism, intimately identified with the domestic sphere, did not interfere with or detract from the arduous task of orienting one's individual life toward securing a place in a competitive social order. As a consequence, while the novels counterpose morality to the dangers of politics, middle-class characters merely fulminate individually against politics. They are tortured by their desire for a state of affairs they can do very little to bring about—a good society divided hierarchically by class in which there are no class tensions.

Of course, the point of examining these novels cannot be to suggest that every middle-class Brazilian believed that morality was a sufficient answer to class conflict.[70] Nevertheless, political moralism, closely consonant with the language, Edenic vision, and glimpsed experience of the middle-class home, was a plausible outlook on politics for middle-class men and women. By recognizing class tensions as the source of social disequilibrium and offering morality as an alternative to class struggle, this vision located politics where the attention of the middle class appears to have been focused anyway—home life. Thus, the potential power of a politically fissile middle class was vested in its role as bearer of a conservatism rooted in the notion that the social world, although far from perfect, was preferable to unbridled class warfare.

BETWEEN HOUSE AND STREET

What is striking about the mid-century, middle-class home as symbol is its capaciousness. In the Brazilian context, it could shelter the changes resulting from the expansion of a competitive social order as well as more resistant cultural forces.[71] The result was an unstable situation in which highly competitive, meritocratic labor markets, a budding consumer culture, and a concern with class divisions mingled with hierarchy, patronage, and a preoccupation with status in the middle-class experience.

The juxtaposition is suggestive, for it hints at the ways in which the new and old interacted to produce a medleyed modernity centered, from a middle-class perspective, on an imagined domestic fastness. Middle-class family men who worked for salaries were not merely atomistic individuals. As heads of families facing budgetary constraints, their ability to maintain a middle-class position could well depend on how their wives managed home life. Even as women's roles were being redefined in terms of their relationship to a market economy, the structural foundations of patriarchy were being reinforced. An important factor binding middle-class men and women together in the home, then, was the shared recognition, or perhaps the palpable hope, that while social hierarchy could properly be reinforced through market outcomes, it could not (or should not) be subverted by them. Hence the stress on morality as an ordering principle for the home—and for politics.

There was in the arcing of morality from domestic to political pole the familiar flicker of *casa e rua* (house and street). A heritage of the nineteenth century, the distinction was a spatial metaphor that, during the twentieth century, came to carry the charge of social difference[72] —and perhaps even of disappointing political experience. At home, *donas de casa* could try to keep the outside world, the street, at bay (although, in fact, the street entered the house in many ways, not least, during the 1930s and 1940s, through consumerism, as I have indicated). Politics was one of the outside forces that impinged on domestic tranquillity, both at home and in society at large. Like the labor market, politics, as seen through the window of the home, seemed to be an arena of amoral individualism dominated by selfish men.[73] This perception fueled the belief that politics needed to be leavened by the morality of *donas de casa,* who were subject to a weakened but sturdy dependence on their husbands.

And so, middle-class men and women could deny themselves an active role in politics while imagining that morality in the private sphere would, or at least should, have a calming influence in the public.[74] But, since morality was to be largely unmediated by collective involvement, and since the home was in fact open to the forces of change on all sides, the influence also ran powerfully in the other direction.

NOTES

This chapter was previously published as, Brian P. Owensby, "Domesticating Modernity: Markets, Home, and Morality in the Middle Class in Rio de Janeiro and São Paulo, 1930s and 1940s," *Journal of Urban History* 24, no. 3 (March 1998): 337–63.

1. Sra. Leandro Dupré, *Eramos seis* (São Paulo, 1943), 240–41. The review was published in *Diretrizes* (5 June 1943), 15. The novel went through eight editions in ten years, was made into a movie in Argentina, and was followed by a sequel in 1944.

2. The concept of *a rua* is discussed in Sandra Lauderdale Graham, *House and Street: The Domestic World of Servants and Masters in Nineteenth-Century Rio de Janeiro* (Austin, 1995); Roberto da Matta, *A casa e a rua: Espaço, cidadania, mulher, e morte* (Rio de Janeiro, 1987).

3. For general context, see Mauricio Font, *Coffee, Contention, and Change in the Making of Modern Brazil* (Cambridge, MA, 1990); and Nicia Vilela Luz, *A luta pela industrialização do Brasil* (São Paulo, 1978).

4. With the breakdown of slave-based patriarchy, skin color became the basis for advantage and disadvantage in the labor market. See Emília Viotti da Costa, *The Brazilian Empire: Myths and Histories* (Chicago, 1985), 234–48. For São Paulo, see George Reid Andrews, *Blacks and Whites in São Paulo, Brazil, 1888–1988* (Madison, 1991); Florestán Fernandes and

Roger Bastide, *Brancos e negros em São Paulo* (São Paulo, 1959, 2nd ed.). For Rio de Janeiro, see L. A. da Costa Pinto, *O negro no Rio de Janeiro* (São Paulo, 1953), 84–5.

5. Florestán Fernandes, "Esboço de um estudo sobre a formação e desenvolvimento da ordem social competitiva," in *A Revolução burguesa no Brasil* (Rio de Janeiro, 1975); Francisco Weffort, "Estado e massas no Brasil," *O populismo na política brasileira* (Rio de Janeiro, 1978). Fernandes's use of the term *competitive social order* accurately distinguishes the Brazilian situation, in which personal relationships and patronage remained strong within a developing market society, from what has been called possessive individualism for Europe and the United States. See Emília Viotti da Costa, "Liberalism: Theory and Practice," in *Brazilian Empire: Myths and Histories* (Chicago, 1985). The danger in drawing this distinction is that of taking possessive individualism for granted in Europe and the United States, without asking what role patronage and relational considerations may have had on the development of a competitive social order there during the nineteenth and twentieth centuries.

6. Any argument regarding the size of the middle class in Rio and São Paulo is hampered by the inaccuracy of census reports from this period as well as by the inherent difficulty of accounting for all of the available white-collar occupations. Perhaps the easiest thumbnail is to note that the service sector of the Brazilian economy, the major source of white-collar job opportunities, expanded from 15 percent of the work force in 1920 to 22 percent in 1950. The percentages for the cities of Rio and São Paulo were higher since service sector jobs were concentrated there. On the whole, the middle class, including white-collar heads of family and dependents, probably accounted for about one-fifth to one-third of the population of Rio's roughly 3.5 million and São Paulo's roughly 3 million people in 1950. See the analysis in Brian Owensby, "'Stuck in the Middle': Middle Class and Class Society in Modern Brazil, 1850 to 1950" (PhD diss., Princeton University, 1994), chaps. 2 and 3.

7. The sociological and theoretical literature seeking to define the middle class is enormous. There is no consensus on an abstract definition. Therefore, I conclude that any a priori definition is pointless and that a nuanced and complex conceptualization of the middle class requires an analysis rooted in the historical and cultural specificities of a given instance.

8. See *O Estado de São Paulo*, 24 May 1936.

9. In May 1932, the average number of advertisements in the "Employees Sought" section of the classified section of *O Estado de São Paulo* was 11. By 1936, the average had grown to 30. In 1940, the average number of such advertisements was 44; in 1944 it was 140; in 1948, 151; and in 1950 the average had risen to about 250.

10. See, for example, Amilcar Cardoso, "No meu cantinho," *União* 4 (January–February 1931): 5; "Estágio e cultura," *Syndiké* 2 (June 1935): 22–3; Sebastiáo Barroso, "A medicina e a profissão médica na atualidade," *Revista do Sindicato Médico Brasileiro* 11 (November 1926), 163; "Até quando," *Revista do Syndicato Odontológico Brasileiro* 1 (August 1936). These citations are only a few examples of the official publications of white-collar associations and unions. See also the letter from Dilermando Xavier Porto to Osvaldo Aranha, 5 May 1938, Fundação Getúlio Vargas, Centro de Pesquisa e Documentação (FGV CPDOC), *Pedidos* folder for 1938.

11. *O Cruzeiro*, 13 May 1950; 24 June 1937; *A Manhã*, 30 June 1935; *Vida Carioca*, 15 (February 1934).

12. See generally *pedidos* in Osvaldo Aranha archive, FGV CPDOC. Women sought patronage for themselves less frequently, although they often did so on behalf of husbands or sons.

13. Franklin de Oliveira, "Comerciarios-A luta pela sobrevivência," *O Cruzeiro*, 19 June 1948.

14. "Os engenheiros são generais na batalha da industrialização," *Diretrizes*, 21 October 1943.

15. Amaldo Nunes, "Contador e literatura," *Revista Paulista de Contabilidade* (January 1945), 10–11.

16. Victor Vianna, "O esforço das elites e a depressão monetaria," *Syndiké* 1 (September 1935), 29.

17. Jodo Lyra Filho, *Problemas das classes médias* (Rio de Janeiro, 1942).

18. See, for example, *Vida Carioca* (February 1934).

19. Susan Besse, *Restructuring Patriarchy: The Modernization of Gender Inequality in Brazil, 1914–1940* (Chapel Hill, 1996).

20. Isabela de Almeida Serrano, *Minha casa* (Rio de Janeiro, 1945), 142.

21. See Revista do Professor (Orgão do Professorado Paulista) 1 (March 1934); Revista da Associação dos Funcionários Públicos do Estado de São Paulo 2 (October–November 1934), 18–19; *O Cruzeiro* (September 1946), 51.

22. Instituto Brasileiro de Opinião Pública e Estatística (IBOPE), "Pesquisa sobre padrão de vida," São Paulo, 1946.

23. *Vida Doméstica* (January 1932).

24. *Vida Doméstica* (July 1935).

25. *Vida Doméstica* (August 1937).

26. José Moacir do Andrade Sobrinho, "Composição do vencimento e níveis do renumeração do funcionário público," *Revista do Serviço Público* 4 (February 1940): 12.

27. Humberto Bastos, "Progresso técnico e padrão de vida," *O Brasil no após-guerra* (conference sponsored by Instituto de Organização Racional do Trabalho, January 1944).

28. IBOPE, "Pesquisa, sobre poder aquisitivo dos leitores da revista O Cruzeiro," Rio de Janeiro and São Paulo, November 1946.

29. IBOPE, "Estudos sobre as condições de vida do comerciário em São Paulo e Campinas," July 1947.

30. IBOPE, "Estudo de mercado para Estabelecimentos Canada," Rio de Janeiro and São Paulo, December 1944.

31. Other IBOPE studies support this view. In one, nearly half of all middle-class people polled who said they planned to buy a home wanted a garage, even though more than 80 percent of them did not yet own cars. Another indicated that the middle class paid closer attention than the rich or the poor to advertisements for cars, tires, and home appliances.

32. *O Cruzeiro*, 26 October 1940.

33. Ruy de Azevedo Sodré, "Em defesa das classes médias, " *Primeiro Congresso Estadual da Familia Cristã* (São Paulo, 1957).

34. "0 salário dos bancários," memorandum to the Congressional Commission on Social Legislation, *Syndiké* (June 1935), 5–9.

35. Sindicato dos Bancários de São Paulo, "As dividas e a estabilidade dos bancários-memorial ao Ministro do Trabalho e Indústria" (December 1939), 13.

36. The implied comparison is that some male manual workers earned more than some male white-collar employees and professionals. It was not uncommon for male workers to earn more than women typists, teachers, or clerks.

37. IBOPE, "Pesquisa sobre padrão de vida," Rio de Janeiro and São Paulo, July 1946.

38. See Gilberto Freyre, *The Mansions and the Shanties: The Making of Modern Brazil* (Berkeley, 1986); Graham, *House and Street.*

39. See Besse, *Restructuring Patriarchy.*

40. *Publicidade* (September 1940).

41. *O Cruzeiro*, 8 December 1945.

42. Serrano, *Minha casa, 25.*

43. Marialice Prestes, *Problemas do lar* (São Paulo, 1945), 17.

44. See Serrano, *Minha casa;* and, *Noções de economia doméstica* (São Paulo, 1954); Prestes, *Problemas do lar.*

45. Dain Borges's evidence of a transition away from a patriarchal toward a more conjugal family among the upper and middle classes in Bahia between 1870 and 1945, especially given the conservatism of Bahian society, is suggestive of what was going on in Rio de Janeiro and São Paulo. See Borges, *The Family in Bahia, Brazil, 1870–1945* (Stanford, 1992).

46. Serrano, *Minha casa,* 170.

47. Serrano, *Noções de economic doméstica,* 33. None of these ideas was new or exclusive to Serrano. They had been talked about for a number of years in magazines of the period aimed at parents, such *as Criança-Revista dos Pais, A Casa, Lar-Revista da Familia* as well as in magazines with wider concerns and larger circulation, such as *O Cruzeiro* and *Vida Doméstica.*

48. Serrano, *Minha casa,* 61.

49. Ibid., 149.

50. Clovis Leite Ribeiro, "A classe média e as eleições de 19 de janeiro," *Digesto Económico* 3 (April 1947): 71–7.

51. Sodré, "Em defesa das classes médias."

52. IBOPE, "Pesquisa de opinião pública sobre materia política realizada nesta capital no mes de setembro 1948." It is worth noting that 53 percent of the rich and 89 percent of the working class gave the same answer. While politics is rarely people's favorite topic, the higher number of the rich claiming interest in politics makes sense in light of the fact that two of the three major parties were dominated by political elites and powerful economic groups and widely perceived as serving their interests. The proportion of the working class down on politics was slightly greater, although it does not seem to have dampened a distinct combativeness, at least among workers involved in organized labor.

53. See chapter 7 in Owensby, "Stuck in the Middle."

54. Paschoal Lemme, *Memórias,* vol. 2 (São Paulo, 1988), 217.

55. See June Hahner, *Emancipating the Female Sex: The Struggle for Women's Rights in Brazil, 1850–1940* (Durham, 1990).

56. Lyra Filho, *Problemas das classes médias,* 67; Sodré, "Em defesa das classes medias," 26.

57. The dominant trend in studies of the middle class has been to concentrate on culture and private life to the exclusion of politics writ large or to deal with public life and politics while bracketing personal and private life aside. Stuart Blumin, *The Emergence of the Middle Class: Social Experience in the American City, 1760–1900* (Cambridge, UK, 1990) is characteristic of the former, and Jaime Covarrubias, *El Partido Radical y la clase media en Chile: la relación de intereses entre 1888–1938* (Santiago, 1990) of the latter. My goal is to suggest the ways in which these two instincts were inseparable, yet in constant tension.

58. Serrano, *Noções de economia doméstica,* 249. Serrano wrote this book, in part, to be used in secondary-school home economics courses.

59. Lyra Filho, *Problemas das classes médias,* 93, 211, 237.

60. As with all literary sources, the issues of production and reception are complicated. In keeping with the social realism of the period, most of these books described the experiences, expectations, and anxieties of people defined by work and home—ordinary people who went to great lengths to lead decent, respectable, and often unremarkable lives. A reviewer said of one best-seller that it evinced a "faithfulness to middle-class types." See review of Dupré's *Eramos seis* in *Diretrizes* (5 June 1942), 15. The authors hailed from backgrounds bespeaking familiarity with the lives they depicted. Their fathers tended to be pharmacists, school teachers, public functionaries, and commercial clerks. Their mothers commonly graduated from normal schools and worked as teachers. All had at least secondary-school education. A number attended university. They earned their livings as teachers, commercial clerks, journalists, lawyers, or public functionaries. All lived in or near a large city. It is impossible to know precisely who or how many people read these books. Some were best-sellers; others were not. Context may be the best guide to the general audience to which they were addressed. They were published during a period of dramatic change in literacy and the book market: see Teresinha A. del Fiorentino, *Prosa e ficção em São Paulo: Produção e consumo* (São Paulo, 1982). Perhaps central to this phenomenon was what one student of the matter has referred to as a "rising middle class" of book buyers, the large number of urban- dwelling, salaried employees and professionals that had emerged over the three decades after the turn of the century. See Laurence Hallewell, *O livro no Brasil (sua historia)* (São Paulo, 1985). Within this new segment of the book market, leisure and a desire to make sense of a postoligarchical, industrializing, urbanizing, class-divided nation led to an "obsessive preoccupation with personal and material matters," causing "the habit of reading to increase dramatically," as one accountant noted in 1936 (Arnaldo Nunes, *Que é a contabilidade,* 24). Or, as Hallewell has put it, the "ascent of a new middle class, preoccupied with its own problems and the problems of the country, were changing the perspectives of the country and creating a whole new market for Brazilian authors." See Hallewell, cited in, Lúcia Lippi Oliveira, "Elite intelectual e debate político nos anos 30," *Dados* 22 (1979): 70.

61. Along these lines for the working class in Britain and the United States, see Pamela Fox, *Class Fictions: Shame and Resistance in the British Working-Class Novel, 1890–1945* (Dur-

ham, 1994); and Michael Denning, *Mechanic Accents: Dime Novels and Working-Class Culture in America* (London, 1987). As in these books, I see the novels under consideration here as entrees to the yearnings, fantasies, and mythologies that so often go unexamined because they escape the sources available for institutional politics. This implies, of course, a vision of class as determined simultaneously by material and discursive processes. See Zachary Lockman, "Imagining the Working Class: Culture, Nationalism, and Class Formation in Egypt, 1899–1914," *Poetics Today* 15 (Summer 1994): 157–90. Thus, the appearance of a linguistic representation of class, of which I am here looking at only a narrow slice, is inseparable from the existence of class as a social and political fact connected to tangible, lived experience.

62. See, for example, João Calazans, *Pequeno burgués* (1933); Jader de Carvalho, *Classe m é dia* (Recife, 1937); Erico Veríssimo, *O resto é silencio* (1943); Dupré, *Eramos seis* (1943).

63. The cynical tone of these novels regarding politics was echoed in the publications of white-collar associations during the 1930s and 1940s. Most criticized self-serving politicians for their failure to address the nation's problems. Further, government bureaucrats and some professionals began to partake of a language of technical competence, in which expertise was seen as an alternative to conventional, collective political activity.

64. On this struggle in São Paulo up to the 1950s, see Joel Wolfe, *Working Women, Working Men: São Paulo and the Rise of Brazil's Industrial Working Class, 1900–1955* (Durham, 1993); and John French, *Workers "ABC": Class Conflict and Alliances in Modern São Paulo* (Chapel Hill, 1992).

65. Democrito de Castro e Silva, *Classe media* (Rio do Janeiro, 1945), 137.

66. Literate women received the franchise in 1932. However, they did not gain prominence within political parties throughout the period from 1930 to 1950.

67. Carvalho, *Classe media;* Calazans, *Pequeno burgües;* Érico Veríssimo, *Crossroads* (1943); Dupré, *Eramos seis;* Veríssimo, *O resto é silencio.*

68. Hélio Chaves, *Uma familia burguesa* (Petrópolis, 1952).

69. More work is needed on the way in which women understood and experienced politics and their own role in society. All but one of the novels treated here, anchoring politics in the domestic sphere, were written by men, although Dupré's *Eramos seis* was a runaway best-seller portraying a long-suffering mother whose mission in life was to hold her family and home together in the face of social upheaval and change.

70. These books do not represent middle-class sensibilities directly. Rather, they are evidence of, among other things, a contest over the role politics was to play in a class-divided society. I see them as glasses against a thick wall that make audible snatches of "the essentially antagonistic collective discourses of social classes" (Fredric Jameson, *The Political Unconscious* [Ithaca, 1981], 76). It is worth noting in this regard that a number of people who purported to speak on behalf of the Brazilian middle class during the 1930s and 1940s made arguments and used language almost identical to that of the novels, referring to the middle class as the "master cross beam of the country's equilibrium," as the key to "social peace," as the "most cultivated, the wisest, the most sensible" segment of the people, as a "powerful factor for equilibrium," and as a force for "moral resistance." See Tito Prates da Fonseca, "Sentido e valor das classes médias," *Quarta semana de ação social do São Paulo* (Rio de Janeiro, 1940), 190; João Lyra Filho, *Problemas das classes médias: Economia, amor, desportos* (Rio do Janeiro, 1942), 101; IBOPE, "Pesquisa do opinião pública realizado no Distrito Federal para O Observador Econômico, coro o objetivo do estudar a atitude do pública realizado no Distrito Federal para O Observador Económico, com o objetivo do estudar a atitude do público em geral e das *chamadas* classes conservadoras, em face das perspectivas do ano de 1946 para o Brasil," Rio de Janeiro, November–December 1945; Clovis Leite Ribeiro, "A Classe media e as eleições de 19 de janeiro," *Digesto Económico* 3 (April 1947): 71–72.

71. By now, a supposed connection between the middle class and some form or other of domesticity is commonplace. Indeed, the link has been sharply criticized, since domestic ideology, broadly understood, can be found among elites as well as among workers. See Wahrman, *Imagining the Middle Class,* 378–80. In Brazil, it would be nonsensical to conclude that domesticity was exclusive to the middle class, since, as Gilberto Freyre (*Casa Grande and Senzala*) argued in the 1930s, family and house were central elements of Brazilian culture across social classes. My concern, therefore, is to indicate some of the ways in which a

domestic ideology crossed with everyday life and political sensibilities among middle-class people. Middle-class domesticity doubtless diverged considerably from that of elites or workers, because of differing advantages and constraints in a market economy and differing class cultures. On the Brazilian working-class home and its relationship to the street in the late nineteenth and early twentieth century, see Sidney Chaloub, *Trabalho, lar, e botequim: O cotidiano dos trabalhadores no Rio de Janeiro da Belle Époque* (São Paulo, 1986).

72. For example, a report issued in 1935 dismissed the idea of vacations for manual laborers because they did not cultivate the "comfort and sweetness" of "home life" but instead spent long hours in the street, prey to "latent vices." This was in sharp contrast to the "intellectual worker," whose home was "welcoming and pleasant," allowing him to avoid "subaltern activities that would alter his moral fabric" (Otávio Pupo Nogueira, *A indústria em face das leis do trabalho* [São Paulo, 1935]).

73. See Da Matta, *Casa e rua*. It might be more accurate to think of this individualism as relational, that is, as an individualism oriented to an expanding labor market in which merit and patronage developed as parallel strategies for personal advancement. See Roberto Da Matta, *Carnivals, Rogues and Heroes: An Interpretation of the Brazilian Dilemma* (Notre Dame, 1991). See text accompanying note 14.

74. While there is considerable overlap between the notions of public-private and house-street, their differences are striking. Whereas in its usual formulation public is identified with the state and private with market and family, house is identified almost exclusively with family intimacy, and street with market and state. At bottom, it is possible to see house-street as characterized by the difference between personal and impersonal spheres, an aspect of what Roberto Da Matta has called the relational universe. Compare Jürgen Habermas, *The Structural Transformation of the Public Sphere: An Inquiry into a Category of Bourgeois Society* (Cambridge, MA, 1989) and Da Matta, *A casa e a rua* and *Carnivals, Rogues, and Heroes.* The distinction is important, for it suggests the ways in which a defining idea of modern society is made problematic by its encounter with Brazilian history and culture.

Chapter Ten

"It Is Not Something You Can Be or Come to Be Overnight"

Empleados, Office Angels, and Gendered Middle Class Identifications in Bogotá, Colombia, 1930–1955

A. Ricardo López

Being middle class is not just a matter of occupation, income, consumption, or lifestyle. Middle-classness, according to Ricardo López, was also rooted in understandings of what it meant to be male or female. Looking at Bogotá, Colombia, from the 1930s to 1950s, López argues that the increasing entrance of women into the office placed the masculinity of male empleados *into some doubt. But white-collar claims to manliness were buttressed by a discourse that likened the office to a patriarchal household, constructed the female "office angel" as a helpmate rather than a worker, and described blue-collar* obreros *as lacking the qualities that made* empleados *"real men." Female employees, for their part, used the "office angel" image and commonly held ideas of femininity to assert their superiority over men in aptitude for service-sector work. While they tended not to challenge the idea of the male* empleado *as principal breadwinner, they argued that it was their contribution, as both model mothers and model office workers, that really secured their families' middle-class status.*

—◄◊◊◊►—

You do not know how difficult to be middle class is. It is a question of . . . you know, every single day you have to feed your status. . . . The motivations, the education, the differences with other people . . . you can see that everywhere. To be middle class, I believe, is a privilege. We are not rich people because we avoid getting crazy for the money. Believe it or not, the obsession for the money can bring you moral problems. We are not *obreros,* because middle

> class is just what you see, it is something difficult to explain, but it is not
> something you can be or come to be overnight. I will tell you something: I
> could not have money in my pocket, not a penny, but I have always been
> middle class and I will always be. Look [at] my daughters; [my husband and I]
> have taught them to be middle class. It is hard, but I think we have succeeded. [1]

A novel published in Bogotá in 1938 tells the story of several fictional men
and women trying, during the first part of the twentieth century, to define
their place in a changing society.[2] Titled *Those in the Middle*, the novel
explored the problems its characters faced amidst the social turmoil produced
by modernization, and the way they imagined their middling position in
society. In one revealing passage, two siblings, Enrique, an empleado (white-
collar employee), and Cecilia, a *mujer de oficina* ("office woman"), discuss
their ideal boyfriend and girlfriend. Although the choice is a matter of great
discussion, Cecilia agrees that what she needs above all is "somebody from
[her] same social status, neither rich nor poor . . . a middle-class man, educated, somebody who plays a role in life, a successful man." Likewise, Enrique
concludes that he also needs "somebody from the same social status, neither
poor nor rich . . . a decent woman, a middle-class lady . . . a real middle-class
woman." After agreeing on the class position of their ideal mate, however,
Cecilia and Enrique comment that although "these wishes are not too much
to ask for, these [ideal] women and men are hard to find."[3]

This passage raises crucial questions about Colombia's middle class.
What historical circumstances enabled the fictional Cecilia and Enrique to
think of themselves as middle class? What did flesh-and-blood employees
and office women mean when they called themselves middle class? Why did
they begin to self-identify as middle class? I address these questions by
tracing how ideas of gender intersected with ideas of class to create a stereo-
typical middle-class male employee (*empleado de clase media*) and middle-
class office woman (*mujer de oficina de clase media*) in early twentieth-
century Bogotá.

My sources include office handbooks and manuals, government publications, employment forms, diaries, private archives, novels, meeting minutes,
and oral histories. I argue that modern ideas of class and gender that gained
currency between the 1930s and 1950s in Colombia promoted the new notion
of a service sector (the office), in antagonistic and hierarchical relation to an
industrial sector (the factory). The creation of this service sector, both as a
real economic phenomenon and as an idea, gave birth to two new historical
actors: the male empleado and the female *ángel de oficina* ("office angel").
Finally, I explore how women and men entering the service sector drew upon
those emerging ideas as they defined and performed new identities as "middle-class women" and "middle-class men."[4]

EMPLEADOS AND *ÁNGELES DE OFICINA*: THE FORMATION OF THE SERVICE SECTOR

Colombia, like most countries in Latin America, changed radically between the 1930s and the late 1950s. Rapid population growth, industrialization, urbanization, and the expansion of the public and private sectors gave rise to a new social order. Insufficiently analyzed by historians of the period is the dramatic growth of the service sector (commerce, government, and transportation). This vital part of the economy expanded as the state became increasingly interventionist. For example, following the 1923 recommendations of the U.S.-sponsored Kemmerer Mission, the Colombian government established the Banco de la República (National Bank) and the Contraloría General de la República (Comptroller General) and supported the creation of banks and other service enterprises such as post offices, tax offices, ministries, and schools. This trend was particularly clear in Bogotá. According to an article published in 1942, the urban service sector comprised 35 percent of the Colombian labor force. Significantly, 46 percent of those employed in the service sector were women.[5]

In emphasizing the importance of the service sector, I do not mean to overlook Colombia's simultaneous process of industrialization. In many ways the expansion of industry and the expansion of the service sector were interrelated processes, each contributing to and helping to define the other. Structural changes in the economy generated occupational diversification, which in turn led to new cultural understandings of different kinds of work. Service sector workers increasingly defined themselves *in opposition to* society's imagined notions of industrial workers.

That construction of a sense of difference was not just a matter of class; it was also shaped in essential ways by ideas of gender. Empleados asserted their identity as middle-class men, *mujeres de oficina* as middle-class women, both with qualities that contrasted with those of their blue-collar counterparts. Employers played an active role in fostering the idea that the service sector belonged to these two special figures. In their employment policies, job requirements, and hiring processes, private and public sector employers constructed empleados as embodying the "masculine traits" a man should have to work in an office; similarly, they constructed *ángeles de oficina* as embodying certain specifically feminine traits.

In various publications, and in the provisions of the *Ley del Empleado* (Employees' Law) of 1936, private sector employers and the municipal government of Bogotá began to distinguish carefully between manual and nonmanual jobs: between people "who work in factories [and] those who work in offices." Empleados were defined as those "men who develop and engage in mental and intellectual work."[6] Empleados had "skills, ability for mental work, morality, a sense of responsibility, hard work, reasoning and patience, loyalty, a desire to be honest and good will and spirit—in contrast to obreros, who were defined as "those lazy, irresponsible [people] doing manual jobs."[7]

A 1942 study that the Contraloria General de la República published for its employees defined several "masculine differences" between obreros and empleados. According to the study, the first requirement for becoming "a real empleado, a man from the service sector," was to work, at the very least, in an office environment, because office work "exalts a man." "Work" in this context meant "work with the head," in contrast to obreros' jobs, which involved working with the hands. "Skill, intelligence," and work in a "peaceful and quiet office" were prerequisites associated with empleados, which made them "broadly different" from obreros, who were perceived as "illiterate, poorly educated, less intelligent, lesser men." After all, "real men work in offices."[8] These constructions did much more than emphasize distinct white-collar job requirements. They established a hierarchical opposition between the industrial sector and the service sector, emphasizing the masculine notions of the imagined empleado working in the office.

Private-sector employers and the municipal government almost invariably spoke of the empleado as a breadwinner, as *jefe de hogar* (head of household), in this way asserting his masculinity. In curricula vitae, job interviews, and labor studies, the empleado was represented as the man who "supported a family, the man who sought a lovely wife and beautiful family with la 'parejita' [two children, a boy and a girl]." Empleados were described not only as patriarchs and breadwinners but also as "real men [who] *enjoy* being good husbands and fathers."[9] Employers and government officials portrayed them as those who "easily eschewed gambling and other rough masculine pursuits" for the "respectable manly" pleasures of an orderly family life. In stark contrast, obreros were imagined as men who, while they might hope to marry, could never achieve "such a difficult manly task" because they allegedly tended to spend their money on alcohol and to "make their families unhappy."[10] Employers in the service sector believed that obreros rarely expected to achieve either a respectable or "manly" future for their families and descendants.[11]

This gendered construction of empleados arose in counterpoint to the creation of the female *ángel de oficina*. Although we are accustomed to expect the invisibility—or omission—of women as historical actors, private employers and municipal government officials *emphasized* women's participation in the service sector. Labor studies, job requirements, and the questions asked in employment interviews in various public and private offices strongly affirmed—indeed, celebrated—women's role in the office. One example among many is a brief account by an employer in the Comptroller General's Office who venerated the "importance" of women's participation in the office's work. In 1946, Mario Carrillo proudly argued, "The office is for our *ángeles de oficina* . . . to those angels that make every day's work easier. . . . What would our offices be without our women, our *ángeles de oficina*? No wonder, without them there would be no offices."[12]

One rendering of this account would lead us to conclude simply that women played a more visible role in the service sector than elsewhere. But there is more to it than that. It is difficult to ignore the language Carrillo is using to insist on the *need* to have women in the office. A deeper interpretation demands that we consider the class connotations and gendered understandings that (male) employers brought to their celebration of women's participation in the service sector.[13] On the one hand, the tasks assigned to women in the office were blurred with, and imagined as an extension of, the traditional duties of women at home, thus casting female office workers in the role of "wives" and "helpers" of the "real men in the office." On the other hand, the male empleados' *actual* wives were described in identical terms, also as "office angels," because they were "the great, exceptional women behind the great men," the ones at home "who [took] care, protecte[d] and . . . made miracles, as good *ángeles*, for their husbands . . . the empleados in the service sector."[14] They were responsible for ensuring the cleanliness of the household, the nutrition and moral rectitude of the children, and the harmony and coordination of the social relationships within the home. Only if empleados' wives properly exercised their role could the family's moral, intellectual, physical, and material well-being "make empleados feel like real men."[15]

A story in a municipal government publication in 1946 for "empleados in the service sector," for instance, shows how ideas of gender and class shaped the notion of the *ángel de oficina*. In this story about the wife of "a modest empleado in a ministry office who had two children," the wife was able to give a "good life" to her husband and family, albeit on a "modest income." Still, it was very difficult, because she had to exercise many strategies "to maintain the social status of the family" and by extension the desired male empleado's status. The wife as *ángel de oficina* not only wanted her family to be middle class but also wanted to "protect [her husband's] status as the best man in the office."[16] She had to use her abilities, intelligence, and organizational skills to accomplish these "feminine tasks." Her daily preoccupation was with "dressing her children, making clothes for her husband with the purpose of making him look like a real man, with a tie and shined shoes, with a clean and well-pressed shirt." She would always be proud of being the wife of the empleado, and in difficult times she had to improve her skills as a wife. If at the end of the month, for example, there was not enough food and the budget was tight, she could miraculously "make these moments less difficult."

By creating, and always protecting, a special environment at home in which even the husband would not notice that his income was insufficient, the wife could make him "feel that he was an empleado that [as a breadwin-ner] could maintain his family as a real man." In one passage in this publica-tion, the wife worried because her husband's salary was not enough "to live well, decently . . . with status." She decided not to tell him, since to do so "would make him so unhappy and . . . he would think he is not a real man." In consequence, she preferred to use "her feminine attributes to make every-thing work in the family." Only in these conditions could the wife as *ángel de oficina* both taste middle-class status and the promise that "the head of the household was the best man in the office." After all, behind an empleado, "a real man in the office," there was always "a real woman, an *ángel de ofici-na*."[17] In short, the construction of the service sector as masculine and the creation of women as "office angels" redrew notions of white-collar mascu-linity. The urban service sector was represented as a masculine space, yet the *ángel de oficina*, a visible yet excluded other, was essential to that sector's functioning.

Significantly, however, as women sharply increased their participation and visibility in the service sector labor force during the interwar years, these gender and class constructions obscured—even erased—female office work-ers *as workers*. Their role as wage-earners went virtually unacknowledged because employers and government officials "never hired a woman worker to work in the offices": instead "they were hiring *ángeles de oficina*."[18] Never-theless, the figure of the *ángel de oficina* enabled women to move into the workplace in unprecedented numbers during those years. Women appealed to traditional gender roles to stake a claim to office jobs, and legitimated their work by manipulating the desired notions of femininity.[19]

As women worked in offices in ever-greater numbers, the discourse of *ángeles de oficina* as "wives" persisted, and took on stronger class connota-tions.[20] In contrast to *obreras,* "irresponsible women who tended to be "ag-gressive, lazy, and with . . . disdain for the rules of the house," *ángeles* would be "real women" who could *help* in the office, showing "the most important feminine obligations, attributes and virtues," namely, "service, patience, kindness, goodness, sympathy . . . and being emotionally supportive."[21]

These feminine attributes had to be revealed in a quasi-domestic environ-ment. Consequently, private employers and municipal government officials constructed and imagined the office, in contrast to the factory, as a space ruled by familial relationships. Rather than being at work, *ángeles de oficina* were ostensibly "helping another family,"[22] not in an "unknown workplace" but in "the office home."[23] They were "exceptional women" capable of con-verting themselves into the "mothers of the office" and seamlessly changing back to the courageous and valiant "mother of the home." Clearly, then, the term *ángel de oficina* celebrated women's moral authority, their extraordi-nary role as wives and helpers, not women as workers. This creation allowed women to move into the service sector in large numbers without transgressing or undermining traditional class and gender roles, because they were seen as merely extending their domestic roles into the office setting. One expert noted, "It is remarkable how these angels [could] help build homes in offices without leaving the homes of their own."[24]

"REALLY, DO WE HAVE WOMEN IN THE OFFICES?" EMPLEADOS, *MUJERES DE OFICINA,* AND MIDDLE-CLASS IDENTITIES IN THE WORKPLACE

Although the increasing entrance of women into office work was as much a result as a cause of the gendered and class-based constructions of "office angels," empleados found themselves experiencing it, in the words of one, as a "strange change." On the one hand, they accepted the entrance of women into the office because it might reinforce their masculinity: after all, "who else [would be] behind the empleados?" *Angeles de oficina* would "help" them to be "the real men in the offices." On the other hand, the very notion of the *ángel de oficina* could also be seen as a "threat to [their] sense of being men."[25] Some interpreted the reality of working shoulder to shoulder with women as a feminization of the office, because now office work—viewed as "help," as service to others—was associated in some ways with the home. Even worse, some empleados saw the entrance of the *ángel de oficina* as a threat to their masculinity not only because those women were taking office jobs from men but, just as importantly, because it might enable other men—namely, obreros—to label white-collar work as "feminine."[26]

Perhaps because of these contradictions and anxieties accompanying the rationalization of office work and the expansion of the service sector during the 1930s and 1940s, empleados began holding meetings where they could gather in a "spirit of camaraderie" and create a new space to deal with what they called "impersonal labor relationships." Although in the mid-1930s these meetings occurred only sporadically, over time they became commonplace in a number of larger Bogotá offices, where they took place on a weekly basis and minutes were recorded.[27] In the meetings, which generally had no organized agenda, empleados discussed different articles published in handbooks, white-collar manuals, and government publications. The minutes sometimes referenced other stories—usually without formal citation of specific publications—that typified empleado experiences, in order to provoke conversation. The men would talk about how those accounts reflected actual experiences. These stories, articles, and discussions mostly dealt with the role that empleados should play as workers at the office and as husbands and fathers at home. Empleados also discussed such issues as the rationalization of office work, job evaluations, and task distribution, as well as various policies being implemented by the Contraloría. Less frequently, but significantly, they discussed matters categorized as "of general interest," such as social life at the office (marriages, births, and informal gatherings) and "personal issues" (advice on the education of children, suggestions about family budgets, and tips on behavior and good manners). [28]

The very structure of these meetings and the minutes they produced speak directly to the anxieties and contradictions that empleados experienced in the face of the expansion of the service sector, the reorganization of office labor, and above all, the increasing employment of women. The minutes show how empleados both responded to and helped to shape those historical changes. Specifically, in the context of the growing "female presence," empleados began developing new strategies to reclaim their place as "the real man in the offices." Some sought to reinforce their masculinity by portraying the office as a source of masculine affirmation: they were still men enough to "reconquer" and dominate the workplace. In contrast to obreros, who "could never think of working in offices," empleados had the potential to take "possession" of the office. [29] They thought that women's presence could reinforce their masculinity, because, as they explained, empleados were "real men with specific tasks." As Hector Alarcón argued in a meeting in 1939: "As soon as women entered into the office, are we doing female jobs? There can be thousands of women, but men have always been over the feminine, and if in the office there are many women . . . the office [is] an active workplace where intelligence, hard work, and discipline is an everyday requirement." [30]

At the same time, however, women's entrance into the office was clearly considered a problem for empleados' definitions of masculinity, as a short story described in the minutes of one meeting illustrates. An empleado was afraid not only of being associated with obreros and thus losing his middle-class status but was also worried about how obreros might view him. One obrero laughed at him for "doing female work . . . a girl's job." [31] The implication was that empleados could barely be considered men because "their daily contact with women in office work could make empleados lesser men." Alfredo Abello, an empleado who commented on the short story, said in 1943:

> Recently, we have seen the massive entrance of women into our offices. We must look at this phenomenon carefully. [It] does not seem to have a solution. There is the danger that it will make us [empleados] seem to be men doing women's jobs. It will make us lose our social status, our until-now well-regarded jobs. We all know that women have always done monotonous and easy tasks, jobs with little importance in the labor force. Sooner or later, our jobs as empleados will be seen, as many have already said, as something related to women's jobs. It would be very sad if we do not do something. [32]

By this logic, women's entrance into the office was a clear threat to the empleados' masculine status because "to work in girls' space could make

[them] sexually suspect, physically weak . . . lesser men" compared to obreros who "were doing masculine jobs."[33]

As Abello suggested, empleados responded to this threat of feminization, mobilizing and resignifying certain definitions of gender and class that circulated in the urban service sector. In this dynamic process they attempted to reassert their masculine distinctiveness and middle-class superiority by positioning the obrero in an inferior place in the imagined social hierarchy and by effeminizing him.[34] Some empleados argued that obreros were the ones who resembled women."[35] In contrast to empleados and their "masculine traits"—knowledge, mental labor, economic security, self-control, decision, and honor—obreros were "passive, weak, sensitive, dependent and subordinated" and, in addition, had "low wages, monotonous jobs, without importance in the labor hierarchy."[36]

These empleados insisted that obreros were inferior not only because they "look[ed] and act[ed] like women" but also because they were inferior even to the *women* employed in office work. If some women could function in offices and obreros could not, it was because obreros were not only less than men but even "less than [these] women."[37] In other words, only the empleado could embody the masculine traits needed to work in service and office jobs. After all, without the "necessary male traits," some empleados argued, "obreros never could be real men, real empleados."[38]

Likewise, empleados portrayed the office hierarchy in ways designed to counteract the notion that "they were doing female jobs."[39] Secretaries, receptionists, and in general anyone who did clerical work should not be called an empleado, because these jobs "could not reach higher status or move up in the work hierarchy."[40] Empleados described women working in the office as having certain positive masculine traits that allowed them to work in the service sector, in effect placing women who could work in office jobs in a sort of intermediate gender. These "[atypical] masculine characteristics," nevertheless, did not rise to the level of the qualities of male employees in "the best and well ranked jobs in the office,"[41] somewhere between the real men (empleados) and *defective men* (effeminized obreros). Office women could have "patience" but never "self-control," "organization skills" but never the "power of decision," an aptitude for mental work but never "intelligence," "morality" but never "superior judgment."[42] This creation of a gendered notion of office women as atypical served to reaffirm empleados' masculinity, because they could continue to ask: "Who can say that office jobs are something for women?" and proudly and emphatically answer: "Nobody."[43]

Empleados elaborated other ways to describe their masculine attributes as "superior" and more "respectable" than those of other social classes. Some argued that "physical strength of the body, muscular capacity, toughness or craftsmanship" should not measure "real manliness (*hombría de verdad*)."[44]

In contrast to common conceptions of working-class masculinity, empleados imagined themselves as "professional and superior," and as "the ones who were worried for their families and women."[45] In several weekly meetings empleados in the Contraloria General de la República commented on a short story about Juan, an empleado, and Pedro, an obrero.[46] Juan, according to the story, always spent his money for family needs and never "hit his wife or children." It was his duty as a "good man" to find a "decent job to support his family." Pedro, in contrast, usually spent his money drinking alcohol and "hit both his wife and children."[47] In their comments on this story, one may see how the empleados remade notions of "middle class manliness," oppositionally related to working class' masculinity.

Whereas several agreed that they "were different [from obreros] in the way of being men," they had diverse notions of how "they should be different." Mauricio Acevedo, for instance, argued that "to be a real man" it was not only necessary to support one's family, but also, and most importantly, to *know* "how to treat both women and persons who [are] weaker." Mauricio claimed that the "key characteristic of being a man" was to have the "ability" to let the weak know that the "real man [was] there to help her, to protect her, to take care of her."[48] As empleado Mario Romero remarked in the early 1940s:

> To be a man is not only to belong to the masculine sex; it is not to have muscles, be strong physically. To be a man is to be aware of the way you act. To be a man is to be a creator of a home; to be a man is to find a decent job; to be a man is to maintain a family; to be a man is to provide your family with some luxury; to be a man is to be able to give children a good education; to be a man is to understand work not as a necessity but as a privilege; to be a man is to be ashamed for hitting weaker ones, women and children. To be a man is to know how to behave with women. These are the real men . . . the real empleado.[49]

These gendered justifications helped empleados to overcome the fear that having "their" women work outside the home might challenge their middle-class masculinity and their role as breadwinner. By mobilizing the idea of "how to treat women well," empleados took credit for *allowing* women to work outside the home.[50] This patriarchal ability to *choose* whether or not the women over whom they had authority might work outside the home served as further evidence of empleados' superior manliness. It was yet another trait that made them different from, and better than, the "little obreros" (*obreritos*) who presumably *needed* women's wages to survive and who did not enjoy the leisure or masculine authority to view women's wage work as a voluntary lifestyle choice.[51]

If women's work was seen as a reflection of the empleados' masculine choice to treat their wives and daughters well by "letting them work," then women's salaries could be defined as pin money: just a little extra to be spent on nice but non-essential things.[52] Whereas women in obrero families had to work to compensate for their husbands' or fathers' insufficient means (and hence inadequate masculinity), empleados who were manly enough to "let women work" continued, by definition, to play the part of breadwinner.[53] Were this not the case, empleados' constructed distinctiveness would run the risk of becoming imperceptible. Their masculinity, therefore, depended upon the creation of at least two opposites—"little obreros" and *ángeles de oficina*—that allowed them to imagine themselves as superior members of a gender- and class-based social order. And empleados tried to *maintain* these hierarchical orders precisely because without the obreros and the *angeles de oficina*, the masculine differences between obreros and empleados "would disappear in time."[54] In this process, empleados' sense of being middle-class men was perpetually in the making.

YES, WE ARE *MUJERES DE OFICINA!*

Office women were by no means passive receptors of male empleados' constructions of them. Although the *ángel de oficina* as an imagined historical actor obscured—and made imperceptible—the crucial participation of women *as* service sector workers, those women entering office jobs could still mobilize the "office angel" image, challenging the hierarchies implicit in the idea to forge identities of their own. They defined new social boundaries, positioning themselves as different from and superior to those they labeled as *obreras*. In so doing they created their own gendered class category: *mujeres de oficina de clase media*.

Like the male empleados, *mujeres de oficina* also held weekly meetings in which they talked about their office experience, as well as discussing articles and stories from various handbooks and government publications.[55] The meetings were similar in structure to those organized by empleados, but the minutes reveal serious thinking about their role *as women* in the office, and especially about the question of how they were to balance office work with their "obligations" at home. In their testimonies, they emphasized the idea that "the opportunity" to *work* was crucial for "being different, for being a middle-class woman."[56] For them, being *mujeres de oficina* meant to "be independent, to earn some money, and to do something different, to do whatever [they] wanted to do."[57] Consequently, they mobilized the "angel of the office" discourse to argue that service work, unlike other available employment, made them more feminine because it "could demonstrate properly feminine virtues and attributes." Service work—serving people and giving attention to others as secretaries and receptionists—was understood to be work well suited to women, because "if they were truly middle-class women, they would be good at service, they would have maternal feelings, they would have the patience to deal with service." Those characteristics not only made excellent women, but also, and above all, "excellent *mujeres de oficina.*"[58]

And yet they always ran the risk of being confused with those *other* "women working outside the home." Perhaps because of this ambivalence, *mujeres de oficina*, like empleados, anxiously discussed their roles. On several occasions they offered explanations of why working in the office was "a job for the perfect women." In contrast to *obreras*, who were seen as "women but acting [like men] and doing men's stuff," *mujeres de oficina* embodied "the proper and [desired] feminine attributes" to do the "exalted service job."[59] Lilia Arellano, for example, argued: "Who could expect *obreras*, who lack the responsibility to take on [proper] female roles, to work in offices?"[60] Moreover, Arellano reasoned, *obreras* had "masculine" traits like "aggressiveness, insubordination, physical strength," that would never allow them "to do service work."[61] Hence, the imagined difference between *obreras* and *mujeres de oficina* was not that some women worked in factories and others worked in offices, but that only the latter were capable of embodying the characteristics of *ángeles de oficina.* They alone could exercise "the most feminine work any woman ever wanted: serving others."[62] To counter the assumption that women working outside the home would inevitably lose their feminine virtues, *mujeres de oficina* imagined the jobs in the service sector as "feminine" and appropriate for "truly middle-class women," while *obreras* "who worked in factories . . . barely deserve to be called women."[63]

Significantly, *mujeres de oficina* also manipulated these ideas to counteract the empleados' assumption that female clerical jobs were of lesser importance than those jobs performed by men. Specifically, they argued that their work "could not be done by anybody else but themselves."[64] Although this conceptualization could have left intact the gendered work hierarchy created by male empleados, *mujeres de oficina* discursively lumped empleados, obreros, and *obreras* all together, depicting them as a homogenous group that "could never have the right feminine attributes to engage in service work."[65] By defining their own "feminine attributes" as superior, these women described empleado masculinity as *incompatible* with office work, because male empleados, like obreros and obreras, lacked the "feminine values" necessary for service work.[66] This lumping together of empleados, obreros, and obreras called into question the masculine prerogatives empleados had created to distinguish themselves from the working classes.

In the minutes of one weekly meeting, Patricia Hernandez asked why obreros, *obreras* and empleados could not do service work, then answered her own question: "They were all the same . . . they were not women."[67] By her statement, it seems, Hernandez wanted to *unmake* empleados as middle-class men since their masculine superiority—which hierarchically positioned empleados over obreros—could be undermined if empleados were, in fact, essentially "the same as obreros."[68] After all, to be imagined and associated with the obrero, even worse to be labeled as an obrero, could make empleados lose their "sense of being a man."[69]

Similarly, although men in the urban service sector imagined the *ángel de oficina* as a wife, *mujeres de oficina* appropriated this discourse to remake their identities as *workers*, in the process creating new notions of middle-class femininity. These new meanings were based upon the assumption that these women, in contrast to "other classes," were the "real women" who exalted "femininity" by being "a wonderful wife, an incomparable worker, and a unique *mujer de oficina*."[70] A story from one *mujer de oficina* handbook, referenced and commented upon in meeting minutes during the early 1940s, insightfully portrayed how these middle-class women were constructing identities of their own.[71] The story depicted three women, "one from lower status, one from the middle status and one from higher status,"[72] and compared their experiences as workers outside the home. Women from the "lower status" were portrayed as "not fulfill[ing] domestic obligations. . . . [they were] terrible wives, terrible mothers and mediocre *obreras*."[73] Their husbands, we are told, almost never came home because "there was no woman, no mother, no wife to see." Their children were "always badly dressed, poorly educated, with no principles, with no maternal education, and [although] they were just five and six they did whatever they wanted to do."[74] Likewise, the "high status women" were represented as "always forget[ting] their obligations as mothers and wives" because they preferred to go out with friends "instead of doing something productive."[75] These women were materially rich because "they had a lot to eat, clothes, money," yet the story warned that "the members of the family ate alone" because there was neither a mother nor wife "to keep the family united."[76] In stark contrast to both groups, middle-class women were portrayed as embodying "perfectly the wifely and maternal obligations in the home." Their children, we are told, "were well-brought up, they [went] to school every day, they had a family life, there was a concerned mother and wife who served her husband and her children."[77]

After reading the story, *mujeres de oficina* discussed a simple yet very suggestive question: "What do you think is the right thing to do?"[78] Interestingly, they agreed that there was no necessity to leave work to be "proper mother and wives." Furthermore, they argued that to be "real women" they needed to be "wife, mother and *mujer de oficina*." If, as Lilia de Gonzalez asserted, one of these three "feminine characteristics was not with you," you would run the risk of "becoming something else."[79] Teresa Acosta constructed these notions as a way to differentiate her way of being a woman from that of "other women."[80] *Mujeres de oficina*, Acosta implied, had a "feminine ability" to make work and home compatible, while those who

lacked that ability did not know "how to be a real woman."[81] In contrast to
upper- and lower-class women, *mujeres de oficina*, Teresa said, "were professional in both office and home."[82] Edna Hernandez said they knew "how
to educate children, how to work, how to be a wife, how to be a mother. . . .
how to be a *mujer de oficina*."[83] Whereas working-class women supposedly
taught their daughters "how to abandon the home very early in life and how
to spend their time working and having fun in unknown and immoral places,"
the *mujeres de oficina* taught their daughters "the duties in life that women
should carry out: to keep the family together, to work in a proper place, and
to exalt the feminine attributes."[84]

Likewise, Sandra Romero questioned "the lack of womanhood" in the
women of higher status in the story. She argued that the "real women" were
those who, although they had to go to work, "would never leave the realm of
the home." *Mujeres de oficina* knew, Romero claimed, how to handle *sirvientas* (maids) "in the running of the home." Having just one servant was
preferable, not only because of the expense but because multiple servants
brought the risk of losing control over the household. Furthermore, ceding
the running of the home to *sirvientas*, as many rich families did, threatened to
bring "moral degradation and *feminine bankruptcy*," because children would
be brought up by maids "and not by their mothers."[85]

Office women did not challenge the discourse of domesticity but rather
manipulated it to construct an identity as middle-class and to differentiate
themselves from "other women." They saw themselves as workers but also
as women. Yet their identification as *mujeres de oficina* depended upon their
embodying specific class and gender characteristics, because otherwise they
could turn into "another type of women without feminine attributes."[86] They
thus emphasized the compatibility of the roles of wife and service-sector
worker as "essential middle-class feminine attribute[s]."[87] They contended,
moreover, that it was always crucial to have that preoccupation of "be[ing]
real women" in both the home and the workplace.[88]

In interviews, *mujeres de oficina* often constructed their narratives around
this "daily preoccupation." Their contradictory testimonies focused on the
idea that they, as middle-class women, had to work "hard to show everyone
[they] were able to maintain the right feminine values and class status."[89]
They had to do "whatever possible" to sustain their economic and social
position, which, they tell us, assured "the differentiation between *obreras*,
rich women and [themselves]."[90] It was the office woman's duty, and nobody else's, to succeed in this difficult task. As Consuelo Fernandez remembered:

> I do not know how I made it, but I did. I woke up at 4:00 in the morning
> always thinking that it was a pleasure to work, to do something for your
> family. I cooked breakfast and lunch at the very same time. Sometimes, I had

someone [i.e., a maid] to help me. Then I took my children to the school and my husband went to his office. I used to do all of these things very quickly. During the weekends I used to do the rest of the stuff, cleaning, laundry. I did well, I was a good mother, I handled everything, and at the office nobody could say that I was a bad worker. . . . It was *the* difference, the *obreras* always could work but they never did one thing right. They did not work . . . and they left their home without mothers.[91]

This testimony shows us not only how women constructed their middle-class femininity, but also their attitude toward one of the pillars of middle-class masculinity: the idea of the male breadwinner. The ways in which women and men constructed their testimonies suggest that this was a dilemma that constantly redefined middle-class masculinities and femininities. On the one hand, women constructed their testimonies to show how important *their* work and *their* salary was to the family's class position. Fernandez, for example, argued that as a "really good worker, mother, and wife," she was the one who "made it possible to enjoy a middle-class status."[92] Furthermore, she went on to argue that on a male empleado's salary alone, they would not have succeeded: "We would have become something else in life." The potential implication was that her husband was not in fact "man enough," because like obreros, he "needed a woman's income to maintain the family."[93] But on the other hand, Fernandez's testimony was contradictory, because at the same time she knew that if she portrayed her husband as an inadequate breadwinner, her own middle-class femininity might be diminished. Consequently she constructed her narrative to demonstrate that, although there were hard times, "her husband was the best father, the best husband, he always gave us everything, he was a really good man . . . a middle-class man, a real man. He was the one who always supported the family. What would we have been without him?"[94]

Mujeres de oficina thought that, without their work either at home or in the workplace, their middle-class status might be imperiled. Yet the negotiation of that significance was crucial, because as soon as *their* men were *demasculinized* or equated with obreros, they feared that by extension their femininity could "become something else." Diana Martinez, for example, like Consuelo Fernández, asserted that her salary "was necessary for the family's income." Without it, Martinez tells us, "we could not have done anything." She did not want, however, to usurp her husband's role as breadwinner, since it was "men's stuff."[95] Hence, in this constant contradiction, middle-class identifications could emerge historically—and in the perpetual (re)definition of this inconsistency, those women and men who considered themselves middle class created and configured their understanding of what they wanted to be. Empleados and *mujeres de oficina* constantly remade the gender and class distinctions that would allow them to imagine themselves superior to those whom, they thought, "should" be placed *below* them in society.

CONCLUSION

The twinned processes of industrialization and the expansion of the service sector between the 1930s and 1950s in Bogotá not only created new work-places and diversified the labor market but also formed modern ideas of class and gender that shaped the lived experience of those men and women enter-ing the world of office work. These people did not just reproduce certain sociological differences created by structural economic changes; instead, the emergence of modern ideas shaping the experiences in the office established two social/historical actors: the empleado and the *ángel de oficina.* The crea-tion of these figures was crucial insofar as they enabled those who were entering into the world of office work to think of themselves as middle-class empleados and middle-class *mujeres de oficina,* and to position themselves in hierarchical opposition to those they labeled obreros and obreras.

Not only were not they simply *different* from obreros and obreras, but my analysis suggests that the very concepts of empleado and *mujer de oficina* depended upon the simultaneous construction of their gender and class ad-versaries (the obrero and obrera) as constitutive yet excluded others that allowed the identifications as middle class to be possible—but also *impos-sible*—historically. Furthermore, for *mujeres de oficina* as much as for em-pleados, it was the imagined obreros and obreras who made possible the very condition of collective middle-classness, distinct from and hierarchically superior to the working classes.

NOTES

Original contribution written for this volume. A. Ricardo López is assistant professor of history at Western Washington University. He is co-editor (with Barbara Weinstein) of *The Making of the Middle Class: Toward a Transnational History* (2012), and co-author (with Mauricio Archila Neira) of *Compensar: 20 años de historia, 1970–1990* (1999).

1. Consuelo Fernández, interviewed by author, Bogotá, Colombia, July 2000, tape record-ing.
2. Augusto Morales-Pino, *Los de en Medio* (Bogotá: Editorial Kelly, 1967 [1st ed. 1938]).
3. Ibid.
4. My understanding of the formation of the middle class has been influenced by Brian Owensby, *Intimate Ironies: Modernity and the Making of the Middle Class in Brazil*(Stanford: Stanford University Press, 1999); David Parker, *The Idea of Middle Class: White-Collar Work-ers and Peruvian Society, 1900–1950* (University Park: Pennsylvania State University Press, 1998); and Michael Jimenez, "'The Elision of the Middle Class and Beyond: History, Politics and Development Studies in Latin America's Short Twentieth Century,'" in *Colonial Legacies: The Problem of Persistence in Latin American History,* ed. Jeremy Adelman (New York: Routledge, 1999). See also Löic J. D. Wacquant, "Making Class: The Middle Class(es) in Social Theory and Social Structure," in *Bringing Class Back In: Contemporary and Social*

Structure, ed. Scott G. McNall (Boulder: Westview Press, 1991); and Pierre Bourdieu "What Makes a Class? On the Theoretical and Practical Existence of Groups," *Berkeley Journal of Sociology* 32 (Fall 1987): 1–18. My approach to the historical relationship between gender and class draws on Joan W. Scott, *Gender and the Politics of History* (New York: Columbia University Press, 1998); and Judith Butler, *Gender Trouble: Feminism and the Subversion of Identity* (New York: Routledge, 1990). See also Ann Farnsworth-Alvear, *Dulcinea in the Factory: Myths, Morals, Men and Women in Colombia's Industrial Experience, 1936–1960* (Durham: Duke University Press, 2000). For the relationship between middle-class and gender identities, see Daniel J. Walkowitz, *Working with Class: Social Workers and the Politics of Middle-Class Identity* (Chapel Hill: University of North Carolina Press, 1999), 1–24. On how language, discourses, and identities work historically, I have been influenced by Miguel A. Cabrera, "On Language, Culture, and Social Action," *History and Theory* 40 (December 2001): 82–100; and Miguel Angel Cabrera, "Linguistic Approach or Return to Subjectivism? In Search of an Alternative to Social History," *Social History* 24, no. 1 (January 1999): 76–90.

5. Rafael Viera Moreno, "Situacion económica de las clases medias," *Mes Financiero Económico* 6, no. 7 (1942): 29–41.

6. Román Pérez Hernandez, *Codificación del trabajo: manual del obrero, manual del empleado, manual del patron* (Bogotá: Editorial Minerva, 1934), 54; Colombia, *Ley del empleados* (Bogotá: Editorial Minerva, 1936), 7.

7. Román Pérez Hernandez, *Codificación del trabajo, 54.*

8. Contraloría General de la República, *Cartilla de empleados* (Bogotá: Ediciones Contraloría, 1942), 15, 17, 23.

9. Archivo Contraloría General de la República (hereafter, ACGR), Box: Selección de personal, folder 2, "Politica de selección de empleados," 32, 1940, typescript. See also Contraloría General de la República, *Cartilla de Empleados*, 31–33, emphasis added.

10. Contraloría General de la República, *Cartilla de Empleados*, 48, 49.

11. For similar arguments, see Karin Alejandra Rosemblatt, "Domesticating Men: State Building and Class Compromise in Popular-Front Chile," and Mary Kay Vaughan, "Modernizing Patriarchy: State Policies, Rural Households, and Women in Mexico, 1930–1940," both in *Hidden Histories of Gender and the State in Latin America*, ed. Elizabeth Dore and Maxine Molyneux (Durham: Duke University Press, 2000), 194–214, 262–90. For Colombia, see Ann Farnsworth-Alvear, "The Mysterious Case of Missing Men: Gender and Class in Early Industrial Medellin, *International Labor and Working Class History* 49 (Spring 1996); Marta Saade and Oscar Calvo, *La ciudad en Cuarentena. Chicha, patología social y profilaxis* (Bogota: Ministerio de Cultura, 2002); Luz Gabriela Arango, *Mujer, religión e industria* (Medellín: Universidad Externado y Universidad de Antioquia, 1991).

12. ACGR, Box 15, folder D47, "Informes de trabajo" 57, 1946, typescript. See also Contraloría General de la Nacion, *Las condiciones económico sociales de la clase media en Bogotá*, (Bogotá : Ediciones Contraloria, 1946), 32–35.

13. In this point, I am drawing on Barbara Weinstein, "Inventing 'A Mulher Paulista': Politics and the Gendering of Brazilian Regional Identities," *Journal of Women's History* 18, no. 1 (Spring 2006): 22–49.

14. ACGR, Box 15, folder D47, "Informes de trabajo" 59, 1946, typescript.

15. Archivo de la Personeria de Bogotá (hereafter APB), Box: Selección de Personal, folder 32, "Politicas de Selección de Personal," 31, 1940.

16. Contraloría General de la República, *El hombre trabaja, la mujer sostiene* (Bogotá: Ediciones Contraloría, 1946) 3; ACGR Box 15, folder D47, "La mujer, la esposa del empleado," 43, 1946, typescript.

17. Contraloría General de la República, *El hombre trabaja, la mujer sostiene, 37.* ACGR, Box 15, folder D47, "La mujer, la esposa del empleado," 43, 1946. See also Zandra Pedraza *En cuerpo y alma. Visiones del progreso y la felicicidad* (Bogotá: Universidad de los Andes, 1999); Armando Ospina, Javier Sáenz Obregon, Oscar Saldarriaga, *Mirar la infancia: Pedagogía, moral y modernidad, 1903–1946* (Bogotá: Uniandes, Editorial Universidad de Antioquia, Foro Nacional por Colombia y Colciencias, 1997); Marta Saade and Oscar Calvo *La ciudad en cuarentena.*

18. ACGR, Box 15, folder D41, "La mujer, la esposa del empleado," 43, 1943, typescript. See also ACGR, Box: Selección de personal, folder 7: "Informes confidenciales de selección," 31, 1940.

19. ACGR, Box 21, folder L31, "Informes de selección de empleados," 67, 1941, typescript.

20. ACGR, Box: Selección de personal, folder 2, "Politicas de selección de empleados," 45, 1940, typescript. See also Contraloría General de la Republica *El costo de vida de la clase media en Bogotá*, 1–3; 79–81; ACGR, Box: Correspondecia Interna, folder 56, "Memo from Carolina Velásquez to Alberto Piedrahita," 10 July 1940, typescript.

21. ACGR, Box: Selección de personal, folder 2, "Politicas de selección de empleados," 41, 86, 1940. typescript. See also ACGR, Box: Selección de personal, folder 7, "Informes confidenciales de selección," 22, 1940.

22. ACGR, Box: Selección de personal, folder 7, "Informes confidenciales de selección," 21, 1940 typescript.

23. Ibid.

24. ACGR, Box 19, folder D41 " La mujer, la esposa del empleado," 43, 1943. See also ACGR, Box: Selección de personal, folder 7, "Informes confidenciales de selección," 31, 1940.

25. Rafael Gomez Picón, *45 Relatos de un burócrata con cuatro parénetesis*. (Bogota: Editorial Minerva, 1941), 57. Carlos Beltran, "Diary," National Library, Colombia, 34.

26. Gómez Picón, *45 relatos de un burócrata con cuatro paréntisis*, 47.

27. I use the minutes of meetings that took place in the Contraloría General de la República and Personería de Bogotá. These are located in the personnel archive of the Contraloría General de la República headquarters in Bogotá, and in the main archive of the Personería. White-collar workers and office women were organizing similar meetings in several other public- and private-sector offices, including the Compañia Colombiana de Seguros [COLSEGUROS]), SEARS, the Banco de la República, and the Compañia de Teléfonos de Bogotá. During the late 1940s and 1950s, these meetings became crucial in the consolidation of middle-class political organizations.

28. Contraloría General de la República, *Cartilla del Empleado*; *Nosotros: órgano oficial de la Federación de Empleados de Bogotá*.

29. APB, Box: Temas varios, folder C41, "Asuntos de interes general, 41, 1939, typescript.

30. Ibid. See also ACGR, Box: Estudios varios, folder A23, "Empleados y obreros," 38, 1943, typescript.

31. ACGR, Box: Estudios de personal, folder L76, "Empleado y obrero," 17, 1943, typescript.

32. Ibid., 42, 1943.

33. Ibid., 49, 1943, typescript.

34. Ibid., 41.

35. Ibid., 47. See also APB, Box: Temas varios, folder C41, "Asuntos de interes general," 41, 1939.

36. ACGR, Box: Estudios de personal, folder L76, "Empleado y obrero," 39.

37. Ibid., 41.

38. Ibid., 42.

39. APB, Box: Escritos de empleados, folder 42, "Quiénes somos?" 13, 1944, typescript.

40. Ibid., 32, 1944.

41. ACGR, Box: Estudios de personal, folder L78, "Empleados y el trabajo," 43, 1943, typescript. See also ACGR, Box: Estudios de personal, folder L77, "Empleados y el trabajo," 10, 1943, typescript.

42. ACGR, Box: Estudios de personal, folder L78, "Empleados y el trabajo," 51, 1943; also ACGR Box: Los empleados, folder "Empleados y el obrero," 41, 1941, typescript.

43. ACGR, Box: Los empleados, folder "Empleados y el obrero," 71, 1941.

44. ACGR, Box: Escritos de empleados, folder 31, "Por qué somos más importantes?" 12, 1941. The word *hombría* is a loaded one that does not translate easily or simply. It certainly denotes masculinity, but it also has connotations of honor and social ascendance.

45. ACGR, Box: Escritos de empleados, folder 31, "Por qué somos más importantes?" 32, 1941. See also *Nosotros, organo de la federación de empleados de Bogotá* (Bogota: Mundo al día, 1934–1937).

46. Similar stories appeared in Contraloría General de la República, *Cartilla para empleados*. See also *Nosotros, organo oficial de la Federación de Empleados de Bogotá*.

47. ACGR, Box: Escritos de empleados, folder 31, "Por qué somos más importantes?" 33–35, 1941.

48. Ibid., 45, 1941.

49. ACGR, Box: Temas de interes general, folder L51, "Nosotros los empleados," 1942, typescript ; ACGR, Box: Temas de interés general, folder 76, "Empleados y obreros," 1943.

50. ACGR, Box: Temas de interes general, folder L51, "Nosotros los empleados," 6, 15, 1942.

51. Ibid., 13, 17, 23 1942.

52. ACGR, Box: Asuntos varios, folder L31, "Nosotros somos empleados," 34, 1943, typescript.

53. Ibid., 41, 1943.

54. Ibid., 11, 1943.

55. Specifically, stories appearing in published form on Contraloría General de la República, *El hombre trabaja y la mujer sostiene*.

56. Carolina Fernandez, interviewed by the author, Bogotá, Colombia, July 2000, tape recording.

57. ACGR, Box 21, "Secretarias de contabilidad," folder 043, "Por qué somos más importantes?" 37, 1943.

58. Ibid., 39, 1943.

59. Ibid.

60. Ibid., 41, 1943.

61. ACGR, Box 21, "Secretarias de contabilidad," folder 043, "Por qué somos más importantes?" 51, 1943.

62. Ibid., 3, 1943.

63. Ibid., 4, 1943.

64. APB, Box: Estudios Generales, folder L91, "Las mujeres que verdaderamente trabajan," 21, 36,89, 1947 typescript.

65. Ibid., 51, 1947.

66. Ibid., 1947.

67. Ibid., 42, 1947.

68. Ibid., 57, 1947.

69. Ibid.

70. ACGR, Box: Correspondencia Interna, 1941–1945, folder L87, "Secretaria un medio para progresar," 32, 17, July 1943, typescript.

71. See Contraloria General de la Republica, *El hombre trabaja, la mujer sostiene*.

72. ACGR, Box: Correspondencia Interna, 1941–1945, folder L87, "Secretaria un medio para progresar," 43–46, July 1943,

73. Ibid., 41, 47, 51, July 1943.

74. ACGR, Box: Correspondencia Interna, 1941–1945, folder L87, "Secretaria un medio para progresar," 53, 55, July 1943.

75. Ibid.

76. Ibid.

77. ACGR, Box: Correspondencia Interna, 1941–1945, folder L87, "Secretaria un medio para progresar," 31, 33, 34, July 1943.

78. Ibid., 6, 63–121, July 1943. It is difficult to discern who specifically gave this question. Usually, during these meetings, any of the participants could actually bring something—stories, questions, complains—to discuss. Although the minutes were specific about who made the comments, they were not very clear on who brought the "material" for conversation.

79. ACGR, Box: Correspondencia Interna,1941–1945, folder L87, "Secretaria un medio para progresar," 66, July 1943.

80. Ibid., 68, July 1943.

81. Ibid.

82. Ibid.

83. Ibid., 75, July 1943.

84. Ibid., 76, July 1943.
85. Ibid., 91, July 1943, emphasis added.
86. Ibid., 63, July 1943.
87. Ibid.
88. Ibid.
89. Consuelo Fernandez, interview.
90. APB, Box: Estudios Generales, folder L91, "Las mujeres que verdaderamente trabajan," 45.
91. Consuelo Fernandez, interview.
92. Ibid.
93. Ibid.
94. Consuelo Fernandez, interview.
95. Diana Martinez, interviewed by author, Bogotá, Colombia, July 2000, tape recording.

Chapter Eleven

Rethinking Aspects of Class Relations in Twentieth-Century Chile

J. Pablo Silva

J. Pablo Silva focuses in this chapter on how analysts of Chilean society imagined the middle class, and the political ramifications of those different imaginings. Drawing on the writings of social scientists and the speeches of political leaders, Silva argues that Chileans' perception of the middle class went through two phases. In the early twentieth century, influential Chilean intellectuals and politicians looked upon the empleados *(white-collar workers), a unionized and often militant group, as quintessential representatives of the middle class. After 1950, however, a new generation of socialist intellectuals and politicians redefined who was middle class and who was not; they now cast entrepreneurs, whose politics were more conservative, as the prototypical representatives of the middle class. Silva argues that although neither empleados nor capitalists had in fact changed their politics, this redefinition of "middle class" became a sort of self-fulfilling prophesy. Believing the middle class to be inherently conservative, the elected Socialist president Salvador Allende in the 1970s marginalized middle-class concerns, thus weakening his appeal and exacerbating the divisions within Chilean society, with tragic consequences.*

White-collar workers staged an illegal general strike in early 1950 that paralyzed the Chilean economy and forced the government to capitulate to union demands. Contemporary observers saw the strike as a defining moment for Chile's empleados (as white-collar workers were termed). In its summary of the strike, the U.S. embassy characterized the outcome as a complete victory for the empleados:

> The final settlement of this strike, which resulted in the downfall of the Cabinet, termination of the Government's coalition with the right-wing Liberal and Traditional Conservative Parties, withdrawal from Congress of a law project

stabilizing salaries, wages and prices, and the revision and passage in a form more favorable to labor of a law project before Congress increasing year-end bonuses for private employees, constituted one of the greatest potential victories won by a labor organization in Chile in recent years. [1]

A noted Chilean sociologist of the period, Amanda Labarca Hubertson, concurred; she characterized the victory as a watershed in the history of Chile's middle class. She noted that "up until recently, only [manual workers, or *obreros*] benefited from agile and combative unions that constantly campaigned for economic betterment. The empleados did not wield that weapon until 1949. So they arrived late to the struggle, but in 1950 they made up much of the lost ground."[2]

For their part, conservatives were appalled by the outcome of the strike. One senator warned that the concessions made to the empleados "constitute the gravest political turn of event of recent times. They signify the breakdown of our juridical and democratic system, the suicide of the political parties, and the adoption on the part of the people's representative of a frank revolutionary syndicalism."[3] The 1950 strike was, in short, one of the most significant labor movement victories in Chilean history.

But by the 1960s, scholars did not associate the Chilean middle class with labor mobilization or radical politics. In fact, they saw the middle class quite differently. In his seminal 1963 article on Chilean class relations (chapter 2 in this volume), Fredrick Pike complained that elitist education had inculcated the Chilean middle class with racist prejudice against the mestizo lower orders and that this attitude had inspired the middle class to ally itself with Chile's traditional oligarchy. Pike's article set the tone for a series of subsequent studies that also condemned the Chilean middle class for slowing social progress. For example, writing just a few years after Pike, the Chilean historian Claudio Veliz repeated the charge that the middle class was an obstacle to social and economic progress:

The middle classes . . . have been responsible for maintaining or even strengthening the traditional structure and for leading some of the major [Latin American] countries into a situation of institutional stability and economic stagnation. . . . Far from reforming anything, they have become firm supporters of the Establishment; they have not implemented significant agrarian or fiscal reforms but have displayed remarkable energy trying to become landowners or to marry their offspring into the aristocracy. [4]

And a few years after Veliz wrote, the political scientist James Petras did not even consider the question of whether the middle class was reformist or reactionary. He simply assumed that the Chilean middle class was reactionary. In his study of Chilean politics, his first question was, "Why are the middle strata oriented toward 'stability' and unconcerned with basic social change?"[5]

In the face of this striking scholarly consensus of the 1960s, we are left with an obvious question: What happened to the radical middle class of the 1950 strike? The answer is actually buried in Petras's research findings from the 1960s. His own survey data hardly confirmed the scholarly assumption that the middle strata were "unconcerned with basic social change." On several issues, segments of his middle class were as reformist as blue-collar workers. In particular, his data show that white-collar workers were generally as "progressive" as blue-collar workers. Of his middle class, only the business owners and the self-employed appear consistently anti-reformist or "reactionary."[6] Apparently, it was more the *perception* of the middle class that had changed since the 1950 strike. At the very least, in the 1960s scholars were emphasizing different component groups within the middle class. Whereas in the early 1950s Amanda Labarca saw empleados as the core of the middle class, by the 1960s scholars were stressing other groups. And as a result, in the 1960s scholars ignored empleados and their union movement when they composed their stinging critiques of the Chilean middle class.

Of course, it is possible that the Chilean middle class had in fact changed substantially in this period, but scholarly opinion seems to have shifted more in response to broader trends in social thought than as a result of any obvious objective shift in the middle class. Between the 1950 empleado strike and Pike's 1963 article, politicians and intellectuals had begun to rethink the role of the middle class in Chilean society. It was this rethinking of aspects of class relations that inspired scholars to imagine the Chilean middle class in a new way. This conclusion follows the example of recent historical research that has argued that classes are constructed in the "social imaginary." This research stresses that public discussions of social reality play an important role in shaping that reality, and in particular, that classes acquire political meaning as they are publicly imagined.[7] In the context of this literature, the 1960s critique of the Chilean middle class is more easily explained. From this perspective, Pike and Petras need to be seen as imagining the middle class as much as describing it, let alone analyzing it. This point is essential because it explains how Petras could assume that the middle class was "oriented toward 'stability' and unconcerned with basic social change," when his own survey data showed that a core component of the middle class was as "progressive" as the working class. In their writings, Pike and Petras were contributing to a rethinking of class in Chile.

If Petras had been writing a few decades earlier, he likely would have put greater emphasis on empleados as the core of the Chilean middle class. In 1913, the Liberal Party added a plank to their platform that called for measures aimed at helping empleados as a way of supporting the middle class. In 1919, Conservative Party congressman Alejo Lira had made the first formal proposal to improve the economic condition of empleados, a proposal that he said aimed to "give some protection on behalf of what is vulgarly called 'the middle class.'" And from that time on into the 1950s, when intellectuals and politicians spoke of the middle class, they usually meant empleados.[8] It was only in the 1950s that perceptions of the middle class began to change; social scientists started to bring their ideas of social class more in line with the Marxist conception that developing societies were principally composed of the traditional land-owning ruling class, an emerging bourgeois challenger to the ruling class, and a lower order of workers and peasants. In this conception, the emerging bourgeoisie was clearly identified as the middle class and given a precise historical role. Pike, Veliz, and Petras wrote in this tradition and essentially ignored the very different conception of the Chilean middle class that had been common a generation earlier.

As the identity of the middle class was being rethought, intellectuals and politicians also reevaluated its political and social role. During the period (from about World War I to the Korean War) when it was identified with empleados, intellectuals and politicians viewed it as a potentially revolutionary group.[9] In this first phase of thinking about the middle class, conservative politicians particularly feared that, as salary earners, empleados might make common cause with manual workers. To preempt this outcome, government policy sought to co-opt empleado unions. After the Korean War, the Chilean middle class was identified with an emerging bourgeoisie and intellectuals, and leftist politicians suddenly began to criticize it for not playing its predicted "historic role." In this second phase, these politicians and intellectuals complained that the middle class had not broken up the old feudal order. It had offered only a weak challenge to the traditional ruling class, and it had certainly not put the country on a more solid developmental path. In short, they complained that the middle class was parasitic instead of progressive, reactionary instead of reformist.

Ironically, in both of these phases, these evaluations did not grow out of a profound analysis of Chilean class relations but instead from ideas imported from abroad about the role of classes in society. In the first phase, politicians were also frightened by the worldwide labor agitation that followed the Russian Revolution and the end of World War I. Thus, in the 1920s and 1930s, they were inspired by corporatist models to adopt policies that would co-opt and restrain different types of workers. Given the preoccupation with workers, it was perfectly natural for politicians in this period to identify the middle class with white-collar workers and to seek interlocutors from amongst the nascent empleado unions.

In the second phase, international Marxism pushed intellectuals to think about the middle class more in light of the orthodox theory of capitalist development and social revolution. From this perspective, middle classes were seen to be failing in their historic role throughout the developing world.

In both phases, Chilean thinkers seemed to accept the foreign theories without testing them against Chilean reality. In the first phase, Chilean elites saw a potential threat at a time when middle-class unions were actually quite weak. And, curiously enough, in the second phase Chilean intellectuals and politicians bought into the increasing condemnation of the "reactionary" middle class just after the country's real-life white-collar movement reached the peak of its radical mobilizational potential, the 1950 strike.

The literature on the Chilean middle class has tended to assume too easily that economic and social conditions are the main determinants of politics and that political ideas faithfully reflect these conditions. But recent historical scholarship on the "social imaginary" warns us that cultural and political trends can actually shape economic and social conditions. I contend that just such a process occurred in twentieth century Chile as politicians and intellectuals rethought class relations. Imported theories led first to competing attempts to co-opt the middle class—attempts that actually helped to foster a growing sense of solidarity among white-collar workers. This solidarity in turn helped to produce a vigorous white-collar union movement. After the 1950s, the conception of a parasitic and reactionary middle class led to a belief on the left that the proletariat and the peasantry faced the implacable opposition of the dominant classes, a belief that contributed to the severe polarization of Chilean politics before 1973. Without a doubt, then, the rethinking of class relations in Chile shaped both the labor movement and class politics of the twentieth century in fundamental ways. As different ideas about the Chilean middle class took hold, they inspired important political players to actions that subsequently changed the reality of Chilean society.

THE MISERY OF THE MIDDLE CLASS

As late as 1913, Chilean class identities remained remarkably vague in the sense that class terms meant different things to different people. Chileans agreed that class status was tied to occupation, but they did not necessarily agree on the occupations that corresponded to each class, variously describing as middle class anyone from a manager or a professional to an empleado or skilled worker.[10] However, the second decade of the century was a watershed for the conception of class in Chile. In these years, political competition between the country's two main parties, the Liberals and the Conservatives, put class relations in the spotlight. As the Liberals began to fear that they were falling behind the Conservatives on the "Social Question," some progressive Liberal politicians led an effort to appeal directly to Chile's white-collar workers as the "class that is most cruelly lashed." Not to be outdone, the Conservatives offered their own proposal "for the protection of the middle class." As a result of these proposals on their behalf, an empleado movement emerged where none had previously existed. The competing proposals would also eventually produce specific social legislation on behalf of empleados. But the most interesting feature of the proposals is that they drew inspiration from Europe as much as from Chile.

In a book on the Social Question, the European philosopher Ludwig Stein wrote about the special needs of the intellectual worker. Stein referred to the "misery of the [intellectual proletariat], whose income is often below the average wage of the aristocrats of labor . . . and who are often more sensitive than [the latter] and more conscious." He asserted that "raising their intelligence also raises their needs as well as the pain that comes with the impossibility of satisfying those needs. The intellectually developed man is incomparably more sensitive, psychically more irritable, and more susceptible to pain than the manual worker."[11]

Jorge Errázuriz Tagle, a young Chilean Liberal associated with the progressive circle around Arturo Alessandri, explicitly drew on Stein's work to justify measures on behalf of empleados.[12] In an obvious paraphrase of Stein, Errázuriz argued:

> It is precisely this social class [the middle class] that is most cruelly lashed by the inequality of fortune because of the gap between its culture, its education [*instrucción*], and its exigencies (which are those of the ruling class or close to it), and an absolute lack of economic means.
>
> This must be an indispensable focus of Political Economy: the support of this middle class made up of empleados of limited income [*escasa renta*] . . . that suffer the full brunt of this inconvenient situation because by habit, education, and the exigencies of their occupations or employment, they must demonstrate decency and decorum; because of their culture and refinement, they must seek domestic comfort, intellectual pastimes, and the progress of their family, and they must also see these legitimate inclinations frustrated by the hard fact that they lack the means to satisfy them. The obrero does not have these exigencies. In proportion to the empleado and small manufacturer, the worker "earns more and needs less."[13]

To be sure, Errázuriz Tagle took some liberties in his interpretation of Stein's words. For example, he chose to interpret the "intellectual proletariat" as equivalent to the middle class and more specifically as equivalent to empleados. But Stein had argued for the special needs of the educated. In those passages, he spoke only of the "intellectual proletariat," "the workers of the spirit," and "the cultivated workers"—he did not mention the "middle class." What is even more interesting is that Errázuriz chose to ignore that section of Stein's book that does refer to the "middle class" and where he makes the much more conventional Aristotelian argument that the middle class deserved particular aid and attention because it helped to stabilize the state.[14] This omission is especially worthy of note because such traditional arguments are completely lacking in subsequent Chilean discussions of the middle class. In this sense, it appears that Errázuriz had an enduring impact on the political discussions on empleados and the middle class in Chile, because for the next thirty years, Chile's middle-class politics would focus on the special needs of the middle class and not on its capacity to stabilize the country.

In the short term, Errázuriz had an impact on the 1913 Liberal Party platform. He sat on the committee that proposed the final language for the platform section on Social Legislation. Under his influence, the committee substantially revised this section from the 1907 version by including an article devoted to the plight of the middle class. Specifically, it called for "urgent measures" aimed at the "protection of the middle class, as in: the creation of housing [*poblaciones*] for empleados so that they can become homeowners, pension or retirement funds for private-sector empleados, [and] community employment offices for the placement of industrial, agricultural, and other empleados."

The measure quite self-consciously sought to extend the scope of social legislation beyond the blue-collar workers (obreros). Instead, the Liberals were aiming to aid "the different social classes." And the committee went so far as to place the article on the middle class ahead of the article on the "clase obrera."[15] To my knowledge this was the first widely publicized call for legislation on behalf of Chile's white-collar workers. But what is most significant here is that the convention provided an explicit justification for empleado class consciousness, a justification based on "the last word in contemporary social-economic science" coming out of Europe.

The Liberal Party had pragmatic political reasons to take a stand on Chile's Social Question. As Tomas Ramírez Frías noted at the 1913 convention, in the minds of most Chileans the social encyclicals of the Catholic Church had put the Conservative Party ahead of the Liberals on the Social Question. Since the Liberals currently had "little support among the people [*pueblo*]," he advised that the party needed to take aggressive steps to catch up to the Conservatives so as to avoid being seen as "oligarchic and anti-democratic." Some of his colleagues urged caution, but others concurred with the idea that it was "indispensable that the [Liberal] Party, which has been labeled oligarchic, study these issues [in order to] attract the most educated elements of the working class."[16] It was this political competition that in subsequent years would help diffuse Stein's idea of a miserable intellectual proletariat with special needs.[17]

The empleados themselves took some time to respond to the Liberals' political overtures. Before 1913, there was no empleado politics to speak of. There were some empleado mutual-aid societies, and some union organizers did make occasional appeals to empleados as workers. But there was no pro-empleado agenda in place, no clear empleado issues, no clearly defined cause to fight for. So there was no call for mass empleado mobilization. Indeed, there is no evidence that many empleados even saw themselves as a coherent group, let alone a "social class" or a core component of "the middle class." But in the wake of the 1913 convention, there were signs that empleados were becoming conscious of themselves as a possible political actor. By 1916, a few empleado unions and newspapers appeared that spoke to empleados in class terms. As a result, the Conservative Party felt compelled in 1918 to offer its own proposal on behalf of the empleados, a proposal that showed clear lines of descent from Stein and Errázuriz.

In September 1918 the Conservative Party convention called for the study of specific measures to help the middle class. By November, the party actually proposed a formal bill in Congress. The Conservatives framed their pro-empleado project in nationalist terms, asserting that Chile's white-collar workers were being excluded from industry and commerce and were thus forced to seek public-sector employment.[18] These assertions matched white-collar union complaints that foreign firms in Chile were hiring from their home countries white-collar workers who had recently been demobilized at the end of World War I. As a remedy, the Conservatives proposed incentives so that firms operating in Chile would employ a minimum percentage of Chilean empleados. They argued that such a measure would help both the middle class and the nation. They also argued that the state had to act on behalf of middle-class empleados because, given their "temperament" and "social position," this group would not resort to strikes. The Conservatives argued that empleados had needs above and beyond those of mere workers, needs imposed on them by their "culture" such as more formal dress, which manual workers did not share.[19] In short, the Conservatives were also echoing the words of Lüdwig Stein.

To be sure, not all politicians equated empleados and the middle class. In fact, the Chilean newspaper *El Mercurio* sponsored an attempt in 1919 to popularize a broader conception of the middle class. Almost as a response to the Conservatives, the paper called for a "Congress for the Welfare of the Chilean Middle Class" that would seek to "improve its situation." The paper explicitly stated that such an effort on behalf of the middle class would demonstrate that the privileged were not a self-interested oligarchy. The congress took place, and from it was born the Federación de clase media. Like the Conservative party champions of the empleados, the sponsors of the Federación publicly asserted that such an organization was needed because middle-class individuals could not rely on unions or political parties to defend their interests and could not use collective action like strikes.

For *El Mercurio,* the middle class embraced a large and complicated social grouping: "public and private empleados; the professionals generally; the owners of small workshops, industries, and factories; the merchants of bazaars, stores, and . . . shops; teachers [*profesores*]; calligraphers; typists;

telegraphers; illustrators; surveyors; contractors; inspectors; traveling agents; and numerous workers already grouped under the first heading of public and private empleados." This was a class composed of "infinite shades . . . useful for maintaining social concord."[20] The newspaper hoped that a formal institution would allow the middle class to "defend itself from the injustices, legal deficiencies, and the abusive and disloyal foreign competition."[21]

With such a broad constituency, however, any organization would find it difficult to formulate a coherent plan of action. And in fact, the Federación de la clase media quickly collapsed under its own contradictions. Soon after its formal foundation, the organization discovered that it had difficulty attracting members; some of its leaders thought that the name limited its appeal.[22] Worse, when the organization did begin to attract more members, the original founders were horrified to see that the empleados among the new cadres wanted to steer the group toward an alliance with militant workers. Rather than see it used against the social order, the founders dissolved the group.[23]

Ironically, the Federación was probably undone by the efforts of the Liberals and the Conservatives. The formal projects to help empleados went nowhere but did serve to inspire some empleados to begin a modest union movement that made pro-empleado legislation a central goal.[24] No doubt it was some of these empleados who tried to take over the Federación. Thus, although the Conservatives and the Liberals had originally sought to co-opt the middle class, they instead lost control of their own pro-middle-class projects and gave life to an authentic middle class mobilization.[25] But the Liberals did bequeath to this movement, at least indirectly, the original inspiration that Jorge Errázuriz Tagle drew from Lüdwig Stein.

This movement eventually saw passage of the so-called Empleado Law of 1924, which in turn powerfully reinforced the idea that empleados constituted a middle class. The law differentiated between three groups—employers, empleados, and obreros—and fit empleados into the middle position. It would not be accurate to credit empleados with passage of the law, since that ultimately depended on the efforts of the junior officers who staged a military coup in September 1924. Nevertheless, empleado unions helped push for enforcement of "their law" and thus deserve some of the blame for the labor code's social and political impact—an impact that went to the heart of Chile's class structure. While such distinctions between empleados and obreros were not unusual in Latin America, they were unnecessarily exaggerated by the sloppily constructed labor code. For instance, the code created completely different types of social security systems for empleados and obreros, and it gave obligatory severance benefits to empleados but not to obreros.[26] Over time these legal distinctions made it natural for Chileans to see empleados and obreros as two quite different and mutually exclusive social categories. And at the time, these distinctions were justified by reference to the special needs of the middle class.

Indeed, by the 1930s, the "miserable" empleados had become firmly identified with the middle class. In this decade, Chilean politicians were once again trying to co-opt the lower classes in an effort to stabilize the social order. The Great Depression had brought on a severe political crisis that led to a series of coups, counter-coups, and failed presidencies. And as they had done in the 1920s when faced with a crisis, some on the right tried to blur distinctions between elites and the middle class to secure support for the social order—this time under the banner of the Unión de clase media. Like the Federación de clase media, this group was yet another ad hoc organization made up mostly of professional men of upper-class background. But unlike the Federación, the Unión de clase media does not seem to have attracted much attention and appears to have quickly wilted on the vine. By the 1930s, there was no constituency for a different definition of the middle class because Chileans had already come to see empleados as the class's essential core. In addition, many empleados had come to realize that they stood to benefit from a discourse that defined them as especially needy. Through their independent attempts to co-opt the empleados, Liberals and Conservatives had begun a process that consolidated the social definitions of the Chilean middle class.

THE RISE OF THE RADICAL MIDDLE CLASS

But further efforts to co-opt the empleados were needed to produce a truly effective empleado movement. Those efforts came in 1933 when President Arturo Alessandri set up semi-governmental commissions that brought together the representatives of workers and employers to negotiate contentious economic issues. In doing so, Alessandri was explicitly borrowing from European corporatist models to try to co-opt the laboring classes and reduce social unrest. In the case of the empleados, he charged a committee with the responsibility of creating legislation "for the improvement of the middle class." In the short term, Alessandri got what he wanted: in early 1937 the Chilean Congress passed a bill that gave empleados dramatic legal privileges, including a minimum salary and mandatory salary increases. Passage of the law was immediately followed by an election campaign for Congress in which the rightist candidates trumpeted their efforts on behalf of empleados and then swept to victory in both houses. But Alessandri miscalculated the long-term effects of pandering to the empleados. Before the 1937 minimum salary law, they were politically quite a weak group; their unions were small and divided, and empleado representatives to the labor ministry could not even agree on basic issues.[27] The minimum salary law changed all that. It gave empleados special privileges that set them above the level of blue-collar workers—privileges they quickly recognized were worth defending and expanding. As a result, empleado unions rapidly became stronger, more influential, and more demanding. Instead of co-opting the middle class as he intended, Alessandri actually helped to radicalize it.

The seeds of this radicalization were sown in the mechanics of the minimum salary law itself. The statutory minimum salary for white-collar workers was unbelievably generous; blue-collar workers did not receive analogous legislation for a minimum wage until twenty years later.[28] But the law also mandated that employers increase the salaries for all empleados making less than five times the minimum salary. Depending on salary and time on the job, these increases ranged from 10 to 60 percent. Although empleados were initially ecstatic, their salary increases were immediately followed by a burst of inflation that ate up all their gains. In response, empleado unions took the position that the government needed to go further: they called for *annual* mandatory salary increases indexed to price increases. The political right refused to allow such a measure so long as it controlled Congress, but at this point the political tide was turning inexorably left and in favor of the new empleado demands. In 1938 the left elected a Popular Front president, and in 1941 the Popular Front Coalition of leftist parties swept Congress from the Conservatives. Never again would the Chilean right control both houses of Congress. The immediate outcome was that empleados got their wish for mandatory annual salary increases.[29]

The new pro-empleado legislation was enough to stimulate the consolidation of a major empleado movement.[30] The main stimulant was the mechanism created to determine the range of annual salary increases. The law did not link salary increases to the inflation rate calculated by the national statistics office; instead, the increases were left to local committees in each province. Made up of union representatives, employer representatives, and a state official to break ties, the committees were in theory supposed to calculate the local salary increases based on food prices. Each committee was supposed to purchase a typical food basket from local retailers to see how much prices had changed. The committees were then supposed to adjust salaries accordingly. In practice, however, both employers and empleados tried to manipulate the data. One former union leader confessed that the empleado representatives intentionally misplaced purchases in order to drive up the apparent cost of the food basket. "I wouldn't say it was done in bad faith," he said. "It's just that we had to lower [the overall weight] because [the employer representatives] would cheat us. For example, they would have [the committee] buy at some place, and the guy [the retailer] was prepared with both the price and the weight. He would give extra weight and charge us less."[31] Such maneuvers made effective unionization vitally important because in practice salary increases became less an issue of measurement and more an issue of negotiation.[32] Empleados quickly realized that effective union representatives directly affected their standard of living.

Over time the system worked to the advantage of the empleados in that their salaries, including the minimum salary, began to outpace inflation (see table 11.1).

Table 11.1. Indices of Minimum Salary and Cost of Living in Santiago, 1937–1955

Year	Minimum Salary for Santiago Pesos/ Month	Index of Minimum Salary for Santiago 1937=100	Index of Average Cost of Living for Santiago 1937=100	Ratio of Indices for (Sueldo Vital/Cost of Living) 1937=100
1937	420	100	100	100
1938	420	100	104	96
1939	455	108	106	102
1940	460	110	119	92
1941	600	143	137	104
1942	815	194	173	112
1943	1,050	250	201	124
1944	1,185	282	224	126
1945	1,320	314	244	129
1946	1,470	350	283	124
1947	1,995	475	378	126
1948	2,400	571	446	128
1949	3,040	724	529	137
1950	3,800	905	609	149
1951	4,670	1,112	745	149
1952	6,070	1,445	910	159
1953	7,550	1,798	1,141	158
1954	11,600	2,762	1,965	141
1955	18,400	4,381	3,442	127

Source: Markos J. Mamalakis, Historical Statistics of Chile, vol. 2 (Westport, CT: Greenwood, 1978–1985), 330; Dirección General de Estadística, Estadística Chilena.

Of course, employers did not see spiraling empleado salaries as good thing and argued that the annual adjustment system contributed to inflation. Conservatives increasingly complained that salary inflation was adversely affecting the economy by increasing costs, reducing profits, and discouraging investment. Eventually even the center left bought into this argument when the last of the Popular Front presidents, Gabriel Gonzalez Videla, agreed in the late 1940s that mandatory salary increases had to be scaled back. To achieve this goal, he appointed the rightist Jorge Alessandri as Minister of Finance. Alessandri was supposed to eliminate the system of annual salary adjustments in order to stabilize prices. In effect, Alessandri, the son of President Arturo Alessandri and a future president in his own right, was charged with the task of undoing the pro-empleado legislation his father had begun.

By this time, however, the empleado movement had gained momentum that could not be easily reversed. The salary-setting mechanism had shaped empleado unions in profound ways. Because the provincial salary committees included only two union representatives, smaller unions had either merged in order to participate in the process or had disappeared altogether. Thus the salary system inspired considerable consolidation among empleado unions at the provincial level. At the same time, because most salary levels came to depend on negotiations and frequent legal action, local unions began to depend on the expertise that only national unions could provide. As a result, they also began to consolidate at the national level. This process culminated in 1948 when three different national confederations formed the Chilean Confederation of Private-Sector Empleados (CEPCh), just in time to challenge Jorge Alessandri and his plans to cut back on annual salary adjustments.

Soon after its formation the CEPCh made clear that it opposed Jorge Alessandri's Economic Stabilization Plan. CEPCh leaders then waited for opportunity to act on their opposition. That moment came in January 1950 when the Chilean Congress debated new profit-sharing rules. Because the proposed rules excluded empleados who worked for major utilities, these empleados walked off the job in protest. But the profit-sharing dispute was just the spark that set off the powder-keg of broader empleado discontent.[33] Once white-collar workers began their illegal strike, CEPCh leaders instructed other white-collar workers to join. The strike quickly divided the government, as the president's own party, the Radicals, panicked over the strike's long-term political implications. When it expanded to public-sector empleados, the Radicals moved to negotiate directly with the strikers. Party leaders then forced Gonzalez Videla to dismiss his cabinet and disavow all plans to impose Jorge Alessandri's Economic Stabilization Plan. In the aftermath of their strike victory, the empleados forced other concessions from both the president and Congress. The strike had turned the CEPCh into a major political force; the U.S. embassy called the it "the strongest [union] in Chile."[34]

The 1950 empleado strike also instilled Chilean politicians with a deep fear of organized general strikes. In this sense, Jacqueline Roddick has asserted that it was "perhaps the single most important strike in the 1920–73 era."[35] But the strike is also a clear indication that empleados had aligned themselves with the political left. In its tooth-and-nail defense of salary adjustments, those in the empleado movement recognized the left wing of the Radical Party as well as the Socialists and Communists as their political allies. They rejected right-wing policies out of hand. Indeed, it is possible to make the case that after 1950 the salary adjustment issue helped define the political polarization between the political right and the left in Chile, with empleado unions firmly on the left.[36] What is certain is that while empleados were recognized as a core constituent of the middle class in this period, they were certainly no allies of the oligarchy. They did not "shun the lower mass . . . to embrace the aristocracy."

THE SOCIALISTS REDEFINE THE MIDDLE CLASS

But if empleados were so clearly on the left after 1950, why is it that soon thereafter leftists and intellectuals began to see the middle class as reactionary? The problem is perhaps best exemplified by the Socialist Party leaders Salvador Allende and Aniceto Rodríguez. In a 1956 senate debate they rose to defend empleados and their privileges, and yet in the same debate they also criticized the conservative tendencies of the "middle class." The answer to the question is that a new discourse was being created about the middle class, in which empleados were no longer seen as the core of a miserable middle class. Indeed, in that 1956 debate Allende explicitly identified the middle class with the "small and medium bourgeoisie."[37] Somehow the left had begun to see the middle class as composed less of white-collar workers and more as a class of property owners allied to the traditional oligarchy. The inspiration for the shift actually appears in the 1956 Senate debate: both Allende and Rodríguez quoted the writings of the Stanford economist Paul Baran as the source for their rethinking of the Chilean middle class. Inspired by Baran, the Socialist Party took up a new definition of the middle class, one that marginalized empleados.

In his seminal article "On the Political Economy of Backwardness," published in 1952, Baran sought to explain why economic development appeared to be limited geographically to Western Europe and some of its colonial offshoots. He argued that the backwards economies were lagging because their middle classes were not following the example of the conquering bourgeoisies of the advanced countries. Baran argued that, instead, "the poor, fledgling bourgeoisie of the underdeveloped countries sought nothing but accommodation to the prevailing order. . . . What resulted was an economic and political amalgam combining the worst features of both worlds—feudalism and capitalism—and blocking effectively all possibilities of economic growth."[38]

According to Baran, "the alliance" of the capitalist middle classes and the landed aristocracy undermined the prospects for capitalist development—first, because it prevented the rise of a capitalist culture of savings and investment, and second, because it polarized backward societies into a united front of the dominant classes on the one hand and the increasingly frustrated "popular masses" on the other. In Baran's view, such social polarization further discouraged investment because it increased political and economic uncertainty: "In such a climate, there is no will to invest on the part of monied people; in such a climate there is no enthusiasm for long-term projects; in such a climate the motto of all participants in the privileges offered by society is *carpe diem.*"[39]

Baran further argued that under such conditions only the primary-product sector would receive investment, but that over time, because only foreigners would have the capital and market contacts needed to fully exploit such natural resources, the strategic economic sector would become "the domain of foreigners."[40]

The article caught the attention of Chilean politicians after the University of Chile published a translation in 1955.[41] Allende publicly referred to the piece first in December 1955 when he recommended it to his Senate colleagues because it was from "a North American professor whose objectivity cannot be disputed. These are not the words of socialists or procommunists." A month later, Rodríguez and Allende both quoted extensively from the article during the debate over yet another austerity bill aimed at freezing the annual adjustment of empleado salaries. Rodríguez used Baran's words to illustrate his contention that by promoting an austerity plan thought up by the foreign consultants of the firm Klein-Saks, the government was demonstrating "the historical incapacity of the dominant groups to understand and resolve the [country's] problems at their root." Allende quoted from Baran's piece to warn the "small and medium bourgeoisie that their civic participation should take a progressive direction, because if that does not happen the insurgency of the popular sectors will turn violent."[42]

Within a few short years, Baran's ideas about economic backwardness and the middle class became a recognizable part of Socialist Party discourse in Chile. The process began when the party republished the piece in pamphlet form as the second in their series "Folletos de divulgación."[43] As a result of Baran's influence, the Socialists began to criticize the weakness of Chilean capitalism. For example, Raúl Ampuero echoed Baran when he declared that "Chile has not even had a healthy and forceful capitalism that has been able to develop on its own, like the capitalism and bourgeoisie in France, England, and the United States."[44] While other Chileans had previously made similar arguments about the weakness of Chile's bourgeoisie, Baran's ideas allowed the Socialists to connect the behavior of the "middle class" to

foreign control of the export economy.[45] For instance, in 1962 the Socialists
described the Chilean economy as follows:

> Chile's sociological configuration follows the basic schema of those countries
> that are semi-colonial or are subjected to imperialist pressure: a) a group of
> large-scale landowners, merchants, industrialists, miners, [and] professionals
> constituted throughout the great expropriating bourgeoisie have held economic
> and political power; b) peasants, . . . low-income public and private emplea-
> dos, artisans, and petty merchants formed the national proletariat.
>
> Between these two great social conglomeration emerged the so-called
> "middle class" or petty bourgeoisie—with greater culture and with a higher
> income than the proletariat—made up of professionals, rural proprietors, me-
> dium-sized industrialists and merchants, public and private empleados, arti-
> sans and skilled workers. By the end [of the nineteenth century], this middle
> class burst timidly into political life under the inspiration of a renovated and
> progressive liberalism and the first socialist ideas that arrived, fighting for
> social demands like the separation of church and state, the eight-hour day,
> obligatory lay education, etc.
>
> Starting in 1920, the Chilean middle class, in accord with the traditional
> parties, achieved some say in the political and administrative direction of the
> country; but, because of those same accords [the middle class] lost its renovat-
> ing impulse and fell into bureaucratism and social-climbing, which today char-
> acterize all the social and political activity of the parties that represent the
> petty bourgeoisie. . . .
>
> [And] the Chilean ruling classes continue . . . surrendering the national
> patrimony over to foreign imperialism.[46]

As this excerpt makes clear, Socialists did not completely forget the historical radicalism of Chile's middle class, but they put it firmly in the past.
Moreover, their middle class ceased to be a class of white-collar workers, but
became instead a servile petty bourgeoisie collaborating with the dominant
classes. This sociological vision added considerable historical detail to Baran's account of a bourgeoisie in alliance with the landed aristocracy, but the
debt to Baran is clear: in both accounts the middle class plays a decisive role
in undermining domestic economic development.

Baran's article might have first caught the attention of Socialists like
Allende because it presented a radical message that bore the imprimatur of
Stanford University—just as Lüdwig Stein's academic prestige had attracted
the attention of Jorge Errázuriz Tagle. But Baran's piece had other virtues to
recommend it to Chilean Socialists. The party had been struggling in the
preceding years. In the 1940s, it had seen the on-again, off-again Popular
Front coalition of leftist and centrist parties break apart when the "middle-
class" Radical Party turned on its leftist allies. Then, the Socialist Party itself
had divided in 1952 when the more middle-class wing of the party had opted
to support the presidential candidacy of the ex-dictator Carlos Ibáñez del
Campo. So when Baran spoke of the failure of the middle classes "to assume

[the] leadership of popular forces and to direct them into the channels of bourgeois democracy," the Socialists must have seen an explanation for their own situation.

Baran's analysis also offered a clear explanation of Chile's economic backwardness. His point about the foreign domination of the export sector seemed to have been written with Chilean copper in mind. His analysis was also appealing because it presented a concise and convincing justification for establishing socialism in backwards countries. Indeed, Salvador Allende seemed to be citing Baran in his first presidential message to Congress when he said,

> The causes of backwardness resided and still reside in the traditional ruling classes with their combination of dependence on external forces and internal class exploitation. They have profited from their association with foreign interests, and from their appropriation of the surplus produced by the workers. . . . Our first task is to dismantle this restrictive structure, which only produces a deformed growth. At the same time, we must build up a new economy so that it succeeds the previous one without continuing it. [47]

In sum, Baran seemed to speak directly to recent Chilean experience and to the dreams of a socialist future. Along with this heady mix, the Socialists as a matter of course also drank in Baran's beliefs about the inherently reactionary character of the Chilean middle class.

SPINNING RADICALS INTO REACTIONARIES

The Socialists were not the only ones thinking about the character of the Chilean middle class in the late 1950s and early 1960s. There was also a growing scholarly literature about the middle class that was sometimes critical of it. In 1949, Eduardo Frei argued that it was playing an increasing role in politics but had nevertheless failed to improve its economic position. A few years later Julio Vega and Amanda Labarca debated the role and weight of the middle class in Chilean society but broadly agreed that it probably served a democratizing function. In English-language scholarship, the major works were by John J. Johnson and Bert Hoselitz. For the most part, however, this early literature eschewed any discussion of "hybrid" classes or class "amalgams."[48] The views that were voiced seem to have been drawn from a varied set of observations and opinions. Because there was no consensus about the typical behavior of the Chilean middle classes, and because the evidence was frequently anecdotal and the research sometimes unsystematic, this literature was vague and contradictory.

Over time, however, scholars began to focus more and more on the relationship of the middle class to the traditional landholding elite and thus came more into line with Baran's article and with the Socialist Party thinking that derived from it. Interestingly, Baran does not appear to have been a direct inspiration: his article is never cited in scholarship on the Chilean middle class.[49] And yet one can identify passages that seem to borrow Baran's language. As a result, it appears that his ideas about middle classes in backwards countries slowly seeped into the intellectual discourse, even without direct inspiration from the original source. It seems reasonable to conclude, then, that Socialist Party discourse on the middle class was the major channel by which Baran's ideas later reached the scholarly literature, and these ideas influenced what scholars saw when they looked at the Chilean middle class.

One can first discern the trend toward Baran's and the Socialists' approach to the middle class in a 1963 report published by the United Nations' Economic Commission for Latin America (ECLA) based in Santiago. In its report on social development in Latin America published in 1964, ECLA approvingly cited the "Hoselitz Hypothesis" and acknowledged Johnson's "optimistic" findings on the middle class, but its conclusions were suspiciously in line with the thinking of both Baran and the Socialists. For example, despite some approving citations of Johnson, the ECLA report ultimately argued that Johnson was describing the region's middle classes as they first emerged in the early part of the twentieth century. The report borrowed from the Socialists to argue that after this progressive phase the middle class lost its renovating impulse. Specifically, ECLA held that after the Second World War, "the new middle classes . . . showed an increasing tendency to identify themselves with the established order and to grasp the opportunity it offered."[50] The report also echoed Baran in specifically arguing that the main social explanation for the lack of economic dynamism in the region was "the assimilation of the middle classes by the traditional system."[51] Although Baran was never cited, and no Chilean Socialist was quoted, it seems reasonable to assume that the authors of the report were familiar with their ideas.

Just as ECLA was writing its report, Pike published his article on the Chilean middle class. Once again Baran was not cited, but the echoes of his analysis are clearly discernible in Pike's description of the "alliance," "amalgam," "merging," and "close association" between Chile's middle class and oligarchy. Baran had argued that in a backward country the middle class and the traditional aristocracy formed an "alliance," (71, 80, 83) an "amalgam," (69), a "coalition," (71, 77), or "a compromise" (80). The overlap between the two articles is not perfect, so there is no reason to conclude that Pike was drawing directly from Baran. But their arguments arrive at the same conclusion, and Pike's vocabulary at least shows that scholars and intellectuals who interested themselves in the Chilean middle class thought about Chilean class relations in a "Baranian" way: they believed that the middle class had cast its lot with the ruling class, that it supported the traditional social order, and that it was thus partly responsible for Chile's lack of economic development.[52]

The high point of this kind of analysis was reached by Fernando Henrique Cardoso and Enzo Faletto in their widely read *Dependency and Development in Latin America.* Writing originally in Chile in 1966 and 1967, the Brazilian sociologist Cardoso and the Chilean historian Faletto argued that class alliances had a decisive impact on the process of development in Latin America:

> We must understand the conflict between social movements that "are set in motion" by social classes in developing societies. . . . An economic class or group tries to establish through the political process a system of social relations that permits it to impose on the entire society a social form of production akin to its own interests; or at least it tries to establish alliances or to control the other groups or classes in order to develop an economic order consistent with its interests and objectives. . . . The traditional dominant groups initially may oppose handing over their power of control to the new social groups that appear with industrialization, but they also may bargain with them, thereby altering the social and political consequences of development.[53]

They hypothesized that a range of class arrangements and outcomes was possible, but after a broad review of many different historical cases they concluded that, typically, Latin American middle classes joined an "alliance" against the popular sectors. In their review of the Chilean case, they argued that early on the national bourgeoisie used state revenue derived from mining to strengthen urban industry, which encouraged the rapid expansion and political ascent of the middle class. Nevertheless, they concluded that the economic development that followed was a *dependent* development—a type that ultimately served the interests of a minority of Latin Americans and foreign capitalists but could not deliver both growth and equity. Therefore they concluded that the Chilean middle class benefited from a development process that inadequately addressed the needs of the broader society.[54]

In a sense, all of these scholarly critiques were accurate: the Chilean middle class did enjoy extraordinary privileges. If one followed the old Chilean convention and defined empleados as the core of the middle class, this middle class enjoyed the benefits of salary readjustments and the special white-collar security funds. But the Socialists and the scholars went wrong when they assumed that the middle class "allied" itself with the ruling class against the popular sectors. Certainly in the case of the empleados there was no "alliance" against the masses. Empleados had to fight tooth and nail to maintain their privileges. In fact, Arturo Valenzuela contends that in the 1960s the fights over salary readjustments were one of the "fundamental" issues of Chilean politics.[55] More to the point, the empleados did not try to keep their privileges the exclusive prerogative of white-collar workers. Quite to the contrary, they favored extending the definition of "empleado" to a growing number of Chilean workers in an effort to expand the political power of the empleado bloc in their constant struggle to preserve and expand their legal privileges. [56]

But to make their arguments about Chilean society, these scholars considered empleados peripheral to the middle class. Essentially, they were redefining the Chilean middle class to fit a preconceived idea about the relationship between the middle class and politics. Their primary concern was to explain the slowness of Chilean development, and thus they were interested in the middle class only insofar as it affected development. They had inherited from Baran and the Socialists a theory of development that saw middle classes in backward societies as dupes of the land-owning aristocracy. Since the radical empleados did not fit this model of middle-class behavior, they became increasingly invisible to the scholarship. Whereas earlier authors like Frei, Labarca, and Hoselitz had all identified empleados as the core of the middle class, the later scholars treated them as marginal actors. When they described the various components of the middle class, they might list the empleados as one segment of it, but for them empleados were not the paradigmatic middle-class group. [57] They could only see the middle class that fit the model. They were looking for a reactionary middle class, and so they found it.

ALLIES AND ENEMIES

We can now see why the middle class came to be seen as reactionary just after the empleados reached the peak of their radical mobilization with the 1950 empleado strike. The empleados had not shifted rapidly to the right; rather the definition of the middle class had shifted. As we have seen, this history began in the aftermath of World War I when some members of the Liberal and Conservative Parties had attempted to co-opt the empleados. These politicians had identified the middle class with empleados because the empleados were a large, easily identifiable group; they occupied the middle space between manual workers and the elite; and both the Liberals and the Conservatives believed that the empleados could be turned into political allies. In this effort they drew at least indirectly on Lüdwig Stein's assertion that intellectual workers had special needs and needed special protection. Labor legislation subsequently codified the "middling" status of empleados by dividing Chilean society into the three hierarchical categories of employers, empleados, and obreros. Empleados retained this middling status until the 1950s and thus, from World War I through the Korean War, were seen as the core of the middle class. That began to change in the 1950s and 1960s, when leftists became preoccupied with the theoretical role of the middle class. Chilean Socialists and like-minded intellectuals inspired by Paul Baran adopted his theory that the middle class was an implicit ally of the landed oligarchy and that this social amalgam of middle class and oligarchy was to blame for the slow pace of Chilean development.

One might assume that the critique of the middle class might have opened up a breach between the empleados and the left, but that is not what happened. On the contrary, leftists continued to see empleados as "intellectual workers" and as a vital constituency. For their part, empleados did not object when leftists disparaged the middle class. Empleado unions continued to see the leftist parties as their critical allies. Moreover, through the 1960s empleados strongly supported a policy of extending empleado privileges to obreros by redefining various blue-collar occupations as white-collar. There is no evidence that empleados were shifting rightwards in their politics. Furthermore, it seems that when leftist intellectuals and politicians criticized the middle class, they had no intention of offending empleados, and empleados did not take offense.[58]

Empleados apparently recognized that when leftists complained about the reactionary middle class, they were not including empleados in that definition. Leftist rhetoric about the middle class was in fact quite careless. The intellectuals and politicians who discussed the middle class would slide from one definition to another. Whenever they sought to precisely enumerate the different segments of the middle class, the leftists would borrow from the older definition of the middle class and list empleados. But when they turned their attention away from precise social categories and tried to imagine the deep structure of Chilean class relations, then they saw a very different middle class—Paul Baran's middle class. This was the middle class responsible for Chilean economic backwardness. These were the entrepreneurs who refused to take risks, the merchants and manufacturers who allied themselves with the elite.

This slippage from one definition to the other reflects the natural imprecision of the term "middle class," but in this case this slippage also came about because these thinkers saw the middle class only as an explanatory variable and were not concerned with the class beyond the scope of their narrow model. This carelessness with definitions explains how scholars could write about a reactionary middle class in the wake of a series of empleado strikes. The focus of these scholars and politicians was not on the precise composition of the Chilean middle class but on removing the obstacles to Chilean development. The middle class was of interest only because Baran's theory tied the middle class to Chilean backwardness.

But while the leftist critique of the middle class may not have alienated empleados, it did have real political consequences. When the Socialists condemned the middle class as the junior partner within the exploiting class, they were clearly casting the middle class as a political enemy. Such arguments helped the Socialists mobilize their most committed supporters, but when Socialist leader Salvador Allende became president of Chile in the early 1970s, his political opponents on the right used this alienating rhetoric to argue that Allende did not see himself as president of all Chileans. Such a portrayal fostered the climate of social and political polarization that arguably played into the hands of those who sought to make the country ungovernable. As the American CIA deployed *agents provocateurs*[59] and extremism mounted on both the right and the left, Chileans came to believe that there was no viable center. The rest of the story is well known. The point made here is simply that by imagining a reactionary middle class that cleaved to the right, the left only made it more difficult for Allende to broaden his appeal beyond his natural constituency. As a result, he found it difficult to fight the centrifugal forces unleashed by his domestic and foreign opponents.

The ironic conclusion of this study is that neither the right nor the left benefited from their attempts to rethink the middle class. That conclusion should give pause to future scholars of the middle class. In both periods studied here, intellectuals and politicians allowed their beliefs to be guided by theories and assumptions that did not necessarily describe the real flesh-and-blood actors who were their declared objects of interest. Indeed, Chilean politicians appropriated foreign social theories that had developed without any consideration of the country's particularities. This process of intellectual appropriation then led to quite unexpected changes in Chilean society. Moreover, the results were not just unexpected: one can argue that Liberals, Conservatives, and Socialists all paid a price for their ways of theorizing the middle class. The Liberals and Conservatives ended up radicalizing the empleados that they had sought to co-opt, while the Socialists left their own supporters convinced that the social order was inherently polarized into hostile camps. The important lesson seems to be that one should approach social theory with a healthy skepticism. Further students of the middle class would do well, then, to either focus on well-defined segments of the middle class or take seriously the process by which the middle class is socially constructed.[60]

NOTES

Original contribution written for this volume. J. Pablo Silva is associate professor of history at Grinnell College, Iowa. Research funding was provided by a Fulbright Fellowship to Chile, and from Grinnell College, a Harris Faculty Fellowship and various grants from the Dean's Office. The author gratefully acknowledges the helpful comments of Mónica Chávez and D.A. Smith. Jessica Beckwith helped transcribe some of the oral interviews.

1. "Annual Review of Labor in Chile 1950," 28 February 1951, 825.06 /2–2851, RG 59, United States National Archive.

2. Amanda Labarca Hubertson, "Apuntes para estudiar la clase media en Chile," in *Materiales para el estudio de la clase media en la América Latina*, ed. Theo R. Crevenna, vol. 6 (Washington, DC: Unión Panamericana, 1951), 83. Unless otherwise indicated, all translations here are by the author.

3. Senado, *Boletín de Sesiones Extraordinarias* (Santiago, 1949–1950), 1117. Looking back on the event a few years later, Jorge Alessandri identified the 1950 strike as one of the two

major events (along with the election of 1938) that had swung Chile to the left. See his letter to Conrado Ríos Gallardo (Santiago, 8 September 1955), Biblioteca Nacional de Chile Archivo de Jorge Alessandri, caja 68, 339.

4. Claudio Veliz, *Obstacles to Change in Latin America* (London: Oxford University Press, 1965), 2.

5. James F. Petras, *Politics and Social Forces in Chilean Development* (Berkeley: University of California, 1969), 2.

6. For instance, his survey showed that an almost equal number of blue-collar and private-sector white-collar workers (93 percent and 94 percent) agreed that Chilean society did not offer equality of opportunity. On the issue of political rights for Communists, empleado support was as strong as worker support: almost an equally small percentage of blue-collar workers (31 percent) and private-sector white-collar workers (33 percent) opposed legalization of the Communist Party. More importantly, white-collar workers were much more reformist than either business owners or the self-employed: a majority of business owners (53 percent) and a large minority of the self-employed (43 percent) opposed political rights for Communists. So, in terms of their politics, white-collar workers were much more similar to blue-collar workers. Land reform was the only question on which white-collar and blue-collar workers profoundly disagreed (with only 27 percent of blue-collars supporting the current system of land tenure versus 68 percent of private-sector empleados). That difference may have to do with the white-collar perception in the 1960s that land reform would lead to higher food prices, against the blue-collar hope that land reform might allow migrants from the countryside to return and acquire land. The question did not, in my opinion, accurately test of overall political inclinations (Petras, *Politics and Social Forces,* 144–52).

7. The path-breaking works here are William H. Sewell Jr., *Work and Revolution in France: The Language of Labor from the Old Regime to 1848* (Cambridge: Cambridge University Press, 1980); Gareth Stedman Jones, "Rethinking Chartism," *Languages of Class: Studies in English Working Class History, 1832–1982* (Cambridge: Cambridge University Press, 1983). For the middle class, see Dror Wahrman, *Imagining the Middle Class: The Political Representation of Class in Britain, c. 1780–1840* (Cambridge: Cambridge University Press, 1995). And for Latin America, the major work is D. S. Parker, *The Idea of the Middle Class; White-Collar Workers and Peruvian Society, 1900–1950* (University Park: Pennsylvania State University Press, 1998); but also see Matthew B. Karush, *Workers or Citizens; Democracy and Identity in Rosario, Argentina (1912–1930)* (Albuquerque: University of New Mexico Press, 2002).

8. Lira's proposal can be found in Cámara de Diputados, *Boletín de Sesiones Extraordinarias* (Santiago, 1918–19), 2671–73. For evidence that politicians continued to identify empleados with the middle class, one need only look at the papers of the "Special Commission to Improve the Condition of the Middle Class," found in Consejo Superior del Trabajo, *Estudios Sobre E.E.P.P., 1934–1942,* Fondo Ministerio del Trabajo, Archivo del Siglo XX (Santiago, Chile).

9. It is a characteristic of Chile, as a dependent economy, that many of the key moments in its domestic political history correspond to key moments in international history. In this case, these international conflicts powerfully affected demand for Chile's major exports, nitrates and copper.

10. For example, the labor leader Luis E. Recabarren spoke in 1910 of a middle class of the most skilled workers and of empleados. See his "A ver, ¿quién puede contradecirme?," *Chile; Discursos con historia* (Santiago: Los Andes, 1996), 56. On the other side, Pike cites Miguel Cruchaga Montt and his image of a middle class in charge of the country's economic development ("Aspects of Class Relations in Chile, 1850–1960," 14).

11. Ludwig Stein, *La question sociale au point de vue philosophique* (Paris: F. Alcan, 1900), 326–27. I cite the French edition rather than the original German because it seems most likely that Chilenas read the French. Today the Chilean Biblioteca del Congreso has this French edition still on its shelves, but not the German.

12. On Errázuriz Tagle and this "Circle of Friends," see Guillermo Feliú Cruz, "Seis claros varones de la generación de 1868: Arturo Alessandri Palma, Alejandro Alvarez, Emilio Bello

Codesido, Ricardo Cabieses, Enrique Matta Vial, y Ricardo Montaner Bello," *Anales de la Facultad de Derecho: Cuarta Época* 8 (1968).

13. *Tercera Convención del Partido Liberal,* 212–13.

14. Lüdwig Stein, *La question sociale,* 292.

15. *Tercera Convención del Partido Liberal celebrada los días 19, 20 i 21 de octubre de 1913* (Santiago de Chile: Sociedad Imprenta-Litografía "Barcelona," 1916), 446.

16. *Tercera Convención del Partido Liberal,* 182–84, 200–24.

17. Parker in *The Idea of the Middle Class* finds a strikingly similar discourse in Peru, but he makes a convincing argument that the language of special needs has domestic roots in that instance.

18. "Informaciones políticas," *El Mercurio,* Santiago, 16 January 1919, 18.

19. Cámara de Diputados, *Boletín de Sesiones Extraordinarias* (Santiago, 1918–1919), 2671–73. See also "Informaciones Políticas," *El Mercurio,* Santiago, 10 November 1918, 21, and 16 January 1919, 18.

20. "La clase siempre olvidada," *El Mercurio,* Santiago, 5 December 1918, 3.

21. "Congreso de la clase media, para su bienestar y protección," *El Mercurio,* Santiago, 6 December 1918, 3.

22. "Federación de la clase media," *El Mercurio,* Santiago, 17 February 1919, 13.

23. On the demise of the Federación de Clase Media, see Patricio de Diego Maestri, Luis Peña Rojas, and Claudio Peralta Castillo, *La Asamblea Obrera de Alimentación Nacional: un hito en la historia de Chile* ([Chile]: Sociedad Chilena de Sociología, 2002), 107–21. Note that my overall interpretation of the Federación differs a bit from de Diego Maestri et al. Where they see the Conservative Party and *El Mercurio* working together to create the Federación, I see the Conservative Party working in a different direction.

24. For a narrative of this early movement on behalf of pro-empleado legislation, see J. Pablo Silva, "White-Collar Revolutionaries" (PhD diss., University of Chicago, 2000).

25. In this sense, Chile offers an interesting contrast to the Argentine case. According to Karush, *Workers or Citizens,* the Argentine elite tried to resist the idea of class politics. In Chile, however, the ruling class instead worked to formalize class distinctions.

26. James O. Morris, *Elites, Intellectuals, and Consensus; A Study of the Social Question and the Industrial Relations System in Chile* (Ithaca: New York State School of Industrial and Labor Relations, 1966), 236, 239–40, makes clear that Chile's original labor code was a soup formed of three competing and contradictory legislative proposals that were passed as a result of an accident of history, the 1924 coup.

27. J. Pablo Silva, "The Origins of White-Collar Privilege in Chile: Arturo Alessandri, Law 6020 and the Pursuit of a Corporatist Consensus, 1933–1938," *Labor* 3, no. 1 (2006): 87–112.

28. According to Albert O. Hirschman, "Chile is probably the only country in the world that instituted a legal minimum salary long before a minimum wage." See "Inflation in Chile," in *Journeys toward Progress; Studies of Economic Policy-Making in Latin America* (New York: Norton, 1973 [1963]), 198.

29. The change came in Law 7064, 15 September 1941, which was modified by Law 7295, 30 September 1942.

30. Interestingly, the Popular Front Coalition began to break up immediately after passing the pro-empleado legislation. As a result, Congress was unable to pass corresponding legislation for workers. Instead, further progressive legislation would have to be negotiated with rightists. Subsequent legislation therefore began to concentrate on industrialization and economic development rather than labor issues. See John Reese Stevenson, *The Chilean Popular Front* (Westport, CT: Greenwood Press, 1942).

31. Author's interview with Marcial Cortés-Monroy (Las Condes, 12 May 2003).

32. There are countless examples of the negotiability of the salary levels, but a particularly clear exposition can be found in Carlos C. Hall, "Annual Review of Labor in Chile in 1949," 10 March 1950, 825.06 /3–1050, RG 59, United States National Archive.

33. This point was made at the time by Senator Ocampo of the Communist Party. See Senado, *Boletín de Sesiones Extraordinarias* (Santiago, 1949–50), 1157.

34. Carlos C. Hall (Counselor of Embassy), "President Faces Serious Problems on Return from United States," 25 April 1950, 725.00/4–2550, RG 59, United States National Archive.

35. "Chile," in *The State, Industrial Relations and the Labour Movement in Latin America* (New York: St. Martin's Press, 1989), 208.

36. The issue was important enough to the left that in 1956 most leftist congressmen actually voted against the law that eventually extended the minimum wage to blue-collar workers precisely because it temporarily put a halt to salary adjustments for empleados. See my "Origins of White-Collar Privilege in Chile."

37. Senado, *Boletín de Sesiones Extraordinarias* (Santiago, 1955–56), 1124–25, 1129.

38. *Manchester School of Economic and Social Studies* 20 (1952): 68–84.

39. Ibid., 77.

40. Ibid., 74.

41. Paul A. Baran, "Sobre la Economía Política Del Subdesarrollo," *Economía: Revista de la Facultad de Ciencias Económicas de la Universidad de Chile* (Santiago) 15, no. 50 (July 1955): 37–50.

42. Senado, *Boletín de Sesiones Extraordinarias* (Santiago, 1955–56), 646, 1125, and 1129.

43. Paul A. Baran, *La Economia de Los Paises Subdesarrolados* (Santiago: Prensa Latinoamericano, 1958). Aside from the slightly modified title and the addition of section headings to replace the original plain roman numerals, the text remains the same as the earlier translation.

44. Raúl Ampuero Díaz, "Alessandri: El hombre de la restauración reaccionaria," in *El clan sagrado (Tres discursos polémico)* (Santiago: Imprenta Universataria, 1960), 10.

45. Compare, for example, the statements to this effect by Eduardo Frei in Alberto Edwards Vives and Eduardo Frei Montalva, *Historia de Los Partidos Políticos Chilenos* (Santiago: Pacífico, 1949), 14.

46. Partido Socialista, Comisión Nacional de Estudios Técnicos, *Esquema Económico de Chile—1962* (Santiago: Prensa Latinoamericana, 1962), 2.

47. *Salvador Allende Reader: Chile's Voice of Democracy,* ed. James D. Cockcroft (Melbourne: Ocean, 2000), 93.

48. One possible exception here might be Jorge Ahumada Corvalán, *En vez de la miseria* (Santiago: Pacífico, 1958), 53, which Pike later cites. But Ahumada discusses the merging of landholders and industrialists, and not the middle class. In addition, his point here is a subsidiary one in a complex argument concerning Chile's social and economic problems, and he does not depend ultimately on the analysis of class relations for his conclusions.

49. Andre Gunder Frank, *Capitalism and Underdevelopment in Latin America* (New York: Monthly Review Press, 1969 [1967]), offers an interesting exception that proves the rule. Frank not only cites Baran but dedicates his book to him. But Frank's analysis of the Chilean economy avoids discussion of the middle class. Frank was interested in the way that Chilean "integration in the world capitalist market . . . allied the most powerful interest groups of Chile to those of imperialism and its interest in maintaining and indeed furthering Chile's underdevelopment" (57). In this line of argument one can see Frank's debt to Baran, but for Frank the analysis worked well using the language of "interest groups" and did not require the reification of "classes."

50. Indeed, according to Parker, *The Idea of the Middle Class*, 4, this historicized vision of the Latin American middle class subsequently became a standard trope visible in classic works on the subject.

51. United Nations Economic Commission for Latin America, *Social Development of Latin America in the Post-War Period* (New York: United Nations, 1964), 10, 89–115.

52. The same idea is evident in the Veliz, *Obstacles to Change,* 1–7.

53. Fernando Henrique Cardoso and Enzo Faletto, *Dependency and Development in Latin America* (Berkeley: University of California, 1979 [1969]), 13–20.

54. Ibid.

55. Arturo Valenzuela, *The Breakdown of Democratic Regimes, Chile* (Baltimore, MD: Johns Hopkins University Press, 1976), 18.

56. Author's interviews with Cortes-Monroy and with Patricio González (Santiago, 8 May 2003).

57. Just to take the main examples presented here, Pike, in "Aspects," esp. 21–22, says that everyone above obrero status was middle class, but his analysis of the middle class seems to concentrate on the nouveaux riches. For Cardoso and Faletto, *Dependency and Development,*

75, the middle class includes "the beginning of an industrial bourgeoisie with the corresponding technically trained professionals, the civil and military bureaucracy, the white-collar workers, and so forth." ECLA, *Social Development of Latin America,* 98, describes how middle classes began to grow from a core of professionals but maintains that public sector workers are now the most representative.

58. Bert Hoselitz, on the other hand, did intend to criticize the empleados. Or rather, he argued that white-collar workers played too important a role in Chilean society. But Hoselitz was no leftist; his whole approach differed from that of Baran, the Socialists, and the scholars that they influenced.

59. We know very little about such activities, but in Peter Kornbluh, *The Pinochet File; A Declassified Dossier on Atrocity and Accountability* (New York: Free Press, 2004), 88, 134–35, there is at least documentation that confirms it existed.

60. Excellent examples of such work can already be found in Patrick Barr-Melej, *Reforming Chile: Cultural Politics, Nationalism, and the Rise of the Middle Class* (Chapel Hill: University of North Carolina Press, 2001); Gabriel Salazar Vergara, "Para una historia de la clase media en Chile" (Santiago: Sur, 1986), working paper; Eugenio Tironi, "La Clase Construida" (Santiago, Sur, 1985), working paper.

Chapter Twelve

We Were the Middle Class

Rodolfo Barros

In December 2001, middle-class people confronting a rapidly deteriorating economic situation rioted in the streets of Buenos Aires. Journalist Rodolfo Barros analyzes this protest in the context of a more general, long-term crisis of the Argentine middle class. The following chapter takes excerpts from his book, Fuimos *("We Were"), the product of interviews and conversations with four Buenos Aires couples who recount their responses to the 2001–2002 crisis and their struggles to maintain a middle-class life. They also ponder more abstract questions about what it means to be middle-class in Argentina, and how this has changed over the past several decades.*

The background to the book: throughout the 1990s, President Carlos Menem adopted a neoliberal development model for Argentina, one of whose key features was the 1991 Convertibility Law, which stabilized the Argentine peso by making pesos fully exchangeable for U.S. dollars. For many in the middle class, convertibility made it easier to travel abroad, to purchase imported products, to get credit, and to save and withdraw their money in U.S. dollars. Ultimately, however, convertibility was not sustainable. Following the election of President Fernando de la Rua in 1999, worries about Argentina's weakening economic fundamentals led to a run on the banks as both Argentine and foreign investors began to withdraw their dollar savings. In December 2001, as it became evident that those banks lacked the dollar reserves to cover the withdrawals, Finance Minister Domingo Cavallo announced a near-complete freeze on all bank accounts; Argentines would only be allowed to withdraw small amounts of their savings at a time, and only in pesos. This policy, which came to be known as the corralito, was the spark that set off the December riots, forcing De la Rua to resign. The corralito was followed by the end of convertibility, the devaluation of the peso, and the forced conversion of U.S. dollar savings into peso accounts.

We have selected five separate but interrelated vignettes from Barros's book. The first is his introduction to the project, in which he discusses his motivation and introduces his interviewees. The second reconstructs the December 2001 crisis and the effects of the corralito *from the perspective of his*

informants. Barros also analyzes the decades-long decline of Argentina's mid-
dle class to put the crisis in context. The third section captures the growing
sense of insecurity among the middle class, as crime rates in the city seemed to
be on the rise. The fourth discusses the middle class's continued preoccupa-
tion with education, even when hard times made private schooling difficult to
afford. Finally, in the fifth section the author invites his informants to his home
to talk about their lives, their problems, and their aspirations, and to discuss
what it means to be middle class in a time of crisis.

PARADISE LOST

"In the past three decades everything in our world has changed," I thought
when I decided to write this book. The middle-class life that my wife and
children and I enjoy is very different from the one I had as a child living with
my parents and my two siblings. Back then—not so long ago—my father
worked as an inspector for the National Institute of Viticulture, and my
mother was a teacher. Between them we had enough money to go to public
school and university and enough to buy clothes that kept us warm during the
winters, even if they weren't brand names. The state-run social security
system covered us in the event of any illness. We could go to the dentist in
the public hospitals, or we could go to private clinics if we didn't want to
wait in line. Because we lived in Mendoza, we vacationed a few times in
Chile. Other times, my parents' Christmas bonuses were enough to put gas in
our 1970 Fiat 1500 to go on a road trip to Buenos Aires or Mar del Plata and
to spend nearly a month in a union hotel or a rented beach house.

In my childhood the state provided a good social safety net. We could
depend on steady employment, decent salaries, and pensions that, although
they were never enough, permitted a certain amount of security after a lifetime of working in the same place. Of course, so much security generated
frustrations.

In those years our sense of certainty held firm even when, from time to
time, explosions of inflation would destroy my parents' real wages, our savings, and everything, it seemed. Sometimes we couldn't even afford the liter
of milk that was delivered to our door in a glass bottle. But these difficulties
didn't last long, because employment was guaranteed, and my parents got
through the harder moments by tightening belts. After every storm came the
calm.

My own family has a very different middle-class status. The only certainty that my wife and I can count on is that we won't retire in the same jobs
that we have today. And even though we contribute to a pension fund, we
don't even know if we'll be able to retire at all. In fact, we started our family
in conditions of insecurity. One month after our wedding . . . my newspaper

fired 50 journalists, myself included. The saying "for better or for worse" became a reality for us as soon as we got married.

For several months we were the "new poor." We ate rice almost exclusively. We had to borrow money (which we could never pay back) from parents and in-laws to pay the rent and to make photocopies of my resume, which I handed out everywhere trying to find work.

Today we are no longer members of the new poor, but we know we could become so again at any moment. We now live in very different circumstances: we bought a house and have high-speed Internet. We are hoping that the public schools remain acceptable so that our children can get a good education. Our lack of security is one of the characteristics of the new middle class. This also generates frustrations.

Like everyone, I lived through the ingeniously grotesque reality of the *corralito*. When Cavallo froze bank accounts and forbade withdrawals in American dollars, I witnessed the line-ups at the foreign consulates, and I felt sadness for those friends who reluctantly left the country, seeking a peace that they never found.

Today's middle class is not only different from the middle class of 30 years ago. In economic terms, it is also much smaller. In the past three decades, nine million members of the middle class joined the new poor. But to define the middle class only by its income or its access to goods and services would be to ignore its most important capital, which it acquired during the era of the welfare state when people of all classes still went to public schools: its symbolic capital.

How, then, could I tackle such a complex theme? The answer was all around me. It was in the people who, with luck, navigated the crisis to their advantage, and it was in the families who fell into an abyss of poverty for which they were not culturally prepared. It was in those who lost their characteristic indifference, and in those who decided to abandon the ideals of progress that they had inherited from their parents and grandparents.

The answer was in people like Claudia and Guillermo Rodríguez, university professors who lived surrounded by poverty in a shantytown on the outskirts of La Plata. They had moved to this city to live the promise of an "easier" life.

It was in the lives of people like Elsa and Gustavo Díaz, who suffered a fall from which they could not recover. Gustavo had two cars and his own business when unemployment hit. They even had to enroll in a make-work welfare program, the *Plan jefes y jefas de hogar desocupados*.[1]

The answer also emerged in the story of Paola and Gerónimo Cabrera, who are stuck in a long court battle to recuperate the money they lost in the corralito. They were in the middle of a real-estate transaction, having sold their old house and just about to close on their new one when bank accounts were frozen. They then spent a long time without a place of their own.

I could also see the adventures and misadventures of the middle class in the experience of Maximiliano Fernández, a well-known businessman in telecommunications. He managed to avoid the different crises by marrying an upper-class woman, in spite of his former militant middle-class ideals. His wife, María, declined my request to interview her, citing security concerns.

In sum, I knew that this book would have to tell the stories of people who are or had been in the middle. I deliberately omitted those on the extremes of the middle class, be they reactionaries, progressive militants, or revolutionaries. I preferred to look for those who were in the middle, those who could be one thing and then, suddenly, become the opposite.

During the past quarter century, middle-class Argentines have been at the center of many decisions, debates, contradictions, and tensions. They have cast their votes thinking about whether they could pay the installments on their blenders, or they have voted against corruption. They have forged their identity as workers and have had to face the abyss when they found themselves unemployed. They have felt rich in some moments and like the new poor in others. They have sent their children to private schools when they would have received a perfectly good education in public school. They have abandoned family-owned shops for supermarkets.

All this was on my mind one night at the end of 2001 when I decided to write this book. And I wasn't alone. That night—19 December 2001—disconcerted citizens emerged from all corners of Buenos Aires, asking themselves why things had gone so poorly without any idea of how to make them better. They took to the streets in anger, in desperation, and with fear for their future. That night thirty people died and the president fled the country.

That was when I decided to interview these different people, each of whom represents a distinct aspect of the middle class—a concept so broad that it's almost impossible to even contemplate. What does it mean to be middle class today? Does it mean owning a car, a house, or having work? Is a family middle class if they have a monthly income of 2000 pesos but live in a poor area on the outskirts of the city? Is the person who finished university but can't find stable work middle class?

The middle class has a new identity. I thought I could understand this new identity by following the lives of these four couples as a participant observer, incorporating my own experience with my observations. Their stories are the stories of millions of Argentines who learned from their grandparents that social mobility was possible; these Argentines want to regain this social mobility for their children.

The events of 19 and 20 December 2001 marked a watershed in middle-class identity. They also offer an entry point into the stories of Claudia and Guillermo, Elsa and Gustavo, Paola and Gerónimo, and Maximiliano.

THE DECEMBER CRISIS

"We are living amidst violence, which endangers persons and property and causes internal commotion. I want to inform all Argentines that, given this situation, I have imposed martial law throughout the country."

President Fernando de la Rúa appears on television and acknowledges the deteriorating situation. The calm before the storm is over. It's hot that night of 19 December 2001.

During the month of December the landscape of Argentine cities has changed significantly. Banks have abandoned their colorful window displays for metal security walls. Taking their hammers to the new fences, account holders try to reclaim their savings. The sounds of the city have also changed. Clanging metal rings through the city streets from the early morning to the late evening; bank customers fill the streets, shouting protests through their megaphones. The banging and the voices are the sounds of desperation. In these days, the reality that had until then been hidden from view appears, breaks out and explodes onto the streets. A smell of burning rubber lingers in the air. Behind these dark storm clouds the *piqueteros*, hungry, put up roadblocks.[2]

"We are living through a difficult time, the culmination of a long process of deterioration, and many Argentines are suffering from economic and social problems," continues de la Rúa. "Some groups, who are enemies of the Republic, have taken advantage of this to sow discord and violence, trying to generate a state of chaos to achieve their political ends."

The air in Buenos Aires was thick with anguish and anger, with impotence and confusion, with fear and uncertainty.

"I understand the penury that many of my compatriots are suffering. I understand it and I suffer with them. Most Argentines know that violence and illegal actions won't solve our problems. We have to face our problems; we are facing our problems."

The speech is obviously recorded. De la Rúa's gestures are rehearsed and forced: he takes off his eyeglasses, as though he were speaking face to face with Argentines, trying to demonstrate his energy: a public relations mistake. Paradoxically, the soon-to-be ex-president wants to pacify the country by imposing martial law.

"They're going to burn everything," I exclaim to my wife, who is speechless. We're both scared. We aren't the only ones.

Maximiliano is swearing at his television in the living room of his Palermo apartment. He curses de la Rúa for not dismissing Cavallo, the economy minister. His children are sleeping and his wife, María, jumps up from the couch and declares: "I'm getting my *cacerola* [cooking pot] and I'm going downstairs."[3]

On the street, the Maximiliano and María run into their neighbors, a journalist and his son. The four of them join the crowd that is gathering nearby. A mixture of joy and fear infuses the crowd. So does that palpable sense of uncertainty that people feel when they take charge of their destiny; or, at least, when they believe they do. A crowd forms in the heart of Palermo: is the mob becoming the citizenry?

Soon the sidewalk can't hold all the people, and the line spills into the road, blocking one lane of traffic. The passing drivers honk in solidarity. Some of the protesters head downtown to the city's main plaza, the Plaza de Mayo. They're angrily chanting *"Que se vayan todos!"* (throw them all out), sweating in their shorts and t-shirts on that hot night.

South of Buenos Aires, Gustavo and his family watch television, amazed at the images of middle-class residents pouring into the streets, marching to the Plaza de Mayo. Gustavo's parents were small farmers and moved to the suburbs of Buenos Aires so that their children could get a good education and leave rural life behind them. Maximiliano's father was a literature professor and a diplomat, and Maximiliano spent part of his childhood and adolescence in Mexico and France. Maximiliano completed a degree in engineering; Gustavo dropped out of the Agronomy program in third year. He had placed his faith in de la Rúa, but now he feels defrauded.

Not too far away from the Díazes, in a neighborhood on the outskirts of La Plata, Claudia and Guillermo Rodríguez listen to the events on the radio; a few months earlier their television had been stolen. But they are hardly even listening to the news. They've had a traumatic year and are only thinking about their upcoming trip to Tres Arroyos, where they were both born.

Claudia is a thirty-six-year-old librarian with three children. She feels a terrible need to get away from the city and go home. The looting, the dismal economic situation, and the generally foul mood of everyone because of the *corralito* all contribute to her distress; the news on the radio only adds to it.

Guillermo is an engineer. He doesn't feel the same way as his wife. Listening to the radio, he doesn't want to escape but to join the protesters. That year he and his children had participated in several marches, to defend public education and in support of teachers and pensioners. At the end of December he is ready to take to the streets again.

About five kilometers away from the Plaza de Mayo, Paolo and Gerónimo Cabrera are having an intimate dinner out to celebrate his birthday. They aren't watching television and don't know that the president is delivering his resignation speech. Instead they're trying to forget about their personal worries, if only for one night. When they found out Paola was pregnant, they sold their apartment, planning to move into a bigger place. But everything went wrong. When they deposited the money from the sale, the *corralito* struck and their money was frozen; they weren't able to buy a place to live. On 19 December, Gerónimo turned thirty-three. He didn't have stable work and was living in his mother-in-law's house.

The sounds of the cacerolas reach them as they finish eating. Paolo and Gerónimo get into their car and drive around Buenos Aires as spectators, astonished at the number of people: entire families wave at them as they march toward the Plaza de Mayo. Though they want to join the crowd, they are concerned about Paola's pregnancy and stay in the car.

They see *caceroleros* on the balconies of their houses, banging on their pots and pans. Others are walking in the streets. Paola and Gerónimo honk the horn in support, and the people cheer them on. Gerónimo thinks that for the first time, Argentine society is waking up, saying: "Enough! We won't take it anymore."

Paola is twenty-seven and has a safe job that gives the couple a modicum of financial stability. But she doesn't share her husband's optimism. Instead, she feels people only act when it hits them in the pocketbook: "We're united, but for what? Is it because we are against all the abuses of those in charge, or only because we can't get our money out of the bank?"

The protests reinforce Gerónimo's idea that he doesn't have the right to be depressed. He thinks, "Why don't the poor get depressed? A poor person doesn't have the opportunity to get depressed because he has to work." As he watches the people flooding into the street, he's comforted and thinks, "We're waking up."

The Fernandezes, the Díazes, the Rodríguezes, and the Cabreras don't know each other, but they have something in common: they're tired and fed up. And on this night, 19 December 2001, they belong to a bigger community that is also angry. They don't ask themselves how long this will last, if it will go beyond catharsis to construction. This night, they don't ask these questions. They're only expressing their anxiety. Each of them, in their own way, says, "Enough."

The next day, 20 December 2001, on the roof of the Presidential Palace, the men approach the helicopter. The president stops and turns to his advisor. "Did you get everything from the bathroom?" "Yes, sir," his aide answers. The president gets into the helicopter, which takes off immediately.

The presidential aide turns to the other men and says, "It wasn't the IMF or the Peronists who forced us out of power; it was the middle class."

Below them, the Plaza de Mayo is packed and Maximiliano is in the crowd.

That morning, the second day of the protests, Maximiliano woke up late, kissed his wife and two girls and went to his office, but he didn't stay long. At midday he decided to walk to the Plaza de Mayo to see what was happening. When he got there the plaza was full of people chanting, "Throw them all out!"

The police arrived and sprayed tear gas into the crowd. As the fumes filled the plaza, it became hard to breathe. The mounted police skirmished with the protesters, beating them with their billy clubs. Rubber and lead bullets shot through the air. Maximiliano ran, leaving and returning several times.

The president's helicopter flew away from the plaza, where the police repression would leave thirty dead.

That same morning, Claudia and Guillermo leave for their vacation. They don't want to get caught up in what's happening. They remember the hyper-inflation and the lootings in 1989—when the prices of milk, bread, and meat climbed hourly—and they tell themselves it's better to stay calm and take the uncertainty in stride. They load up their car and head for Tres Arroyos.

When they arrive at Guillermo's parents' house, they learn the extent of the crisis. For the next several days they're glued to the television. They watch as de la Rúa escapes by helicopter and the Peronist senator Ramón Puerta takes over as interim president. Adolfo Rodríguez Saá, who follows Puerta, announces that Argentina will default on its debt and not pay its international creditors; he then resigns after barely a week in office (23 to 31 December). During their New Year's Eve dinner, Guillermo's family watch as the country's political leaders try to determine who will take over as the next president, a job no one seems to want.

As they eat lunch on New Year's Day, they watch as the fourth president in less than two weeks, Eduardo Duhalde, promises that those who deposited pesos in the bank will receive pesos and those who deposited dollars will receive dollars.

Claudia and Guillermo are determined to escape from the crisis. They take their children on a four-day canoe trip. They don't meet another person, and they don't hear any news. A few days later, however, back in Tres Arroyos at Claudia's parents' house, they watch on television as some 3,000 people in Buenos Aires wait in line at the Spanish Consulate, seeking visas or recognition as dual citizens. There are similar lines at the Italian Consulate. Meanwhile, realizing there aren't enough dollars left in the banks, Duhalde reneges on his promise: those who deposited dollars will only receive pesos.

It's now Sunday, 3 February. The new Minister of Economy appears on television and announces that the banks will be closed on Monday and Tuesday while dollar accounts will be converted to pesos. The peso, which prior to the crisis was exchangeable with the dollar one-to-one, will subsequently float on the open market. As the bank holiday is extended to a week, everyone waits anxiously for the banks to reopen, to get access to their funds and to learn how bad the devaluation will end up being. When the banks reopen, savers find that dollar accounts have been converted to pesos at 1.40 pesos/dollar, while the dollar's free market price hovers around 2.10 pesos. The courts are flooded with legal appeals by dollar account owners, who demand compensation for the forced conversion of their savings into devalued pesos.

Paola and Gerónimo first try to wait things out. But then their situation changes: Paola's mother suffers from a chronic illness in her spine, and they need to pay her hospital bill and buy medicine, in the midst of shortages and skyrocketing prices. Everyone in Paola's family has money trapped in the banks. The corralito has even destroyed family networks: there's no one to ask for a loan.

Gerónimo goes to Citibank where he had deposited the money from the sale of their house into an American dollar account. After waiting for over an hour he gets to the teller, to whom he tries to give a written complaint to put in his file in protest of the conversion of his dollars to pesos. It states that he has no choice but to withdraw his money on the bank's terms because of his mother-in-law's illness.

"Listen, man," the bank teller says, "it's like this: if I accept this paper from you I have to start a file and bring it to the main branch where they make these decisions. And I should tell you that I've sent hundreds of these and haven't had a single answer."

Extremely reluctantly, Gerónimo accepts conversion at 1.40, while the dollar is up above 2.20 on the free market.

———*ʊʋʊ*———

During the crisis, sales of brand names plummeted, as consumers started to make decisions based more on cost. Elsa and Gustavo Díaz had switched in 1998 from the top names to supermarket labels; with the outbreak of the 2001 crisis they turned to cheaper brands of unknown quality. Then they switched from the supermarket to the local market. And they started shopping weekly instead of doing one big shop per month. They also tried to save in other areas. They switched their regular phone line to a pre-paid card system and limited themselves to one 20 peso card per month for the entire family. [These were typical responses to a particularly intense moment of crisis for the middle class, but viewed from another angle, they were also a manifestation of the class's long-term decline.]

In 1974 the middle class received nearly 42 percent of Argentina's national income. By the end of 2001 they could claim only 33 percent. During that same time, the share of the upper class increased by 10 percent. In 1974, 6.5 of every 10 Argentines belonged to the middle class; in 2001, before the December crisis, 5 of 10 remained middle class. In 2005, it's only 4 of 10. And these 4 belong to a very different middle class than existed in 1974. There's much greater income variation within the class. It is no longer a harmonious group.

At the end of 2004, economists from the Institute of Fiscal and Economic Studies (IEFE) proposed new categories and sub-categories to describe the middle class: salaried middle-class; self-employed; and salaried workers. But sociologist Artemio López prefers to talk about upper middle classes, middle middle classes, lower middle classes, and the new poor. The new poor are members of the middle classes who suffered in the crisis and today have an income of 200 pesos or less. "From 1974 to 2001 the middle class transferred the equivalent of 15 billion dollars per year to the upper classes," says López. By the end of 2004, 53 percent of the poor had originally been middle class.

In 1952 Argentina had the highest standard of living in Latin America, and by 1954 workers received the highest portion of the national income in history: 50.8 percent. This begs the question: How did the country that invented the ballpoint pen, fingerprinting, and the bus, a country with enormous natural resources, Nobel prizes, and the best education system on the continent—how did this country destroy its middle class?

During the first two governments of Juan Domingo Perón (1946–1952 and 1952–1955), in the context of favorable external conditions, Argentina underwent massive industrialization, and workers joined the middle classes. With their salaries and end-of-year bonuses they owned cars and enjoyed vacations. Their prosperity stimulated consumption and contributed to a growing number of good jobs.

But this golden age ended.

———◦◦◦———

VIOLENT TIMES

Like Claudia and Guillermo Rodríguez, many Argentines shut themselves up in their houses and tried to isolate themselves from what they perceived to be an increasingly hostile environment. They began to feel afraid. They began to look over their shoulders before opening their front doors or getting into a taxicab. They wouldn't let their children play in the street.

Fear itself—rather than the actual experience of robbery or assault—led many Argentines in 2001 to tell opinion polls that the lack of security was the most pressing national problem.

People felt they lived in violent times. Scholars argued that the violence wasn't due to poverty, but to the growing inequality between rich and poor. The crisis had accelerated the concentration of wealth that had begun in the 1970s. In forty years, Argentina went from having a distribution of wealth similar to European countries to one more like Brazil's—the most unequal country in Latin America.

Violence increased in tandem with the growing gulf between rich the poor. Claudia and Guillermo understood this well: their house, in a once-rural neighborhood that had subsequently been turned into a squatter settlement, had been robbed four times.

Maximiliano also suffered from the increased violence. In mid-2002 he was victim of a botched express-kidnap job. These express-kidnappings were direct results of the *corralito*. Because Argentines didn't carry much cash, petty thieves organized themselves by necessity into gangs that kidnapped their victims for several hours and forced them to withdraw cash from their bank machines.

After his assault, Maximiliano was terrorized by the fear of being kidnapped. He fantasized about what he would do in different situation: he was determined to not let the kidnappers take control of the situation. His imaginary scenarios could well appear in an action movie:

Scene 1: Outside, late afternoon

Maximiliano is in a rush. He wants to get home early. He's tired after a business meeting. He hails a cab. He doesn't pay attention to whether or not the taxi belongs to a dispatch service. A tall man with wide shoulders, he gets into the taxi with some difficulty. He gives the driver directions to his home.

He doesn't notice that the taxi moves slowly. Suddenly, a strong young man opens the door beside Maximiliano. The driver warns him, "Stay calm." Maximiliano shouts, "No" and closes the door, locking it. But another young man jumps into the back seat from the other side. The first man gets into the front seat.

The taxi speeds up. In the back seat, Maximiliano struggles with the man beside him. He tries to open the door, succeeds, and the man shuts it. The driver is getting nervous and shouts, "Throw him out."

Maximiliano opens the door again but stops for a second; how can he jump out of a moving vehicle? He curls himself into a ball and throws himself onto the cement. The taxi speeds away as Maximiliano rolls onto the road. He jumps up and takes stock. He has ripped his shirt, but there are no broken bones. He looks around and sees a bar.

Scene 2: Inside the bar

Almost every table is occupied. Some of the patrons look up at Maximiliano, surprised. He's disheveled, sweating, and agitated. He scrutinizes everyone around him. Anyone could be an enemy. He's convinced they're going to kidnap him again. He sits at an empty table. When the waiter approaches, Maximiliano looks at him suspiciously and orders a coffee.

Maximiliano would not be surprised if something like this happened to him. And others who might be less well off share his fears. This collective paranoia, this feeling of insecurity, increases faster than the crime statistics.

Since the 1960s mass media has contributed to this distortion by producing exaggerated images of violent crime. The images feed public opinion and have very real psychological consequences: people tend to be more isolated and less trusting of strangers, seeing the world as hostile and dangerous. They then demand greater security and lend their support to the "forces of law and order."

The Center for Public Opinion at Belgrano University in Buenos Aires studied the disparity between instances of crime and a more general sentiment of insecurity. They found that in some months between 2001 and 2004, crime actually declined. But during these periods the main national newspapers ran emotional stories about everyday victims of crime, allowing their readers to identify with these victims and their terrible dramas.

This tendency culminated in August 2002 when several testimonies and photo essays documented a "wave of kidnappings." The coverage focused principally on a few leading cases, especially the kidnappings of several minors from middle-class families, one of whom was murdered by his kidnappers. In August 2002, insecurity appeared as the theme of 31.6 percent of headlines, followed by discussion of the upcoming 2003 presidential elections, with IMF negotiations in third place.

———✦———

"YOU CAN'T PHOTOCOPY SHOES"

In the same way that they led the move into gated communities, the middle class led the shift from public to private education. It's odd. Even during the 2002 crisis, when they needed to save pesos, the middle class didn't sacrifice private schooling for their children. A study on the effects of the crisis revealed that unemployment hurt every social class equally and lack of income forced most people to change their consumption patterns, cutting corners wherever they could. But this study found no evidence that families switched their children from private to public schools.

Gustavo tells me that he's considering switching his four children into the same private school because it offers a multi-child discount. The teachers in private schools are trained in the same programs as public school teachers. Gustavo is considering spending 140 pesos per month for this school when his monthly income is only 800 pesos. At this moment 725 pesos a month is the official minimum cost of living for a family of four

What Gustavo and Elsa don't know is that although students in private schools spend more hours in class, they score the same in testing as their public school peers.

Instead of giving up private education, families cut back on scholastic expenses in more creative ways. According to one survey, six of ten middle-class homes significantly reduced their purchases of school materials. Gustavo, for instance, became an expert at photocopying books. "The books for English classes are the most problematic," he explains, "because they're in color." Instead of buying the books, he pays a little every day for the copies. "The problem is that when classes begin, it's not only about the books. It's also about the clothes, shoes, and backpacks. On average, one pair of shoes for my kids costs 40 pesos. Because I also have to buy them slippers, I have to spend over 300 pesos on footwear. And you can't photocopy shoes."

While some middle-class families struggle heroically to keep their children in private school, the dropout rate in high school for middle-class students is one in three. In desperation, some of these kids leave school to help support their families, but end up in only temporary jobs, making food deliveries, for example. In other words, these adolescents abandon their studies to contribute to family finances, only to end up in short order without education *and* without work. Education was once the last safety net for parents and the state to keep these teenagers from falling into social marginalization or even crime. As society suffers crisis after crisis, people's hopes and illusions deflate, and the achievements of a hundred years of social mobility begin to unravel.

———*๛*———

THE DINNER

The Rodríguezes, the Díazes, the Cabreras, and Maximiliano Fernández have a lot in common, things that they all deem middle-class characteristics. They all have grandparents or great-grandparents who were immigrants, who began a process of upward social mobility that allowed their children or grandchildren to attend university. They all believe that education is the key to upward mobility; they all believe in hard work. They are also connected to one another by their fears.

They don't know each other, and I've invited all of them for a dinner in my apartment, to share their fears and their opinions. Everyone has accepted readily, eager to meet one another and discuss the new identity of the middle class.

All my guests concur that the middle class is destroyed. They all believe that the middle class will never again be what it was, whatever they each mean by that.

Gustavo takes up one of the principal questions: Can the middle class be reconstituted?

"It's that we're moving from one extreme to another," said Gerónimo. "Before Peronism, it was the businessmen who imposed the conditions, and everyone on the bottom had to accept what they were given. Then we went to the other extreme, when workers determined the conditions and the entrepreneurs had to accept. It's as if the middle ground doesn't exist in Argentina. We went from a chaotic administration to a military dictatorship that controlled everything."[4]

Maximiliano invokes his personal utopia of Buenos Aires in the 1980s: "There was a feeling of satisfaction. We didn't have the latest things, we were still drinking our milk from glass bottles when all the other countries used plastic, but we lived in tranquility."

Though it wasn't without problems, the Argentina of the 1980s was a much more just society. Wealth was distributed more equitably. The trains, though they often arrived late, went to many more places, places that today, with the privatization of rail service, have become ghost towns. Unemployment was low: there was work. And no one talked about poverty, not because it didn't exist but because it wasn't increasing. All of this was held together by a big state, with its public companies in which one could make a career. At least in terms of the distribution of wealth, returning to the 1980s is a progressive proposal.

Toward the end of the meal, Gerónimo declares: "The middle class is a bag of cats. In terms of economics, it includes those who make 750 pesos and those who earn 3000 pesos.

"It's a question of subtlety," says Guillermo. "People don't behave that differently depending on their income. Sure, there are some differences—but not many—between those who earn 2800 pesos and 3200."

"The middle class is defined by culture, especially after the last crisis. It's the middle class that has the tools to do something different tomorrow," intervenes Paola. She's thinking of the households in which people have a certain level of education and can hope to be middle class even if they earn fewer than 700 pesos a month.

Claudia doubts that education and hope are enough to climb out of poverty. Gerónimo disagrees; he believes that education guarantees social mobility.

"But I have more education than my parents, and they're doing better than me," insists Claudia.

"Upward mobility is not about the individual but about society as a whole," adds Maximiliano. "In the 1990s, for instance, the salaries of scientists were cut, and since then they've been moving downwards, not upwards. This was a message: "It doesn't matter if you study hard and become a scientist."

"That's what I'm saying," says Claudia, "I've done better than my parents, culturally, but they are still financially better off. Society was set up for their success: they had better paying jobs and social security; they were able to save for the future. As far as I'm concerned, we don't have the same opportunities to move ahead."

"If the economy improves, we might also have better jobs," hopes Gerónimo.

"The middle class has aspirations, they want their children to attend university. They believe in education as a means of social mobility, even when it is in doubt," says Maximiliano.

"Yes, you believe that it's better for your son to continue his studies instead of starting work at 17," affirms Claudia.

Everyone agrees.

"I tell my children that even though their father, an engineer, doesn't have a great job, this doesn't diminish the value of education," Claudia says. "I would never tell them: 'Don't study, go out and work as a taxi driver and you'll earn more.'"

"It's hard to convince your children to keep studying," says Maximiliano. "Sometimes it sounds as if you're preaching the truth of an outdated belief, and they tell you about a guy they know who has eight unemployed engineers working for him in his Internet cafe. Our parents didn't have to preach to us about the value of education because the benefits were real: if you studied, you would have a better life. In today's economy this calculation is no longer true, but we stick to it nonetheless. This is one of the great things about Argentina: even though we have the GDP of Bolivia, we have this fantasy expectation of being like Europe. Though this makes us a bit arrogant, it's a positive trait because we never believe that we're at the end of the road."

It seems that to be middle-class is to have hope and to believe in a utopia of progress, whatever progress means. What is the nature of this hope?

Guillermo believes that hope is not the same as waiting for good fortune to fall from the sky. It comes from personal virtues, from having basic tools at one's disposal and using them.

I tell those at the table that the Díaz family presently earn an income only 40 pesos above the poverty line. Maximiliano senses where I'm going with this and contends that other families, who are economically on the same plane as the Diazes or might even earn 100 pesos more, are in fact much poorer, "because there are things that you lose. There are those who no longer tell their children to keep studying. What sustains the middle class is the same as what the slave Kunta Kinte[5] said to his children, and those children to their children, and so on: that they had dignity, that they had once been free and someday they would be free again. This kind of talk only begins to make sense generations down the road, because the guy who said it in the first or second generation was a lunatic, a crazy dreamer. The same thing with the middle class: it is sustained precisely by those lunatics, those who insist that you need to get an education despite the fact that the immediate reality says, 'Why waste money and effort educating your kids when they'll make more money starting an internet café?'"

Paola emphasizes that this preoccupation with schooling is a middle-class phenomenon. Maximiliano adds that it also exists in households of professionals who earn good money but spend a disproportionate amount on education: "It's a very typical fear. In face of doubt, they opt for the most expensive education. It's a form of terror. And I'm saying this, I who send my children to private school even though I think the public ones are superior in many ways, including academically. It's a fear about class."

According to Maximiliano, this fear leads many parents to project their own frustrations onto their children: "We want them to be financially successful, so they should learn Chinese but not stop taking typing, English, and computer classes."

"So," I ask, "is Gerónimo right? Is the middle class a bag of cats?"

"Well," says Claudia, "you've got rich people who live in gated communities and country clubs but share the mentality of the middle class. In the middle class you have the nouveaux riche, the sons and granddaughters of workers, and members of the middle class who are now on the *Plan jefes y jefas de hogar desocupados*."

"It's a question of culture, a drive to get ahead, for oneself and one's children," synthesizes Gustavo. "The poor are resigned, but when one has expectations, he or she belongs to the middle class."

"To be middle class is to have expectations," concludes Maximiliano.

My guests have gone and I'm tired, but I can't stop thinking: Are these families so different from one another? Does something that can be defined as the middle class still exist in Argentina? I have no doubt that it does, but it's a very different middle class from forty years ago.

The middle class existed. It was a compact among income, a society that opened its arms, and aspirations. It grew under the protection of a strong, big state that guaranteed social mobility. After a series of economic crises, middle-class hopes hang solely on individual resources, be they symbolic or material. The middle class today is a decimated class. Statistically, it has been cut in half. More than just smaller in size, though, it has found itself alone, without protection. It is no longer a part of the national project when once it was the ideal.

The middle class is sustained by lunatics, Maximiliano said. He's right — crazy dreamers who continue to believe in a future. Expectations, like hope, are the last thing we lose; at the end of the day, they are what keep us in the middle class. At the very least, these expectations will keep us from getting stuck worrying about what we *were* and, maybe, we start thinking about what we *will be*.

NOTES

This chapter was previously published as, Rodolfo Barros, *Fuimos: aventuras y desventuras de la clase media* (Buenos Aires: Aguilar, Altea, Taurus, Alfaguara, 2005), excerpted from 11–23, 28–33, 35–36, 67–70, 113–14, 117. Translated and edited by Louise E. Walker.

1. To redress unemployment. The state paid heads of households for work in community service, construction, or maintenance and sometimes provided basic training.

2. *Piqueteros* are protesters who put up roadblocks (*piquetes*) to call attention to a particular political issue or demand.

3. By getting her *cacerola*, María intends to participate in a *cacerolazo*—a political tradition in many Latin American countries wherein citizens, generally women, bang on their pots and pans to protest economic crisis. The empty pots symbolize the difficulty of providing food for a family.

4. Here Gerónimo synthesizes twentieth-century Argentine history in broad strokes. He refers to the pro-worker policies of president Juan Perón (1946–1955), to the "chaotic" administration of Isabel Perón (1974–1976), and to the military dictatorship (1976–1983).

5. A reference to *Roots,* the 1977 American television miniseries based on the Alex Haley epic tracing an African American family over the generations from Kunta Kinte's sale into slavery to his descendants' eventual emancipation.

Bibliography

SELECTED WORKS IN ENGLISH

Adamovsky, Ezequiel. "Aristotle, Diderot, Liberalism and the Idea of 'Middle Class': A Comparison of Two Contexts of Emergence of a Metaphorical Formation," *History of Political Thought* 26, no. 2 (2005):303–33.

Angell, Alan. "Classroom Maoists: The Politics of Peruvian Schoolteachers under Military Government." *Bulletin of Latin American Research* 1, no. 2 (May 1982):1–20.

Barr-Melej, Patrick. *Reforming Chile: Cultural Politics, Nationalism, and the Rise of the Middle Class.* Chapel Hill: University of North Carolina Press, 2001.

Becker, David G. *The New Bourgeoisie and the Limits of Dependency: Mining, Class and Power in "Revolutionary" Peru.* Princeton: Princeton University Press, 1983.

Bell, David A. "Class, Consciousness, and the Fall of the Bourgeois Revolution." *Critical Inquiry* 2–3 (2004):323–51.

Bledstein, Burton J., and Robert D. Johnston, eds. *The Middling Sorts: Explorations in the History of the American Middle Class.* New York: Routledge, 2001.

Blumin, Stuart. *The Emergence of the Middle Class: Social Experience in the American City, 1760–1900.* Cambridge: Cambridge University Press, 1990.

Bourdieu, Pierre. *Distinction: A Social Critique of the Judgment of Taste.* Cambridge: Harvard University Press, 1984.

———. "What Makes a Class? On the Theoretical and Practical Existence of Groups." *Berkeley Journal of Sociology* 32 (Fall 1987):1–18.

Braun, Herbert. *The Assassination of Gaitan: Public Life and Urban Violence in Colombia.* Madison: University of Wisconsin Press, 1986.

Butler, Tim, and Garry Robson. *London Calling: The Middle Classes and the Re-Making of Inner London.* Oxford: New York: Berg, 2003.

Cabrera, Miguel A. "Linguistic Approach or Return to Subjectivism? In Search of an Alternative to Social History." *Social History* 24, no. 1 (January 1999):76–90.

———. "On Language, Culture, and Social Action." *History and Theory* 40 (December 2001):82–100.

Chakrabarty, Dipesh. *Provincializing Europe: Postcolonial Thought and Historical Difference.* Princeton: Princeton University Press, 2000.

Ching, Erik Kristofer, Christina Buckley, and Angelica Lozano-Alonso, eds. *Reframing Latin America: A Cultural Theory Reading of the Nineteenth and Twentieth Centuries.* Austin: University of Texas Press, 2007.

Corfield, Penelope J., ed. *Language, History, and Class.* Oxford: Basil Blackwell, 1991.

Crossick, Geoffrey, ed. *The Lower Middle Class in Britain, 1870–1914.* London: Croom Helm, 1977.

Davidoff, Leonore, and Catherine Hall. *Family Fortunes: Men and Women of the English Middle Class, 1780–1850.* Chicago: University of Chicago Press, 1991.

Davis, Diane E. *Discipline and Development: Middle Classes and Prosperity in East Asia and Latin America.* Cambridge: Cambridge University Press, 2004.

Eineigel, Susanne. "Revolutionary Promises Encounter Urban Realities for Mexico City's Middle Class, 1915–1928." Paper presented at the 12th Conference of Mexican, United States and Canadian Historians, Vancouver, 4–8 October 2006.

Fox, Pamela. *Class Fictions: Shame and Resistance in the British Working-Class Novel, 1890–1945.* Durham: Duke University Press, 1994.

Furbank, P.N. *Unholy Pleasure, or the Idea of Social Class.* Oxford: Oxford University Press, 1985.

García-Bryce, Iñigo. *Crafting the Republic: Lima's Artisans and Nation Building in Peru, 1821–1879.* Albuquerque: University of New Mexico Press, 2004.

Garguin, Enrique. "Los Argentinos Descendemos de los Barcos: The Racial Articulation of Middle-Class Identity in Argentina (1920–1960)." *Latin American and Caribbean Ethnic Studies* 2, no. 2 (Sept. 2007):161–84.

Gilbert, Dennis. "Magicians: The Response of Middle-Class Mexican Households to Economic Crisis." *Journal of Latin American Anthropology* 10, no. 1 (2005):126–50.

———. *Mexico's Middle Class in the Neoliberal Era.* Tucson: University of Arizona Press, 2007.

Glassman, Ronald M. *The New Middle Class and Democracy in Global Perspective.* New York: St. Martin's Press, 1997.

Guano, Emanuela. "A Color for the Modern Nation: The Discourse on Class, Race, and Education in the Porteño Middle Class." *Journal of Latin American Anthropology* 8, no. 1 (2003):148–71.

Gunn, Simon. "The Failure of the Victorian Middle Class: A Critique." In *The Culture of Capital: Art, Power, and the Nineteenth-Century Middle Class,* edited by Janet Wolff and John Seed. Manchester: Manchester University Press, 1988.

Hoselitz, Bert F. "Economic Growth in Latin America." In *First International Conference of Economic History, Stockholm, August 1960,* 87–101. Paris: Mouton and Co., 1960.

Hyman, Richard, and Robert Price, eds. *The New Working Class? White-Collar Workers and Their Organisations.* London: Macmillan, 1983.

Jiménez, Michael F. "The Elision of the Middle Classes and Beyond: History, Politics, and Development Studies in Latin America's 'Short Twentieth Century.'" In *Colonial Legacies: The Problem of Persistence in Latin American History,* edited by Jeremy Adelman, 207–28. New York: Routledge, 1999.

Johnson, Dale L. *Dependence and Underdevelopment: Latin America's Political Economy.* Garden City, NY: Doubleday, 1972.

———, ed. *Middle Classes in Dependent Countries.* Beverly Hills and London: Sage, 1985.

Johnson, John J. *Political Change in Latin America: The Emergence of the Middle Sectors.* Stanford: Stanford University Press, 1958.

———. *The Military and Society in Latin America.* Stanford: Stanford University Press, 1964.

Johnston, Robert. *The Radical Middle Class: Populist Democracy and the Question of Capitalism in Progressive Era Portland, Oregon.* Princeton: Princeton University Press, 2003.

Jones, Gareth Stedman. *Languages of Class: Studies in English Working Class History, 1832–1982.* Cambridge: Cambridge University Press, 1983.

Joshi, Sanjay, *Fractured Modernity: Making of a Middle Class in North India.* Delhi: Oxford University Press, 2001.

Joyce, Patrick, ed. *Class.* Oxford: Oxford University Press, 1995.

Karush, Matthew B. *Workers or Citizens: Democracy and Identity in Rosario, Argentina (1912–1930).* Albuquerque: University of New Mexico Press, 2002.

Kocka, Jürgen. *White-Collar Workers in America, 1890–1940.* London: Sage, 1980.

———. "The Middle Classes in Europe?" *Journal of Modern History* 67 (1995):783–806.

Kocka, Jürgen, and Alan Mitchell, eds. *Bourgeois Society in Nineteenth-Century Europe*. Oxford: Berg, 1993.

Koshar, Rudy. *Splintered Classes: Politics and the Lower Middle Classes in Interwar Europe*. New York: Holmes and Meier, 1990.

Lewis, Oscar. *Five Families: Mexican Case Studies in the Culture of Poverty*. New York: Basic Books, 1959.

Ley, David. *The New Middle Class and the Remaking of the Central City*. Oxford Geographical and Environmental Studies. Oxford and New York: Oxford University Press, 1996.

Liechty, Mark. *Suitably Modern: Middle-Class Culture in a New Consumer Society*. Princeton: Princeton University Press, 2002.

Lieuwen, Edwin. *Arms and Politics and Latin America*. New York: Praeger, 1961.

———. *Generals vs. Presidents: Neo-Militarism in Latin America*. New York: Praeger, 1964.

Lockman, Zachary. "Imagining the Working Class: Culture, Nationalism, and Class Formation in Egypt, 1899–1914." *Poetics Today* 15 (Summer 1994):157–90.

Lomnitz, Claudio. "The Depreciation of Life during Mexico City's Transition into 'the Crisis.'" In *Wounded Cities: Destruction and Reconstruction in a Globalized World*, edited by Jane Schneider and Ida Susser, 47–69. Oxford: Berg, 2003.

———. "Times of Crisis: Historicity, Sacrifice, and the Spectacle of Debacle in Mexico City." *Public Culture* 15, no. 1 (2003):127–47.

Lomnitz, Larissa Adler de, and Ana Melnick. *Chile's Middle Class: A Struggle for Survival in the Face of Neoliberalism*. LACC Studies on Latin America and the Caribbean. Boulder, CO: L. Rienner Publishers, 1991.

López, A. Ricardo, and Barbara Weinstein, eds., *The Making of the Middle Class: Toward a Transnational History*. Durham: Duke University Press, 2012.

Mayer, Arno. "The Lower Middle Class as a Historical Problem." *Journal of Modern History* 47 (1975):409–36.

Maza, Sarah. *The Myth of the French Bourgeoisie: An Essay on the Social Imaginary, 1750–1850*. Cambridge: Harvard University Press, 2003.

Mills, C. Wright. *White Collar: The American Middle Classes*. New York: Oxford University Press, 1953.

Minujin, Alberto. "Squeezed: The Middle Class in Latin America." *Environment and Urbanization* 7, no. 2 (October 1995).

Moreno, Julio. *Yankee Don't Go Home! Mexican Nationalism, American Business Culture, and the Shaping of Modern Mexico, 1920–1950*. Chapel Hill: University of North Carolina Press, 2003.

Nelson, Lowry. *Rural Cuba*. Minneapolis: University of Minnesota Press, 1950.

Nun, José. "The Middle-Class Military Coup." In *The Politics of Conformity in Latin America*, edited by Claudio Véliz, 66–118. London: Oxford University Press, 1967.

———. *Latin America: The Hegemonic Crisis and the Military Coup*. Berkeley and Los Angeles: Monthly Review Press/Institute of International Studies, 1969.

O'Dougherty, Maureen. *Consumption Intensified: The Politics of Middle-Class Daily Life in Brazil*. Durham: Duke University Press, 2002.

Owensby, Brian. *Intimate Ironies: Modernity and the Making of Middle-Class Lives in Brazil*. Stanford: Stanford University Press, 1999.

Parker, D.S. *The Idea of the Middle Class: White-Collar Workers and Peruvian Society, 1900–1950*. University Park: University of Pennsylvania Press, 1998.

Petras, James. *Politics and Social Forces in Chilean Development*. Berkeley: University of California, 1969.

———. *Politics and Social Structure in Latin America*. New York: Monthly Review Press, 1970.

Prasad, Bhagwan. *Socio-Economic Study of Urban Middle Classes*. Delhi: Sterling Publishers, 1968.

Reddy, William. *Money and Liberty in Modern Europe: A Critique of Historical Understanding*. Cambridge: Cambridge University Press, 1987.

Rosemblatt, Karin. *Gendered Compromises: Political Cultures and the State in Chile, 1920–1950*. Chapel Hill: University of North Carolina Press, 2000.

Scott, Joan W. *Gender and the Politics of History.* New York: Columbia University Press, 1998.

Sewell, William H., Jr. *Work and Revolution in France: The Language of Labor from the Old Regime to 1848.* Cambridge: Cambridge University Press, 1980.

Silva, J. Pablo. "White-Collar Revolutionaries: Middle-Class Unions and the Rise of the Chilean Left, 1918–1938." PhD diss., University of Chicago, 2000.

———. "The Origins of White-Collar Privilege in Chile: Arturo Alessandri, Law 6020 and the Pursuit of a Corporatist Consensus, 1933–1938." *Labor* 3, no. 1 (2006):87–112.

Smith, Peter. *Labyrinths of Power: Political Recruitment in Twentieth-Century Mexico.* Princeton: Princeton University Press, 1979.

Stearns, Peter N. *Paths to Authority: The Middle Class and the Industrial Labor Force in France, 1820–48.* Urbana: University of Illinois Press, 1978.

———. "The Middle Class: Towards a Precise Definition." *Comparative Studies in Society and History* 21, no. 3 (1979):377–96.

Thompson, E.P. *The Making of the English Working Class.* New York: Vintage Books, 1966.

———. "Time, Work-Discipline, and Industrial Capitalism." *Past and Present* 38, no. 1 (1967):56–97.

Veliz, Claudio. *Obstacles to Change in Latin America.* London: Oxford University Press, 1965.

Vidich, Arthur J. *The New Middle Classes: Life-Styles, Status Claims, and Political Orientations.* New York: New York University Press, 1995.

Wacquant, Loic J. D. "Making Class: The Middle Class(es) in Social Theory and Social Structure." In *Bringing Class Back In: Contemporary and Social Structure,* edited by Scott G. McNall, 39–64. Boulder, CO: Westview Press, 1991.

Wahrman, Dror. *Imagining the Middle Class: The Political Representation of Class in Britain, c. 1780–1840.* Cambridge: Cambridge University Press, 1995.

Walker, Louise E. *Waking from the Dream: Mexico's Middle Classes after 1968.* Stanford: Stanford University Press, 2013.

Walkowitz, Daniel J. *Working with Class: Social Workers and the Politics of Middle-Class Identity.* Chapel Hill: University of North Carolina Press, 1999.

Wallerstein, Immanuel. "The Bourgeois(ie) as Concept and Reality." In *The Essential Wallerstein,* edited by Immanuel Wallerstein, 324–43. New York: New Press, 2000 [1988].

Watenpaugh, David. *Being Modern in the Middle East: Revolution, Nationalism, Colonialism, and the Arab Middle Class.* Princeton: Princeton University Press, 2006.

Weinstein, Barbara. *For Social Peace in Brazil: Industrialists and the Remaking of the Working Class in São Paulo.* Chapel Hill: University of North Carolina Press, 1996.

Whetten, Nathan L. "The Rise of a Middle Class in Mexico." In *Materiales para el Estudio de la Clase Media en la América Latina,* ed. Theo R. Crevenna, vol. 2, 20–27. Washington: Pan-American Union, 1951.

Wolfe, Joel. *Working Women, Working Men: São Paulo and the Rise of Brazil's Industrial Working Class, 1900–1955.* Durham: Duke University Press, 1993.

Wright, Eric O. *Classes.* London: Verso, 1985.

Wynne, Derek. *Leisure, Lifestyle, and the New Middle Class: A Case Study.* London and New York: Routledge, 1998.

Zeitlin, Maurice. *The Civil Wars in Chile (or the Bourgeois Revolutions That Never Were).* Princeton: Princeton University Press, 1984.

SELECTED WORKS IN SPANISH OR PORTUGUESE, BY COUNTRY

General

Crevenna, Theo R., ed. *Materiales para el estudio de la clase media en la América Latina.* Washington: Pan-American Union, 1951.

De Galíndez, Jesús. "Revolución socio-económica en Iberoamérica." *Cuadernos Americanos* 13, no. 2 (March–April 1954):7–18

Visacovsky, Sergio Eduardo and Enrique Garguin, eds. *Moralidades, economías e identidades de clase media*. Buenos Aires: Antropofagía, 2009.

ARGENTINA

Adamovsky, Ezequiel. "Acerca de la relación entre el Radicalismo argentino y la 'clase media' (una vez más)." *Hispanic American Historical Review* 89, no. 2 (2009):209–51.
———. *Historia de la clase media argentina: apogeo y decadencia de una illusion, 1919–2003*. Buenos Aires: Planeta, 2009.
Arizaga, Cecilia. *El mito de la comunidad en la ciudad mundializada: estilos de vida y nuevas clases medias en urbanizaciones cerradas*. Buenos Aires: El cielo por asalto, 2005.
Garguin, Enrique. "El tardío descubrimiento de la clase media en Argentina." *Nuevo Topo: Revista de Pensamiento Crítico* 4 (Sept.–Oct. 2007):85–108.
Germani, Gino. "La clase media en la cuidad de Buenos Aires: estudio preliminar." *Boletín del Instituto de Sociología* 1 (1942):105–26.
———. "La clase media en la Argentina con especial referencia a sus sectores urbanos." In *Materiales para el estudio de la clase media en la América Latina*, ed. Theo R. Crevenna, vol. 1, 1–33. Washington, DC: Unión Panamericana, 1951.
Jauretche, Arturo. *El medio pelo en la sociedad argentina*. Buenos Aires: Corregidor, 1996 [1st ed. 1966].
Mafud, Julio. *Sociología de la clase media argentina*. Buenos Aires: Distal, 1985.
Minujin, Alberto, and Eduardo Anguita. *La clase media, seducida y abandonada*. Buenos Aires: Edhasa, 2004.
Svampa, Maristella. *Los que ganaron: la vida en los countries y barrios privados*. Buenos Aires: Biblos, 2001.
Wortman, Ana. *Pensar las clases medias: consumos culturales y estilos urbanos en la Argentina de los noventa*. Buenos Aires: La crujía, 2003.

BRAZIL

Saes, Décio. *Classes médias e sistema político no Brasil*. São Paulo: T. A. Queiroz, 1985.

CHILE

Covarrubias, Jaime. *El Partido Radical y la clase media en Chile: la relación de intereses entre 1888–1938*. Santiago: Andrés Bello, 1990.
Hubertson, Amanda Labarca. "Apuntes para estudiar la clase media en Chile." In *Materiales para el estudio de la clase media en la América Latina*, ed. Theo R. Crevenna, vol. 6. Washington, DC: Unión Panamericana, 1951.
Salazar Vergara, Gabriel. "Para una historia de la clase media en Chile." Working paper. Santiago: Sur, 1986.
Tironi, Eugenio. "La clase construida." Working paper, 2 vols. Santiago: Sur, 1985.
Vega, Julio. "La clase media en Chile." In *Materiales para el estudio de la clase media en la América Latina*, ed. Theo R. Crevenna, vol. 3. Washington, DC: Unión Panamericana, 1951.

COLOMBIA

Pinto Saavedra, Juan Alfredo. *La hora de la clase media: bases para la movilización política de los grupos intermedios en Colombia*. Bogota: Artepel Impresores, 2006.

ECUADOR

De la Torre, Carlos. *El racismo en el Ecuador: experiencias de los indios de clase media.* Quito: CAAP, 1966.

MEXICO

Camacho, Manuel, Juan Sánchez Navarro, et al. *Sociedad: las clases medias.* Mexico City: Instituto Nacional de Estudios Históricos de la Revolución Mexicana, 1986
Careaga, Gabriel. *Mitos y fantasías de la clase media en México.* Mexico City: Editorial J. Mortiz, 1974.
———. *Biografía de un joven de la clase media.* Mexico City: Editorial J. Mortiz, 1977.
Coral, Emilio. "La clase media mexicana, 1940–1970: entre la tradición, la izquierda, el consumismo y la influencia cultural de los Estados Unidos." *Historias* 63 (2006):103–25.
Cuevas Díaz, J. Aurelio. *El Partido Comunista Mexicano: la ruptura entre las clases medias y el Estado fuerte en México.* Mexico City: Editorial Línea, 1984.
De Garay, Graciela, ed. *Modernidad habitada: multifamiliar Miguel Alemán; ciudad de México, 1949–1999.* Mexico City: Instituto Mora, 2004.
González Cosío, Arturo. *Clases medias y movilidad social en México.* Mexico City: Editorial Extemporáneos, 1976.
Loaeza, Soledad. *Clases medias y política en México: la querella escolar, 1959–1963.* Mexico City: Colegio de México, 1988.
Loaeza, Soledad, and Claudio Stern, eds. *Las clases medias en la coyuntura actual: seminario llevado a cabo en el Centro Tepoztlán, A.C., Tepoztlán, Mor., 26 de septiembre de 1987.* Mexico City: Colegio de México, 1990.
López Cámara, Francisco. *La clase media en la era del populismo.* Mexico City: Miguel Angel Porrúa, 1988.
———. *Apogeo y extinción de la clase media mexicana.* Cuernavaca: UNAM, 1990.
Porter, Susie. "Espacios burocráticos, normas de feminidad e identidad de la clase media en México durante la década de 1930." In *Orden social e identidad de género. México siglos XIX y XX,* edited by María Teresa Fernández Aceves, Carmen Ramos Escandón, and Susie Porter. Guadalajara: CIESAS, 2006.
Schwartz, Rami, and Salomón Barbaz Lapidus. *El ocaso de la clase media.* Mexico: Grupo Editorial Planeta, 1994.
Tarrés, María Luisa. "Del abstencionism electoral a la oposición política: las clases medias en Ciudad Satélite." *Estudios Sociológicos* 4, no. 12 (1986):361–90.

PERU

Basadre, Jorge. "La Aristocracia y las clases medias civiles en el Perú republicano." *Mercurio Peruano* 44 (1963):466–67.
McEvoy, Carmen, ed. *La experiencia burguesa en el Perú, 1840–1940.* Frankfurt and Madrid: Vervuert/Iberoamericana, 2004.
Nugent, Guillermo. *Peru hoy: la clase media ¿existe?* Lima: DESCO, 2003.
Parker, David S. "Los pobres de la clase media: estilo de vida, consumo e identidad en una ciudad tradicional." In *Mundos Interiores: Lima 1850–1950,* edited by Aldo Panfichi and Felipe Portocarrero. Lima: Universidad del Pacífico, 1995.
Portocarrero, Gonzalo, ed. *Las clases medias: entre la pretensión y la incertidumbre.* Lima: SUR/Oxfam, 1998.
Sabogal Wiese, José. "Las clases medias en el Perú," *Economía y Agricultura* 2, no. 8 (Oct. 1966): 343:44.

Index

About the Contributors

Rodolfo Barros is an Argentinian journalist, and economics editor at the newspaper *Perfil*. He also teaches at the Universidad Nacional de la Plata. He is the author of two books, *Fuimos: Aventuras y Desventuras de la Clase Media* (2004), and *La Marca y el Deseo: Manual para no Caer en las Trampas del Marketing* (2006), and has published several papers in Argentina and Brazil on journalistic best practices.

Mario Benedetti (1920–2009) was a Uruguayan poet, novelist, and essayist. He wrote for the literary-cultural-political magazine *Marcha* until 1973 when he was exiled. His best known works include the novels *La Tregua* (1960, made into an Oscar-nominated 1974 film), *Gracias por el Fuego* (1965), *Primavera con una Esquina Rota* (1982), and *La Borra del Café* (1993), the short story collection *Montevideanos* (1959), the essay collection *El País de la Cola de Paja* (1960), and numerous books of poetry.

William E. French is associate professor of history at the University of British Columbia. He is author of *A Peaceful and Working People: Manners, Morals, and Class Formation in Northern Mexico* (1996), and editor of two essay collections: *Rituals of Rule, Ritual of Resistance: Public Celebrations and Popular Culture in Mexico* (1994, with William Beezley and Cheryl Martin), and *Gender, Sexuality and Power in Modern Latin America* (2006, with Katherine Bliss). His current work is on love, courtship, and the law in Mexico between the 1860s and 1930s.

John J. Johnson (1912–2004) was professor of history at Stanford University from 1946 to 1977, and also served stints as acting chief of the South American branch of the research division of the U.S. State Department, managing editor of the *Hispanic American Historical Review*, Latin American Studies Association president, and director of Stanford's Center for Latin American Studies. His works include *Political Change in Latin*

America: The Emergence of the Middle Sectors (1958), *The Military and Society in Latin America* (1964), and *Latin America in Caricature* (1980).

Francisco López Cámara (1927–1994) was professor of political and social sciences at the Universidad Nacional Autónoma de México (UNAM). He authored several books on liberalism in nineteenth-century Mexico and the middle class in twentieth-century Mexico, including *La génesis de la conciencia liberal en México* (1954), *Qué es el liberalismo?* (1962), *El desafío de la clase media* (1971), *La clase media en la era del populismo* (1988), and *Apogeo y extinción de la clase media mexicana* (1990).

A. Ricardo López is assistant professor of history at Western Washington University. He is co-editor of *The Making of the Middle Class: Toward a Transnational* History (2012, with Barbara Weinstein), and co-author of *Compensar: 20 años de historia, 1970–1990* (1999, with Mauricio Archila Neira). He is currently completing a book entitled *Makers of Democracy: The Transnational Formation of the Middle Class in Colombia, 1958–1982.*

Brian P. Owensby is professor of history and former chair of the History Department at the University of Virginia. He is author of *Intimate Ironies: Making Middle-Class Lives in Modern Brazil* (1999) and *Empire of Law and Indian Justice in Colonial Mexico* (2008). His current research examines the nexus between law, commerce, religion and politics in the mid-eighteenth century Ibero-American world. He is also working on Sérgio Buarque de Holanda's *Raizes do Brasil* and the problem of writing history from beyond the horizon of European historiography.

David S. Parker is associate professor of history and former chair of the History Department at Queen's University, Canada. He is author of *The Idea of the Middle Class: White-Collar Workers and Peruvian Society, 1900–1950* (1998), and articles or book chapters on topics ranging from public health reform to images of social climbers in Chilean fiction to dueling among journalists and politicians in Uruguay.

Fredrick B. Pike was professor of history at Notre Dame University. His wide-ranging scholarly work includes *Chile and the United States, 1880–1962* (1963), *Hispanismo, 1898–1936* (1971), *The United States and the Andean Republics* (1977), The *Politics of the Miraculous in Peru: Haya de la Torre and the Spiritualist Tradition* (1986), *The United States and Latin America: Myths and Stereotypes of Civilization and Nature* (1992), and *FDR's Good Neighbor Policy* (1995).

J. Pablo Silva is associate professor of history and chair of the History Department at Grinnell College in Grinnell, Iowa. He is author of "The Origins of White-Collar Privilege in Chile," published in the journal *Labor: Studies in the Working-Class History of the Americas* (2006), and is finishing a book on the creation of a radical middle-class movement in twentieth-century Chile.

Charles Wagley (1913–1991) was a cultural anthropologist and Brazil specialist. He taught at Columbia University, where he founded and directed the Institute of Latin American Studies, and later at the University of Florida. His books include *Amazon Town: A Study of Man in the Tropics* (1953), *An Introduction to Brazil* (1963), *The Latin American Tradition* (1968), *Welcome of Tears: the Tapirapé Indians of Central Brazil* (1977) and the collection *Race and Class in Rural Brazil* (1952).

Louise E. Walker is assistant professor of history at Northeastern University in Boston. She is the author of *Waking from the Dream: Mexico's Middle Classes after 1968* (2012). She is currently co-editing a special dossier on Mexico's recently declassified secret police archive for the *Journal of Iberian and Latin American Research* (2013, with Tanalís Padilla). Her research projects also include the history of conspiracy theories.

Andrew H. Whiteford (1913–2006) was professor of anthropology and curator of the Logan Museum at Beloit College, Wisconsin, until his retirement in 1976. A pioneer in Latin American urban anthropology, he wrote *Two Cities of Latin America* (1960) and *An Andean City at Mid-Century* (1977). Whiteford was equally recognized for his work on the native art and archaeology of the American southwest, for which he received a Lifetime Achievement Award from the Native American Art Studies Association.

Made in the USA
Columbia, SC
27 April 2020